INFIBULATION

INFIBULATION

Female Mutilation in Islamic Northeastern Africa

Esther K. Hicks

Transaction Publishers
New Brunswick (U.S.A.) London (U.K.)

Library of Congress Catalog Number: 92-24753
ISBN: 1-56000-077-5
Printed in the United States of America

Library of Congress Cataloging-in-Publication Data
Hicks, Esther K.
Infibulation : female mutilation in Islamic northeastern Africa / Esther K. Hicks.
  p. cm.
Includes bibliographical references and index.
ISBN 1-56000-077-5
  1. Infibulation—Africa, Northeast. 2. Africa, Northeast—Social life and customs. 3. Women, Muslim—Africa, Northeast. I. Title.
GN650.H53 1992
392—dc20

92-24753
CIP

This book is dedicated to A.J.F. Köbben
in recognition of a debt of gratitude.

Contents

Figures, Maps, Plots, and Tables

Figures

Maps

Plots

Tables

Appendix

Preface and Acknowledgments

Infibulation, the most extreme form of female circumcision, is primarily practiced by those populations inhabiting Islamic northeastern Africa. For these populations, circumcising young girls and boys is an important part of their normative socialization process. For outside observers such operations are more often perceived as a mutilation of young children. In recent years this perception has received considerable publicity as increasing attention has been drawn to the various forms of female circumcision. Moreover, such practices have all too often been exploited in the media as portraying a specific, albeit symbolic, example of man's inhumanity to woman. This is especially so with respect to infibulation: the justification of its perpetuation is perceived as having its basis in the manipulation of holy writ.

But is this, in fact, the case? Or is infibulation but one of a myriad of cultural traits developed, over time, by individual social systems to define and circumscribe the social role of those members most pivotal to its structural survival? In this case, women. And why do we refrain from politically platforming the rights of young boys? Is the traditional symbolic basis of circumcising young children of either sex really so different? Or is the primary difference between the circumcision operation for boys and girls one of degree and not kind; that is, infibulating young female children can have serious immediate, and long-term, medical consequences, whereas the circumcision of young boys leaves primarily invisible scars? Perhaps of equal relevance is the question of what the (small) war waged by feminists and the various international interest groups against all forms of female circumcision tells us about our own cultural biases and insecurities. Would we not be better served by first determining the importance and embeddedness of this practice in the social systems within which it occurs?

It was with these questions in mind that I undertook the writing of this book. However, the paucity of reliable and extensive field studies, indeed of any information on this practice, necessitated a historical approach. On the one hand, this aided the determination of (1) the original geographic and cultural (population) distribution of infibulation; (2) the potential historical function(s) of this practice; (3) the reason for the

xiii

current distribution of this practice across the entire pastoral-rural-urban continuum. On the other hand, it resulted in a considerably more conservative delineation of the geographic distribution of this practice than that indicated by other studies (academic or otherwise). Similarly, and in the interests of historical continuity, the traditional (geographic) provincial designations were retained throughout this study (especially for Sudan).

Because this book has been through two stages of development over the past five years, I would like to thank colleagues and friends in somewhat chronological order. For their substantive assistance in the preparation of the initial version of this volume, I am indebted to Jan Berting, and especially to Wim Kers, for volunteering his services for the HOMALS analysis of my data. I am equally beholden to my friend, Leslie K. Hunt, who unfailingly read and commented on innumerable early versions of the various chapters, and whose friendship did not once flicker and dim in all that time. Most especially, I am obliged to André Köbben, to whom this book is dedicated, for his support when it was sorely needed, his constructive, but firm criticism, his kindness, and his ultimate resignation to the fact that I would never learn to spell. Finally, I wish to thank my husband, Wouter van Rossum, who suffered through, and constructively criticized every single 'final' version of this book, and who continues to be my best friend and confidant in spite of it all.

Introduction

The formulation of problems . . . should include explicit attention to a range of public issues and of personal troubles; and they should open up for inquiry the causal connexions between milieux and social structure.
—C. Wright Mills, *The Sociological Imagination*

Qualifying a given problem as social does not make it so. Infibulation (the most extreme form of female circumcision) is a case in point. Generally speaking, relevant national governments have publicly exhibited a desire to eliminate this practice (see e.g., Boddy, 1982:696n; Grassivaro-Gallo, 1986, personal communication). However, it is unclear whether this "desire" has emanated directly from indigenous governments or indirectly, via external sources at the governmental level, or primarily reflects the wishes of the indigenous population. The distinction is crucial. In the past, for example, it was the colonialist mandate powers that strongly "suggested" (and more often implemented) legal measures forbidding this practice. Nevertheless, even though "Pharaonic" circumcision (infibulation) was made criminal in the Sudan by Penal Code S.284A (1946), and again in 1969, there is no record of prosecutions for this crime. Farran has attributed this both to a chronic lack of witnesses and to the failure of police to report it (1963:17n).

The situation remains largely unchanged. Nevertheless, infibulation continues to be defined, prima facie, as a "social problem" and treated as a public issue by both government and relevant interest groups. This position is also reflected (and stimulated) by relevant international organizations and associated field researchers.

This view is not, however, shared by the vast majority of the female population in infibulation-practicing regions: for them, not being infibulated would be the social problem. It seems, then, that indigenous governments—including national committees—have seriously underestimated the importance of understanding the rigid retention of this practice, which is more integrally (socially) functional than it at first appeared to be. That infibulation plays an important role in the life of females in Islamic northeastern Africa is clear; why and how it does this has never been clear.

1

Of course, explaining the original function and form of individual culture traits for any given society is an almost impossible task. Given that most traits are embedded in a historically traditional milieu, often the best we can do is determine their hierarchical position and importance in the cultural network, and the functions they fulfill in the immediate cultural environment. Unfortunately, available research addressing the general question of female circumcision is minimal, and studies concerned with the practice of infibulation are almost nonexistent. Those that do exist represent either anthropological or medical research involving area-specific populations. Although such information can facilitate limited case-specific analyses, it is insufficient in quantity to allow either extensive cross-cultural analysis or a clear evaluation of the relevant functions of infibulation in the broader social context. Moreover, the conjoining in the literature of all types of female circumcision has impeded an analysis of how the various forms are integrated into the social sphere.

As a consequence, and in order to understand the traditional cultural imbeddedness of the practice of infibulation, a diachronous approach was taken for this study. It is in this context that the social importance and function of this practice is delineated and evaluated. Moreover, as is usual in such an approach, the behavior patterns of the *group or population* are considered, rather than that of individuals (Hofstee, 1976:107).

The findings of this study indicate that, historically speaking, infibulation was primarily practiced by pastoral and agro-pastoral (see chapter 2) populations in northern Sudan and the Horn of Africa. Its later diffusion to riverine agriculturalists, and the urban populations of northern Sudan, Djibouti, and Somalia, can be related to the traditional socioeconomic interdependence of pastoral-rural-urban populations (chapter 2). In the present study, the area where infibulation is currently practiced has been designated "Islamic northeastern Africa". This area, which includes northern Sudan, Eritrea, Djibouti, the coastal region of Ethiopia, and northern Somalia, is a somewhat revised version of those regions designated 'northeastern Africa' by Trimingham (1952:1; see also chapter 2, this volume).

Among all of the populations included in this area, infibulation constitutes a rite of passage for female children. It initiates them into womanhood and makes them eligible for marriage, the only status position available to women in these societies. In Islamic northeastern

Africa, both the structure of marriage and the social status of females has been codified, if not de jure then de facto, by traditional Islam. It is in this context that the practice of infibulation must be considered.

Although the existence of this practice predates the introduction of Islam into the Sudan and northeastern Africa, the latter has been instrumental in embedding infibulation into the structural nexus of marriage, family, and social honor. It is also for this reason that infibulation can be found across the full spectrum of socioeconomic configurations in these regions. Thus, while the web of developmental growth may have economically affected the urban setting, its influence on the sociocultural ethics of this population has been primarily superficial. This would explain the perplexing manifestation, especially among the urban elite, of a drive for rapid and often radical economic change and the concomitant retention of traditional practices such as infibulation. It is in this context that we can speak of a pastoral-rural-urban continuum in these regions. In short, it is highly possible that the combination of Islamic tradition and the socioeconomic pastoral-rural-urban interdependence that has continued despite the developmental growth of the last decades has facilitated the perpetuation and diffusion of infibulation.

Clearly, the importance of understanding the rigid retention of cultural traits (such as the practice of infibulation) must not be underestimated, especially with respect to the process of change involving growth and development. Thus, while an exploration of the potential reasons for its continued practice might not provide us with answers about how to eliminate infibulation, it might give us some hints about how *not* to try to effect social change. Similarly, we must remember that, regardless of how barbaric we may find it, in certain geographic areas infibulation remains an important part of the female existence and, as such, cannot be treated in isolation as a single issue destined for elimination. In fact, this practice is but a symptom of the wider-reaching problems involved in effecting social change in Islamic northeastern Africa. Indeed, long-term programs generating large scale socioeconomic and political changes may well have the equally long-term end result of eliminating the need for this practice.

Unfortunately, the elimination of female circumcision (to include infibulation) is no longer only an issue involving Islamic northeast African societies. In the course of the last decade, existing problems in this region became compounded by drought and civil and political strife.

This has generated an increasing influx of refugees from this region into various European countries, including France, Great Britain, and the Netherlands (Bartels and Haaijer, 1992). As a consequence, European governments are now also confronted with the problem of how to deal with female circumcision as a domestic, albeit a minority, issue.

Objectives and Limitations

Although the research presented in this study is specifically concerned with those populations practicing infibulation, it does not represent the results of a field study. The reasons for this are threefold.

1. Upon initiating this project, it was unclear exactly where infibulation was practiced and by whom. A search of all available literature on female circumcision did not solve this problem. Indeed, the situation proved somewhat analagous to that of Prime Minister Salisbury who, when delineating French shared "spheres of influence" between the Mediterranean and Lake Chad, noted that, while he and the French ambassador were giving away mountains, rivers, and lakes to each other, "we have only been hindered by the small impediment that we never knew exactly where those mountains and rivers and lakes were" (MacMichael, 1954:57). This comment represents a state of knowledge about the general geography of northeastern Africa that continued well into this century. It also represents the state of knowledge about all forms of female circumcision throughout Africa right up to the present. Consequently, an initial and primary objective of this study was to inventory indigenous populations, differentiating between those traditionally practicing infibulation, and those for whom it represented a more recent adaptation.

The more recent source materials indicate a considerably more widespread occurrence of infibulation than is given in the present study. Although the majority of these studies do include those areas for which infibulation can be documented, other areas for which there is less evidence are also listed, for example, all of Somalia, northern Nigeria, parts of Upper Volta, eastern Chad, southern Egypt, parts of Mali, etc. (see for example, Hosken, 1982; McLean/Graham, 1985; Levin, 1980; Oldfield-Hayes, 1975). This is not to imply misrepresentation, but is more probably related to a heavy dependence on unreliable secondary sources (e.g., other studies on female circumcision), which are all too often based on guesswork or guilt by association. Equally important in this context is the fact that infibulation is a cultural, rather than a geographic phenomenon, confined to ethnic groups that are not necessarily geographically circumscribed.

Unfortunately, there are few anthropological studies available that address the social structure and cultural traits of individual tribal populations in Islamic northeastern Africa. Most of the more recent anthropological studies of the northern Sudan, for example, have concentrated more on political and/or economic structures than on other aspects of social structure. Conversely, although there is (relatively speaking) considerable information available about the southern Sudan, populations in that area do not currently practice, and are not historically known to have practiced, infibulation. Similarly, although Lewis's studies of Somalia are invaluable for the northern Somali, no accurate comparative analysis can be made with southern Somali populations, due to insufficient information. Even the more recent literature concerned with infibulation in Somalia does not specifically delineate all infibulation-practicing populations or their social and cultural complexion (e.g., Dualeh, 1982; Grassivaro-Gallo, 1986).

As a result, an imposition of national boundaries upon this practice (although difficult and undesirable) was necessary in order to determine where and among which populations infibulation occurred. Geographically speaking, I was only able to substantiate the occurrence of infibulation—*as a cultural rather than an individual or isolated group phenomenon*—in most of northern Sudan, Eritrea, the (primarily) coastal area of Ethiopia, and northern Somalia.[1] Although there is also evidence of infibulation being practiced in the Chad regions of Wadai and, to some extent, Bornu, I was only able to verify its occurrence among populations that either originated in (relatively recent immigrants), or were spillover populations from, the Sudan. It is for this reason that Chad has not been included as a separate geographic region in this study. Where infibulation occurs among populations in the Chad area, it has been noted under the individual population listings in the appendix. Although Eritrea and Djibouti also fall into this category, both have been considered separately due to the extent to which infibulation is practiced in these areas. Both Eritrea and Djibouti have, however, been dealt with more briefly than other areas (and to some extent have been combined with Ethiopia). Map 1 indicates the general geographical areas covered in this study.

MAP 1—General Regions Where Infibulation Occurs (outlined)

2. In order to determine the possible historical functions of the practice of infibulation, it was necessary to gain insight into the historical socioeconomic and cultural milieu in which infibulation has traditionally occurred. This also provided a basis for evaluating existing academic and indigenous views about the reasons for the existence and vehement retention of this practice.

3. The question of whether infibulation-practicing populations manifest composite attributes that significantly distinguish them from those that do not infibulate dictated an (historical) exploratory approach. This was also necessary because of the wide distribution of this practice

throughout Islamic northeastern Africa. Moreover, in order to address this question it was necessary to delineate and determine the distribution of the sociocultural and economic attributes that were historically common to infibulation-practicing populations (but that were only minimally present or completely absent in noninfibulating populations).

This information provided the basis both for the qualitative and quantitative analysis of the function of infibulation in the social nexus, and a determination of the potential reasons for the retention of this practice in otherwise "developing" social systems. It also aided in the development of field-testable hypotheses (see pp. 161–62, chapter 5), the research results of which could provide additional information about the nature of the embeddedness of infibulation and assist in estimating short- and long-term strategies for the constructive elimination of this practice.

Chapter 1 describes the operation of infibulation and outlines indigenous and academic explanations for this practice. Chapter 2 delineates the geographic and demographic distribution of this practice, presenting reasons for its proliferation across the pastoral-rural-urban continuum. Chapter 3 considers the "closedness" of Islamic northeastern African societies and considers infibulation in this context. Chapter 4 outlines the methodological approach chosen (HOMALS), and provides information about the study and control samples, together with the total variables found to be associated with infibulation. In chapter 5 the sociocultural variables that were found to be associated with infibulation are qualified and analyzed, and propositions are proffered with respect to the structural function of infibulation. Chapter 6 briefly considers the future of infibulation. Chapter 7 contains concluding remarks on the practice of infibulation in the geographic regions in which it traditionally occurs, and among political refugees and immigrant populations in the European context. The appendix presents an overview of the geographic regions considered in this study, the distribution of Islam, and specific demographic information.

Note

1. See maps 10, 11, 12. Although the populations are primarily identified and qualified in the appendix, relevant supplementary information has also been incorporated in the chapters.

1

Infibulation:
Description, Function, and Diffusion

Although Pharaonic circumcision, generally referred to as "infibulation" by Western researchers, is claimed to have originated in Egypt, there is no direct evidence of its having been practiced there. Clitoral excision does, however, appear to have been practiced by both the ancient Egyptians, and Arabian peninsula tribes (in the pre-Islamic period) (Ghalioungui, 1963:95–97; Levy, 1962:252).

Barclay, in his study of Buurri al Lamaab, Sudan, describes "infibulation" as an operation that is generally performed on young girls between the ages of four and eleven years (1964:238). It involves the removal of much of the labia majora, the mons veneris, the labia minora, and often the clitoris, using razors, knives, or other sharp objects (see figure 1.1): "a reed, tube or match stick is inserted into the vaginal opening in order that after the wound heals a small hole may remain for the passage of urine and menses. The girl's legs are strapped together for forty days to allow the wounds on the two sides to heal together by contact. In a few tribes thorns are used to suture the wounds and these are held in place by threads wound round their projecting ends" (Barclay, 1964:238). There are numerous descriptions of this operation in the available literature, however, with only minor exceptions, they follow the one given above.

When the young girl is married, a "midwife" or her mother usually has to be called in to "defibulate" her in order to facilitate intercourse. Although, ideally, it is the husband who deflowers the wife, the pain and size of the opening often make this impossible. Dualeh, in her study of infibulation in Somalia, enumerates some of the consequences when a husband attempts to force the opening with various objects, in order to avoid the shame of calling in the girl's mother or a midwife for assistance (1982:24).

9

FIGURE 1.1
Vulva (External Genitalia) Pre- and Post-Infibulation

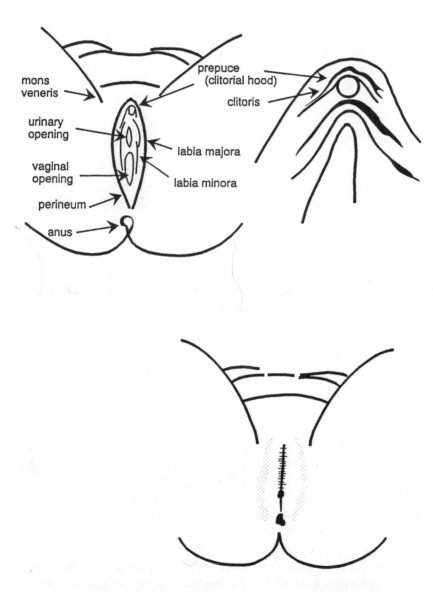

When and if the girl becomes pregnant, she must be "defibulated" to facilitate birth, and restitched thereafter. Although there is an indication that Sudanese women are "reinfibulated" (i.e., the opening is returned to its originally infibulated size) after childbirth, Dualeh stresses that this is not done in Somalia, where "infibulation takes place only once: before marriage" (1982:5). Grassivaro-Gallo disagrees, pointing out that postpartum reinfibulation is the norm (1986:74 and personal communication).

It is of course possible that, given the general inaccuracy of available information concerning infibulation, postpartum restitching (closure of what, in fact, is an open wound) has inadvertently become interpreted as "reinfibulation." Moreover, the degree to which a woman is "reinfibulated or restitched" will undoubtedly vary from population to population, indeed, from individual to individual.

The physiological consequences of such an operation are numerous. And, although there would seem to be a low death rate associated with the operation, deaths are often not reported. There are, however, numerous cases of chronic infection, sterility, tetanus or septic anemia, hemorrhage, long-term gynecological and obstetrical complications, cysts, keloid and fistula formation, etc. Nevertheless, the operation and its consequences have changed very little, with the exception perhaps of urban core areas (see, for example, Oldfield-Hayes, 1975; Levin, 1980; Dualeh, 1982; Grassivaro-Gallo, 1986; W.H.O. Chronicle, 1986).

While there are many variations of the operations of excision and "infibulation," only in the more recent literature have these variations, at least to some extent, been defined (e.g., El-Dareer, 1979; Sanderson, 1981; Cook, 1979). In summary, the various views (modified according to a communication from L. Sanderson) delineate roughly three categories of female circumcision:

1. Clitoridectomy: the partial or complete removal of the clitoris, or the removal of only the prepuce of the clitoris.

2. Pharaonic circumcision (infibulaton): which includes excision of the entire clitoris, the adjacent parts of the labia minora, (often) all of the external genitalia, parts of the labia majora, and a subsequent sewing up or joining together of the roughened (or partially amputated) remnants of the labia majora.

3. Clitoridectomy and excision of labia minora: less severe than Pharaonic in the sense that the labia minora and all or part of the clitoris are removed, but without the subsequent joining or closure of the vulva area.

In actual practice, the above three types occur with considerable variation, but the paucity of specific data does not allow a more exact or detailed delineation. Consequently, in the present study, "infibulation" refers to both 2. and 3. above. Form 3. (clitoridectomy and excision of labia minor) seems to be more prevalent among the westernmost populations, for example, among many of the Baggara tribes in western Sudan and eastern Chad. Because of the lack of precise data however, and since these populations are noted in the literature as practicing "infibulation," they have been qualified, in this study, as infibulation-practicing.

The reason for the scarcity of information about infibulation may relate to the initial, and often only, reaction of many researchers to this practice, which is to view it as an act of violent and unnecessary mutilation of female children. Another (and perhaps more valid) reason may be related to the gender of researchers—which until recently has been primarily male. It need hardly be mentioned that male access to women in Moslem societies is taboo for all but the closest relations. And, as Oldfield-Hayes points out in her study of infibulation in modern Sudan,

> Very few studies or reports of this practice even exist. Those that do are limited in their explanatory value for a number of reasons. Previous investigators have been content to treat the operation as a cultural retention of ancient times, which has persisted because civil and religious authorities had ignored it until about a generation ago. Moreover, most reports are almost exclusively descriptive and are the works of non-social scientists, such as British nurses and colonial administrators . . . and the strict seclusion of Sudanese females from unrelated males, especially European or any other non-Sudanese males has almost completely prevented male social scientists from interviewing female informants on the subject. . . . Sudanese society is also closely knit. These facts make it difficult for even female investigators to collect data on infibulation. (1975:617)

Similar difficulties of data collection apply to the Horn region (Grassivaro-Gallo, 1986, personal communication). In addition, colonial governments apparently felt that the passing of a penal code would suffice to eliminate the problem. This has not been the case. Complicating the issue still further is that the literature available either deals with the issue of infibulation only in passing, or no attempt is made to separate and analyze infibulation from other, milder, forms of female circumcision (e.g., partial or complete excision of the clitoris). However, all of the literature, without exception, views infibulation as an extreme form of female genital mutilation.

Function: Indigenous and Academic Perspectives

Indigenous explanations of the purpose of infibulation can be summarized as follows: (a) it has religious significance; (b) it preserves virginity until the time of marriage; (c) it is hygienic and purifying; (d) it curbs the (potentially) excessive sexuality of females; (e) it promotes fertility; and (f) it maintains general body health (e.g., Bullough, 1976:219–20; Gruenbaum, 1979:45; Oldfield-Hayes, 1975:624; Brehm, 1975/1853:-136; Lewis, 1973:430; Hayder, 1979:105; Kennedy, 1970:181; Boddy, 1982:685 and 1989:55; Koso-Thomas, 1987:5).

Indigenous concepts about both female sexuality and Islamic tradition seem to play an important part in indigenous perspectives on infibulation. Bullough, for example, recalls a Sudanese who stated that

> circumcision of females releases them from their bondage to sex, and enables them to fulfill their real destiny, as mothers. The clitoris is the basis for female masturbation; such masturbation is common in hot climates; the spiritual basis of masturbation is fantasy; in fantasy a female broods on sexual images; such brooding inevitably leads a female to spiritual infidelity, since she commits adultery in her heart, and this is the first step to physical infidelity, which is the breaker of homes. (1976:219–220)

Burton's translation of the "Perfumed Garden" (1982 referenced reprint) illustrates numerous anecdotes expressing a similar, albeit "Middle Eastern" view of female sexuality (see for example pp. 76, 97, 109-10, 112n, 164, 204, 224–25, 251).

Forni qualifies the popular explanations for the practice of both excision and infibulation as relating to Islamic religious tradition, and the express desire of men. "What is quite sure is the fact that very few men would marry a girl who has not been excised and infibulated, which does not give women any choice in the matter (1980:26).

Various academic theories have, of course, also been posited as to the function of infibulation. Nadel, for example, categorizes female circumcision of all kinds as paralleling and symbolizing a balance with males and male circumcision:

> Female circumcision never appears by itself in the Nuba Mountains: it accompanies or succeeds the adoption of juvenile male circumcision. It thus comes to express the conception of a balance of the sexes . . . that female life should parallel male life . . . where female circumcision appears, this conception of balance is deeply rooted in the social structure. (1947:487)

Whether or not we accept Nadel's viewpoint (here restricted to a study of the Nuba), it is certainly true that I have not been able to find a single case of female circumcision (excision or infibulation) without the concomitant practice of male circumcision.

A. de Villeneuve considered infibulation a precaution against rape in nomadic societies (Widstrand, 1964:122), whereas Courtecuisse (1971:108) thinks that it might have begun as a way to "depreciate" females, thereby decreasing the risk of them being taken as slaves. Rüssegger (1843:497) was of the opinion that this "sewing up" was primarily done to slave women to keep them virginal prior to selling them; earlier, Larrey (1803:414ff.) also indicated that the Turks infibulated female slaves prior to their sale. Of the more recent literature, Oldfield-Hayes makes a distinction between "manifest and latent functions." Included in the manifest functions (and as related by informants) were the notions that the honor of the group is preserved by protecting females from their own inherently oversexed natures, as well as from potential male assailants. In addition, uncircumcised females are viewed as prostitutes, and therefore are socially condemned (1975: 624). Of the latent functions, she qualifies the economic contribution such as the sums of money paid to the midwife for the initial and subsequent infibulation and reinfibulations. Moreover, their status/role would be seriously undermined "if the practice were dispensed with, and no other exclusive practice of comparable magnitude were provided for the midwives" (Oldfield-Hayes, 1975:628).

Infibulation has also been seen as an effective means of controlling population growth in an area of very restricted carrying capacity (this is considered in greater detail in chapter 3) (Oldfield-Hayes, 1975:619).

In his analysis of infibulation, Kennedy expresses the importance of the marriage factor, and suggests that circumcision and excision represent necessary preliminaries to marriage, which in turn establish the individual's position (status and role) within the community:

> Marriage had extreme importance in the lifecycles of individuals by validating adult status and ushering each person into full social standing. Islamic sanction backs this notion in the saying that 'marriage completes one's religion.' Until marriage, a Nubian is not considered fully Muslim, and thus in a real sense is not a complete social being. Men have no vote in community affairs, and women cannot validate their maturity and social worth by bearing children until they have crossed this all important threshold. Being pre-requisite to marriage, and in many ways rehearsing it, circumcision and excision are implicated in this validation of full adult standing and community membership. (1970:182)

Finally, Boddy interprets infibulation as predominantly functioning to qualify sexual identity and enclose the womb, which "protects a woman's fertility, her potential and, ultimately, that of her husband . . . the womb of an infibulated woman is an oasis, the locus of appropriate human fertility" (1982:695; 1989:chap. 1).

These various views are considered below, and again in chapter 5, in the context of the sociocultural variables which were found to be associated with infibulation.

Diffusion

The Historic Geographic and Demographic Distribution of Female Circumcision in Northeastern Africa and the Sudan

In Seligman's consideration of female mutilation (excision and infibulation) he points out that

> the geographical distribution of the custom of mutilation in Africa and the East indicates that it arose in the Hamito-Semitic area in the neighbourhood of the Red Sea. It is distributed round this area in just such a manner as might be expected if it had at first remained more or less localized among the peoples sprung from a common stock, and had then been carried far afield by the great wave of Semitic influence that followed the birth of Islam. Thus, while its distribution eastwards is sporadic, as though carried by trade and isolated colonies, it radiates from the shore of the Red Sea westwards and southwards across Africa with ever diminishing intensity. (1913:639–45)

And additionally, that

> the geographical distribution of "mutilation" fully bears out the contention that the custom is not originally Mohammedan or even Arab. . . . But since the rite existed in ancient Egypt, and is found at the present day over so great a part of Africa east of the Nile . . . it follows that the custom must be either indigenous or due to physical or cultural contact with a people who practised it and at one time or another, directly or indirectly, exerted their influence over the whole of the area under consideration. . . . If the view that mutilation is a survival from a period of undifferentiated Hamito-Semitic culture be accepted, we may conjecture that the different grades of severity of the operation prevailing in the Sudan are merely local variants of the common widely spread rite, and that the operation has, on the whole, tended to become more and more severe as it was found that it assisted to safeguard the chastity of women. It is indeed probable that among the half-bred Semites and semiticized Hamites of Eastern Africa the preservation of chastity became the whole, or at least the avowed, object of the operation at a comparatively early date, as it is at the present day among the Mohammedan tribes of the Anglo-Egyptian Sudan. (1913:639–45)

Although Seligman is here referring to all forms of female circumcision, this study generally bears out his conclusions. Map 2 indicates that the prime intensity, and most generalized distribution of infibulation occurs among nomadic Red Sea coastal area populations; as well as in the area of (historical) major trade activity and trade route intersections. (Also see map 3, chapter 2.)

Population and Cultural Diffusion

Until the end of the first millennium the Beja were the only independent pastoralists in Africa. After this time pastoralism was adopted by the 'Afar, Somali, and Galla populations (Murdock, 1959:318). The first to do so were the 'Afar, "who moved north into the Danakil semi-desert and adjacent coastal Eritrea. The second were the Galla" (Murdock, 1959:320). Cassanelli (1982:23), Trimingham (1952:9), and Jensen (1947:790) also qualify the autochthonous Galla/Oromo along the Somali frontier as cattle herding pastoralists (or possibly agro-pastoralists).

Somali pastoralists (originally only in the northern regions) are today widely distributed throughout (and outside) the Somali territory. Indeed, when considering the practice of infibulation in Djibouti (among the Somali Esa, and the 'Afar), Ethiopia (occurring primarily in Harar Province), Eritrea (among the Beni 'Amer, Beja), or its occurrence among some Galla groups in northern Kenya, we are in fact dealing with Somali related populations.[1]

It has been hypothesized that these populations originated in southeastern Ethiopia, whence they expanded to the east, south, and north by the sixteenth and seventeenth centuries. Although the Galla appear to have occupied northern (and perhaps also central and southern) Somalia prior to the Somali themselves, Murdock points out that, once the Somali expansion began, "it proceeded apace. Carrying Islam . . . the Somali expanded eastward to the Horn and southward. . . . During the fourteenth and fifteenth centuries they occupied the entire valley of the Shebelle River, reducing the agricultural Bantu inhabitants to the status of serfs" (1959:320). Also see, for example, Lewis, 1960:all; Lewis, 1965:chap. 2; Lewis, 1966:all; Lewis, 1969:45–46; Cerulli, 1957, vol. 1:60–61; Cassanelli, 1982:35–36, 78ff.; Paulitschke, 1893, vol. 1:20 ff.; Murdock, 1959:chap. 41.

H. Lewis, while agreeing that the Galla, Somali, 'Afar, and Saho probably originated in southern Ethiopia, additionally contends that perhaps we should view

> these groups as having diverged from a generally similar parent culture rather than . . . ascribing shared traits to more recent borrowing . . . the northern Somali bias towards pastoralism and their distinctive lineage system might be viewed as an adaptation to the extreme poverty of their environment, while the Rahanwin and Digil Somali, who practise mixed agriculture and do not stress lineage relations for political purposes, may be closer to the original Somali pattern. Lineage does not serve as the basis for sociopolitical life among most of the Eastern Cushitic peoples of southern Ethiopia and northern Kenya. It may be the northern Somali, therefore, who are divergent and require a special explanation, rather than the Rahanwin and Digil. (1966:42–43)[2]

These migrating populations are thought to have displaced a considerable portion of the population in the southern part of what is now Somalia (Lewis, 1965:18–20; 1969:13,41–45). By the end of the seventeenth century, the Galla had lost all their territory to the north of the Juba River to the Somali, and groups of Dir (Bimal) began reaching the southern regions, eventually establishing themselves in their present location, near Merca. Lewis informs us that the extant ethnic complexion of southern Somalia had already fairly well been established by the eighteenth century (1965:28–29).

By the early part of this century, the Darod (Somali) had conquered the Galla along the Juba, and were attempting to dominate the entire southern region as far south as the Tana River. The remaining Zengi, and some Galla, became the clients of the Darod. With the exception perhaps of such minority client groups, the Somalis represent a homogeneous population, sharing an ethnic identity with Somalis in the three adjoining states of Ethiopia, Djibouti, and Kenya.[3] This high degree of homogeneity is due primarily to their consistent "occupation of nearly four hundred thousand square miles of contiguous territory; a common language . . . a shared Islamic heritage; a widespread belief that all Somalis are ultimately descended from a small number of common ancestors; and a way of life that is overwhelmingly pastoral" (Cassanelli, 1982:3–4).

This pastoral life-style, historically traditional among Somali (and many Galla/Oromo) populations, has resulted in a decentralized (mobile) society, with no fixed territorial boundaries, having a segmentary lineage structure, with political relations based on genealogy and a system of political contracts that cut across genealogical lines, thereby allowing minorities to form alliances without necessarily being genealogically assimilated (Lewis, 1960:25; Cassanelli, 1982:5; Lewis, 1969:14; Hunt, 1951:chap. 9, 152; Lewis, 1965:4-7).

MAP 2 - General Distribution of Infibulation and Major Historical Trade Routes

•   GENERAL DISTRIBUTION OF INFIBULATION
·····   MAJOR HISTORICAL TRADE ROUTES

Today, as in the past, the majority of the population, especially in the north, remains pastoral (Silberman, 1959:559). Although several types of livestock are kept by all pastoralists in Somalia, specific regions are more conducive to breeding and rearing particular animals. In the northern and central regions (dry plains) camel breeding predominates in combination with sheep and goats, whereas cattle predominate in much of the southern region (between the Juba and Shebelle Rivers) and to some extent in the northwest, near Borama. The latter groups (cattle-breeding) are primarily agro-pastoral, and thus have more circumscribed, permanent pastures than do camel-breeding populations. This results in patron-client relationships, especially in dry seasons and cases of extreme drought, when large numbers of camel nomads become the pastoral clients of those populations with access to more stable grazing and water resources. Cassanelli points out that this type of pastoral clientship (one of three in Somalia) is

> more widespread in southern Somalia than elsewhere in the Peninsula. This has generally been interpreted as a reflection of the high degree of heterogeneity in clan composition characteristic of the southern interriver region, which has long been a refuge area for nomads fleeing environmental pressures . . . in the lands to the north and north west. From a strictly socio-anthropological perspective, clientship can be viewed as a way of incorporating lineage segments of diverse origins into larger political confederations; it is seen as a way of increasing the strength and cohesion of social groups in a region where agnatic ties are weak or diffuse (1982:75-78).

This genealogical heterogeneity, characteristic of southern Somalia, distinguishes it from the rest of the country.

The population of Somalia is composed of two principal parts, the Somali and the Sab, with the majority of the pastoral population belonging to the first group (Lewis, 1969:15).[4] Each of these divisions is represented by several major "clan-families," which are further subdivided into numerous clans and subclans, and primary lineages, with the latter functioning as corporate political units. These units often combine to form what is known as a "dia" (bloodwealth) paying group, to whom they owe their principle loyalty (the membership size of these dia-paying units varies from group to group) (Lewis, 1961:4-7; Lewis, 1980:243; Cassanelli, 1982:17-19).[5]

> All lineages which act corporately do so first because of their agnatic basis, and secondly through an explicit treaty defining the terms of their collective unity. In a formal sense, contract operates structurally as at once a unifying and dividing principle within the various spheres of extended agnation. Genealogies represent generally the widest range of possible political unity by dividing and uniting groups of kinsmen according to the ancestors from whom they stem. Contract galvanises the diffuse and manifold bonds of kinship at any point and through any ancestor, giving rise to opposed political units. (Lewis, 1961:3)

This segmentation is thus relative, and by no means represents permanent divisions. Those groups functioning as a unit on one occasion may represent mutually hostile units on another. Because the area inhabited by Somali pastoralists and their relations in similar habitats in adjacent nation-states provides only sparse grazing resources, there exists a constant competition for access to pasture and water. This results in frequent feuding, and it is here that agnatic solidarity becomes imperative (Lewis, 1962a:6). The combination of an extremely harsh environment and the concomitant need for an extensive support network is also related to the practice of clan exogamy among Somali pastoralists.[6] Here, even though (exogamous) affinal (marriage) ties in this (patrilineal) system are, and remain, secondary to agnatic ties, they nevertheless produce the alliance formations necessary for purposes of defense, strategic resource sharing (and the co-operative management of herds), as well as provide an extensive support network necessary in times of crises (e.g., during periods of extended drought).

> Clans were typically the largest exogamous units in Somali society: marriage outside the clan was encouraged because it helped to widen the circle of potential allies that could be called up in time of need. The clan was also a territorial unit. There were certain grazing areas associated with each clan and "home wells" to which clan members returned during the dry season. However, because nomadic movements were conditioned by unpredictable and widely scattered rains, and because pasture was regarded as a gift from God to all Somalis, herding units from different clans were often interspersed in the same district. Clansmen were often widely separated from one another through much of the year. (Cassanelli, 1982:19)

The territorial expansion of the pastoral populations (outlined above) and the trade related expansion (considered below) may together have generated the expansion both of Islam and infibulation. Of course, this presumes (1) that the intensity and range of the practice of infibulation was, historically, greatest in the neighborhood of the Red Sea; (2) that the practice of infibulation has historically been primarily practiced by nomadic pastoralists living at minimal subsistence level; (3) that ecological conditions remain such that complex alliances must be forged at all levels of social structure in order to maintain subsistence level for herds and humans alike; (4) that these same ecological factors conditioned a history of population mobility and expansion together with the development of patron-client relations; and (5) that these same pastoralists were, historically, indispensible to, and engaged in, trading, thereby further extending their physical presence and influence.

Trade Routes and Slavery

By the tenth century, traders (and Islam) were entering the interior of Africa along three primary routes (see map 2): (1) *North Africa*: Of the three primary caravan routes through this area, two are relevant for the distribution of infibulation: the central route, from Tunisia toward Chad, and the eastern route, along the Nile valley to Darfur and Kanem; (2) via the *Red Sea coast*; (3) via the *ports of the Indian Ocean.*

Because all of the main trade centers were strongly influenced by Islam, they acted as a vehicle for the dissemination of this faith. Caravan traders also played a crucial role in the spread of Islam, especially the large camel-owning non-Arab nomads such as the Berbers of northwestern Africa and the Somali and 'Afar of northeastern Africa (Lewis, 1980a:20). Lewis points out that Islam made its

> earliest, most concerted inroads in the Eastern Sudan and the Horn of Africa. While the southern part of what is today the Sudan Republic, with its largely Nilotic and negroid populations remained until recently for the most part shielded from any intensive Muslim influence, the north was from early times subject to Islamic penetration . . . from the seventh century onwards Arab immigrants began to move south into the northern Sudan in an ever increasing tide. (1980a:4)

This Arab influx did not occur in either Ethiopia or the Horn of Africa, and Islamic influence in this region was primarily effective among the "Saho, 'Afar (Danakil), and Somali, and more recently . . . with less . . . success . . . the Oromo. . . . In this region as a whole the main gateway for Muslim influence has been the Red Sea and the Indian Ocean coasts" (Lewis, 1980a:6).

Islamic northeastern Africa (and especially the Sudan) has not only been the site for trading goods, but has also historically been raided for slaves. Arab traders exported large numbers of these slaves to the Moslem world, as Islamic law does not permit the enslavement of Moslems (Hasan, 1967:46; Ashtor, 1976:106; Lapidus, 1988;531–35). Hasan informs us that in Abyssinia, "even . . . the inhabitants stole the children of one another and sold them to merchants" (1967:47). Although it is difficult to speak in numbers and to differentiate percentages of males and females taken into slavery in any given period, there is some indication that certain populations were preferred for given tasks. Nubian females, for example, were popular as midwives and nurses, and the more attractive ones served as concubines. In fact, both Nubian and Abyssinian females appear to have been in high demand even in the earlier stages of Islamic history (Hasan, 1967:49).

Although there is some indication that infibulation was carried out on these female slaves by Turkish slave traders in order to prevent their getting pregnant, this cannot actually be substantiated (Cloudsley, 1981:86). However, it is noteworthy that the

> distribution of infibulation in the Sudan in the 19th Century appears to correspond with the north-south caravan route to the 'interior' of Africa, which linked Sennar with Egypt by way of the Nile; and the east-west caravan route traversing the Wadia (Tchad) and then across the western desert of Sudan through Kordofan, so linking Darfur with Suakin on the Red Sea Coast and thence to Massawa the port of Eritrea. Likewise, the caravan route to Ethiopia followed the Blue Nile from Sennar and centred on Gondar (the ancient capital in western Abyssinia). These were also the slave trade routes to the South and Bahr al-Ghazal in south-western Sudan. (Cloudsley 1981:86; also see Beachey [Collection of Documents . . .], 1976:53ff)

Although infibulation might have been carried out on female slaves by the slave traders themselves, this does not explain why it remains a "women's" affair today. Courtecuisse is of the opinion that those populations directly and extremely affected by the slave trade (especially by the loss of their women and female children) might have infibulated their female offspring very early in life to discourage their being taken as slaves (1971:108). On the other hand, Hayder points out (in his study of the Shaiqiyya) that circumcision for both males and females "denotes Islam and Arabism," and that to be noncircumcised "denotes mean origin, as only slaves and some non-Moslem people were not circumcised" (1979:105).

As can be surmised from the above, there is insufficient data to determine any actual association between slavery and infibulation; yet it is curious that the main slave-supply sources comprised noninfibulation-practicing populations, while the main slave-receivers (in the Sudan) comprised infibulation-practicing populations (see McLoughlin, 1962:360–61 for a listing of both supply sources and receivers).

Also of potential interest here is the question of the universality of the practice of infibulation in those regions where it is known to occur. Specifically, I have not been able to determine if "client" populations, related to primary infibulating groups, also practice infibulation. In Somalia for example, client groups, known collectively as "sab," are distinguished from the 'noble' Somali. The former provide primary services for the latter, to include specialized crafts such as metal and leather working, and hairdressing. The women of one of these groups (the Midgan) also function as midwives, and are called upon to perform the operation of infibulation (Lewis, 1961:14, and 1969:53).

If it is the case that the women of these client groups are not infibulated (nor were so in the past), then infibulation may function as a direct status indicator. If infibulation did indeed differentiate status in the past, then it is also possible that Turkish slave traders infibulated southern women (and any others from pagan, noninfibulation-practicing regions) in order to *increase their value, by increasing their status through mutilation* (i.e., infibulation). Although we cannot adequately research this question historically, it would theoretically be possible to determine whether or not women from these client populations are currently infibulated. Field research could be initiated to explore this question.

The Role of Islam

As was pointed out above, the geographic area penetrated by Islam coincides with the general distribution of infibulation, and all populations known to practice infibulation are (to one degree or other) of the Islamic faith. Even non-Islamic populations (in the same geographic area) who adopt this practice do so concomitant with their conversion to Islam (both of which are usually a result of pressure from their Moslem neighbors). This is not to imply that the practice of infibulation is condoned by Orthodox Islam; on the contrary. However, those populations practicing infibulation have regularly interpreted it as being in keeping with the traditions of the Islamic faith.

It is not possible to substantiate either a direct historical association between Islam and infibulation, or the existence of infibulation prior to the incursion of Arab populations into the area. Interestingly, however, although some of the (indigenous) pagan populations of southern Sudan, as well as some Galla (Oromo) populations (who migrated into Somaliland and Ethiopia [Lipsky, 1962]) practice partial or total clitoral excision of females, none (unless recently influenced by Islam [e.g., Nadel, 1947:223]) appear to have (had) a tradition of infibulation.

That infibulation (to date) has been found only among Moslem populations, and that it does not seem to occur among groups considered to be indigeneous to the area, does not imply that a direct correlation exists between Islam and infibulation. There is some indication (e.g., Seligman,

1913) that most (if not all) infibulation-practicing populations have traditionally practiced female excision, and that infibulation represents, at best, an aberration of excision. As such, infibulation would only be an indirect correlate of conversion to Islam. One example of how such an aberration of a traditional practice can occur is provided by L. Leakey in his study of the Kikuyu problem (in parts of the Kikuyu Reserve in Kenya). He observed that, although the circumcision operation varied from district to district, initially it involved "a simple clitoridectomy . . . that in some parts . . . was accompanied by cuts on the upper part of the labia majora" (1931:278).

There had also been a traditional custom (besides the sex organ operation at initiation) involving the making of "a number of small cuts on the pubic area of young girls prior to initiation. These resulted in a number of small keloids, which were supposed to give increased pleasure to the sexual act when performed, later, in married life. . . . A similar custom is common in parts of the Congo" (1931:279). Leakey maintains that Christian missionaries (in the area) were instrumental in forcing this practice underground, through their determined campaign against female circumcision. This was complicated by a (local) misinterpretation of the "virgin" in "Virgin Mary," (which was probably related to a lack of concise instruction, definition, and clarity about this subject on the part of missionary teachers). Specifically, the concept "virgin," even when referencing the Virgin Mary was locally translated (and interpreted) to mean essentially "an unmarried girl who has been through the initiation ceremony, and who has therefore undergone the operation of the sex organs" (1931:279). One result of this confusion was that, whereas

> in the old days the operation on the girls at initiation could only be performed by professional operators (aruithia) who had served a long period of apprenticeship before being allowed to perform the operation themselves, recently, especially in or near the townships, women who style themselves aruithia, but who have had no real training in their adopted profession, perform the operation, and it is certain that they have increased its severity through lack of skill and knowledge. (1931:280)

Leakey argues that what began as clitoral excision inadvertently developed into a practice more closely resembling infibulation, and that the increased severity of this operation was the result of Christian missionary activity. The dubious level of orthodoxy of both the Islamic religion and the Arabic language (among the inhabitants of northeastern Africa and Sudan), may have resulted in a similar "creative" indigenous, linguistic, and/or social (interpretive) rendering of such terms as seclusion (isolation), protection, clean, pure, virginal, honor.

Even though it is not inconceivable that erroneous interpretations might have been made during the interaction between early Islamic traders and the local population, we have no way to test such a hypothesis at this time. It would, however, partly explain why the severity of the infibulation operation is geographically variable, being most extreme among Red Sea coastal populations (who were the first to be influenced by Islam), and diminishing in extremity in its dispersal westward, where it usually constitutes a fairly recent adoption. Further field research would be necessary in order to determine the exact regional and "operational" variability of this practice. Nevertheless, while Islam is hardly the cause of infibulation, it is not incompatible with the persistent retention of this practice:

- it perpetuates, and often amplifies a low status position for females, as well as prescribing their physical and/or symbolic seclusion; although complete physical seclusion of women is usual only among sedentary populations;

- it supports the view that women have an uncontrolled sexual nature (from the onset of menstruation to menopause), and interprets the sexual purity of women as representing the "honor" of the family; and finally,

- its encouragement of polygamy perpetuates, and may exacerbate, male absenteeism (especially among nomadic and seminomadic populations). It may also function to trigger infibulation among populations already excising their females. Thus, where Islam introduces, or reinforces

the practice of female excision or clitoridectomy among a people who traditionally carry out such other genital mutilations as infibulation, this conjunction may serve to add new weight, though quite without warrant, to the latter. To some degree this is apparently the case in those parts of the Sudan Republic, Ethiopia, and the Somali Republic where women are regularly infibulated. (Lewis, ed., 1980:69)

Because Islam permeates, and indeed regulates all levels of the social, political, and legal system, its tenents are deemed sacrosanct. Consequently, as an institutional structure, it is virtually imperviousness to the effects of external exposure; especially where only a small proportion of the population is confronted with conditions outside their immediate environment. As such, Islamic northeast African societies can be conceived as closed systems. This position is considered in chapter 3.

Notes

1. In "Peoples of the Horn of Africa" (1969 reprint of 1955 publication:11) Lewis points out that the Somali, 'Afar, and Saho are very closely related and "belong, with the Galla and Beja, to the Southern Cushitic peoples." They exhibit both a common culture and uniform material culture. All are pastoral, primarily camel nomadic (although some also keep cattle), and all are Moslems. In "A Pastoral Democracy", he qualifies this: although the Somali no doubt share certain affinities with the

> South Eastern Cushites (or Hamites)—the 'Afar, Saho, Galla, and Beja, they display marked differences in social and political structure. Thus, the 'Afar . . . who occupy similar country on the northwest frontier of Somaliland and whom Somali raid and despise and rarely marry, have a different territorial and apparently more formal system of government . . . those 'Afar institutions (such as the true levirate) which differ from their own, excite ridicule. Similarly, while Somali again recognize some degree of relationship with the Galla tribes . . . who border them to the west and south, and whom they also raid and scorn, they do not share their age-set system. This was . . . to some extent adopted by the Daarood to the south of the Juba River and historically at least distinguishes them from their northern clansmen. (1961:10-11)

2. Further discussion of this position (and further delineation of the variability of these populations) can be found in, for example, I. M. Lewis (1960:21,25,27,36-38; 1960a:227-28; 1961:7-13; 1965:4-7 and chap. 2; 1969:45ff.); and Cassanelli (1982:78ff.) Relative to the 'divergence' of the northern Somali, it is interesting to note that by the sixteenth-seventeeth century, the present distribution of northern Somali was already evident, their expansion into the south being of more recent date: "I found no record in British Somaliland today of any of the other Somali groups who traditionally came from Northern Somaliland to settle in the south, except in the case of the Hawiye of whom a small group, the Rer Fiqi Sinni, are found amongst the Dulbahante (Darod) clan of the east of the Protectorate" (Lewis, 1960:37). Thus, although the autochthonous Somali may indeed have been agro-pastoral, neither their immediate nor long-term aim seems to have been the occupation of a region conducive to this type of subsistence base.

3. See Lewis (1969:13-55, 155-60, 174-76) and Paulitschke (1893, vol. 1:41-68) for a general overview of demographic distribution. The following index was taken from Silberman (1959:560).

TABLE 1.1: Estimated Total Somali Population, and Percentage and Distribution of Nomads

Territory	Est. Somali Population	% age Nomadic	Est. no. Nomadic
Italian Somalia	1,300,000	66	867,000
British Somalia	600,000	85	514,000
Ethiopia Ogaden Region	300,000	85	257,000
French Somalia (Bjibouti)	27,000	20	5,000
Kenya	70,000	80	56,000
Total	2,297,000	74	1,699,000

These areas together comprise the entire area of current Somalia, Djibouti, northeastern Kenya, and the easternmost region of Ethiopia (Ogaden). The major tribal groupings occupying these areas are the Somali, Sab, and Darod (see the appendix for primary subdivisions).

4. See I. M. Lewis (1969) and Paulitschke (1893) for a more detailed delineation of the tribes and their affiliates in the Horn. Also, "Conformity and Contrast in Somali Islam" (Lewis, 1980:240–52) provides an excellent overview of the structural differences between northern and southern populations. Specifically contrasted are the dia-paying groups of the north in contradistinction to the lineage confederations of the south (which are territorially based, noncorporate political units).

5. Cassanelli (1982:19–20) defines the dia-paying groups as "the mobilization of kinsmen for joint military action or resource management. . . . This was a group within a clan of patrilineal kinsmen, usually from the same or several closely related lineages, who agreed to work and fight together and, most important, to pay the dia, or blood-wealth, in common." Lewis (1962a:1) also informs us that a person usually acts as a "member of a 'dia-paying group' . . . within the segmentation of his primary lineage." It is the dia-paying group which is the "basic jural and political unit of northern Somali society." See I. M. Lewis, "Peoples of the Horn of Africa" (1969a), "A Pastoral Democracy" (1961), and Lewis (1980:243–45) for a more detailed discussion relative to dia-paying groups (and a delineation of the major clan-families (and their subdivisions).

6. Clans are divided into a "series of component patrilineages. . . . Within the clan the largest most clearly defined subsidiary group can conveniently be termed a 'primary lineage.' This unit usually represents the limits of exogamy; amongst its segments marriage is forbidden, although not considered incestuous, and most marriages are between people of different primary lineages" (Lewis, 1962a:1).

2

The Socioeconomic Distribution
of Infibulation

A primary problem in analyzing the function of infibulation is its current occurrence among populations at all subsistence levels, that is, populations currently practicing infibulation are distributed all along the pastoral-rural-urban continuum. Consequently, of preeminent concern for this study was a determination of the geographic and demographic distribution of infibulation-practicing populations, together with their historical subsistence mode(s).

Geographic Distribution: The search for the geographic distribution of infibulation was initiated by surveying all available literature generally concerned with the practice of female circumcision, and all available historic and current demographic sources. Compositely viewed, these sources indicated that the general geographic area *in which the practice of infibulation constitutes a widespread phenomenon* includes the northern Sudan (and related populations in eastern Chad), the coastal regions of Ethiopia, Eritrea, Djibouti, and northern Somalia (i.e., Islamic northeastern Africa).[1]

Demographic Distribution: Since demographic information is geographically (or nationally) delineated, a discussion of infibulation must, perforce, be within the context of its geographic or "national" occurrence.[2] As close an examination as the literature allowed was made of the actual populations occupying the region demarcated as Islamic northeastern Africa, to determine the presence or absence of the practice of infibulation. The appendix represents a listing of those populations about which sufficient information was available to have warranted inclusion and does not, consequently, represent a complete listing of all the tribal populations in these regions. It does, however, include all those populations known to practice infibulation. Because infibulation was

29

found to have no tradition in either the southern Sudan or the highland areas of Ethiopia, these regions have been excluded from this study (although some of the major population groups are mentioned in the appendix).

Unfortunately, demographic and ethnographic information for the geographic area covered by this study is limited in quantity, and usually incomplete. Consequently, the information provided below and in the appendix has been compiled from a variety of sources, dating from the last century to the present; earlier, albeit sporadic accounts were also used when accessible. Although this method facilitated a preliminary identification of those populations known to have traditionally practiced infibulation, *general census data limitations precluded any numerical estimation of the current, or historical, extent of this practice.* Similarly, some of the populations listed as practicing infibulation may, in very recent years, have opted for a less severe form of circumcision for their females. The converse may also be the case. Wherever corroborating information was available, both the past and present forms have been mentioned (see the appendix).

Subsistence Modes: Much of the literature concerned with infibulation assumes a greater socioeconomic variability among populations practicing it than in fact exists (e.g., Oldfield-Hayes, 1975; Levin, 1980; Hosken, 1982). And, although it certainly is true that infibulation is practiced by urban, village, seminomadic, and nomadic populations, and that an increasing number of the latter are (or are becoming) sedentarized, most of these populations have either a (relatively recent) pastoral origin, or have maintained kinship or economic associations with pastoral populations (see below). Indeed, even the majority of the populations currently practicing infibulation are either pastoral (nomadic or seminomadic) or agro-pastoral, or were so until very recently. Consequently, this chapter includes a general overview of the various forms of pastoralism, and urban-pastoral interaction patterns prevalent in the geographic areas under consideration. Individual geographic areas and, where possible, their populations, can be found in the appendix. Map 3 indicates the distribution of infibulation according to subsistence patterns.

Pastoralism in Northeastern Africa and the Sudan

Generally speaking, pastoral nomadism constitutes a primary dependence upon livestock and a way of life that is based on population mobility in response to the pasturage needs of herds and flocks.[3] A group may be considered "more" or "less" nomadic, however, depending on the degree of necessary mobility, which brings us to the problem of qualifying a given pastoral population as nomadic, seminomadic, agro-pastoral, or other.

Since the intention here is not to provide a treatise on pastoralism, the following constitutes only a brief overview of the forms of pastoralism relevant to this study, and as they prevail throughout eastern Africa (following Brandstroem et al., 1979).

- *Nomadic pastoralists* include only those totally dependent upon their livestock, being wholly nomadic, and living in portable dwellings. This does not preclude their consumption of agriculture products, it simply means that they are not the producers of these products. Such populations may be camel, sheep and goat, cattle or horse breeders, or all of these, either in seasonal or annual migratory movement in search of pastures.

- *Semi-nomadic* are similar to those above, with the exception that they practice minimal cultivation (usually at a base camp), and usually migrate seasonally.

- *Agro-pastoral* inhabit areas less arid than either nomadic or seminomadic pastoralists. They are village dwelling agriculturalists, with animal husbandry an important supplementary activity. Herds may, however, have to be separated from the main households during a dry period, and moved to seasonal camps.

Although nomadic pastoralists represent a highly mobile population, they must not be viewed as completely isolated populations. Carlstein notes that "a close contact between pastoralism and agriculture persists; if not through the direct participation of nomads in cultivation activities, then through raiding, trading, or other forms of interaction" (1982:104). And Brandstroem et al. point out the interdependence of all types of pastoral and sedentary societies.

> There are no pastoral societies which subsist exclusively on pastoral products, although there may be groups within a society which during certain periods consume no vegetarian food . . . On the contrary, there are even pastoral nomads, for which cereals constitute the bulk of the food consumption . . . the specialized production of pastoralists and the subsequent deficiency in grain necessitate the production of a pastoral surplus which can be sold or bartered in exchange for cereals. It follows that the existence of societies producing an agricultural surplus is a necessary condition for pastoral specialization. (Brandstroem et al., 1979:12) (The Kababish are a northern Sudanese example of pastoral nomads whose primary dietary consumption is in the form of cereals [Asad, 1970:30].)

MAP 3 - Distribution of Infibulation According to Subsistence

1   NOMADIC (camel/cattle) PASTORALISTS
2   SEMI-NOMADIC PASTORALISTS (cattle)
3   AGRO-PASTORALISTS
4   AGRICULTURALISTS WITH HUSBANDRY DEPENDENCE

Generally speaking, "nomadic" pastoralists in northeastern Africa are primarily camel, rather than cattle herders (although many cattle herders have both, strict camel nomads in these geographic regions have only sheep and goats in addition to camels). Cattle herders more often fall into the category of seminomadic (although there are exceptions to this, e.g., the Baggara, Masai, Samburu, Beni Amer). Cattle are also often kept by sedentary, agricultural populations. Brandstroem et al. (1979:10) point out that societies labelled as being "pastoral" often include (a) primary herders who practice secondary agriculture (e.g., the Jie and Karimojong); and (b) primary herders who practice minimal or no agriculture (e.g., the Masai and Samburu). Similarly, populations whose main subsistence activity is agriculture (with secondary animal husbandry), are also usually qualified as "pastoralists." Brandstroem et al. have clarified this ambiguity to some extent, retaining the qualification of (a) and (b) above as pastoralists, while defining agiculturalists practicing secondary animal husbandry as agro-pastoralist (1979:10). Maps 4 and 5 generally indicate the subsistence potential of the regions under discussion in this study.

Pastoral-Rural-Urban Interaction and Infibulation

Since infibulation-practicing populations currently comprise pastoral, agro-pastoral, rural, and urban populations, any study of the perpetuation of this custom must take pastoral-rural-urban interaction patterns into consideration.[4] Although many infibulation-practicing populations currently inhabit towns or are agriculturalists or migrant laborers, all appear to have either a recent history of pastoralism, a continued close association with pastoralists, or are historically (genealogically) related to pastoral populations. In this sense these populations differ from those occupying Middle Eastern towns (see below) (Trimingham, 1949:81ff.; Kesby, 1977:51ff., 244, 250; Adams, 1977:54ff.; Lipsky, 1962:6ff.; Lewis, 1961: introduction; Lobban, 1977:3).

An important factor in the historical interaction between the rural and pastoral sectors lies in the negative attitude toward working the land; cultivation is viewed as a demeaning activity. In the Sudan, for example, prior to both the Mahdiya and Condominium periods of the latter nineteenth and first half of the twentieth century, animal husbandry was of primary importance as the major source of wealth, and cultivation was accomplished mainly by slaves. Slavery was eliminated during the Condominium period of British occupation (see, e.g., McLoughlin, 1962: especially 355–59, 361, 377–78).

MAP 4 - General Distribution of Agriculturalists, Agro-Pastoralists, and Pastoralists

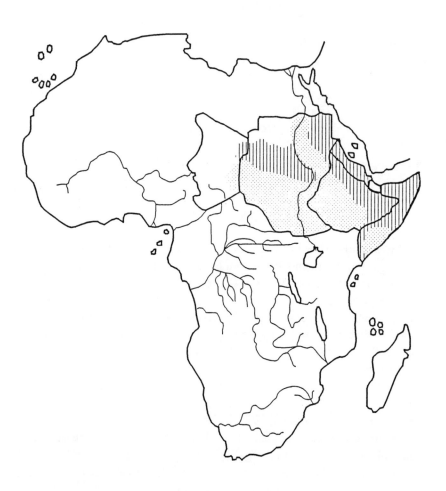

AGRO (pastoral)

PASTORAL (all)

MAP 5 - General Distribution of Pastoralists

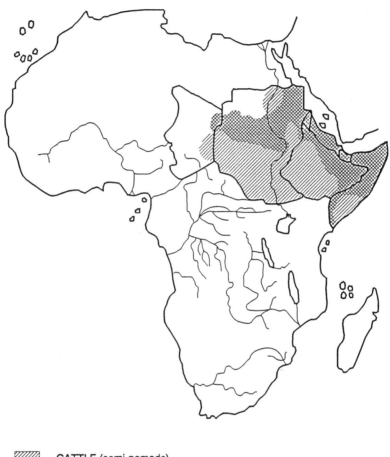

▨▨▨ CATTLE (semi-nomads)

▨▨▨ CAMELS (sheep/goats - nomads)

The Sudan

The population of the Sudan, according to the 1973 census, has been estimated at between 16 and 18 million. Of this number, about 12 million inhabit the six northern provinces. The majority are Moslems. The other 4 million, who trace their origins to black Africa, inhabit the three southern provinces (see map 6) (Nelson, 1973:2; U.S. Dept. of State, 1982:1; UN Econ. and Social Council, 1981:3; Statistik des Auslandes, 1982:13).[5]

MAP 6 - Provinces of the Sudan and Population Density

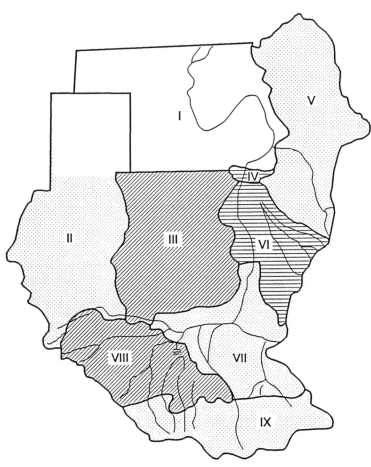

PROVINCES

I   NORTHERN
II   DARFUR
III   KORDOFAN
IV   KHARTOUM
V   KASSALA
VI   BLUE NILE
VII   UPPER NILE
VIII   BAR EL GHAZAL
IX   EQUATOIRA

APPROXIMATE POPULATION DENSITY
per km^2

less than 3

3 to 5

6 to 10

35 to 81

Source: Adapted from 'Statistik des Auslandes 1982'

Essentially the Sudan is an agricultural and pastoral country, and its economy is on that basis (MacMichael, 1954:172). In the northern Nile valley area irrigation farming, apart from government mechanized projects, is accomplished by small-scale subsistence farmers. Approximately 50 percent of the rest of the population of the northern provinces are either nomadic herders or move seasonally. In the southern provinces, the populations practice mixed subsistence (e.g., agriculture, husbandry, or cultivation, cattle herding, etc.).

Industrial development generally remains limited, and cities and towns are few. Of the ten cities and towns with populations exceeding twenty thousand only the tri-city area of Khartoum, Khartoum North, and Omdurman (excepting perhaps industrialized Arbara and Port Sudan), resemble modern cosmopolitan centers (Nelson, 1973:2). The inhabitants of other towns, while formally subservient to central authority, still maintain a primary attachment and dependence upon family, tribe, or region (Nelson, 1973:3).

Of course, it must be kept in mind that "urban" centers constitute not only a relatively recent development (late ninteenth and twentieth centuries), but are essentially foreign enclaves; their most important officials and many of their residents being non-Nubian (Adams, 1977:55). Moreover, while it is probably the case that "all areas defined as urban have a relatively high population density, not all high population concentrations possess urban characteristics" (Geiser, 1967:145).

Indeed, in most of the urban centers in the geographic regions included in this study, the proportion of peasants usually outweighs that of actual "urbanites" (Sjoberg, 1955). Similarly, there is a gap between strict rural agriculture and husbandry dependent agriculturalists. Adams points out that, although the majority of Nubia's population remain peasant farmers to the present day, they can be distinguished from Egyptian peasants by their greater dependence on animal husbandry (1977:53). This is related not only to subsistence necessity, but also to the reversion of sedentary populations to pastoralism during periods of political or migratory stress (especially during the major periods of Arab tribal migration into the area, e.g., the fifteenth and sixteenth centuries).

> Historically, the importance of the pastoral element in Nubian life cannot be overstated. It was the earliest basis for sedentary life, and has continued to provide both a supplement and an alternative to farming in all later times . . . the Nubian could and at times did abandon the pursuit of agriculture and revert to a pastoral way of life when natural resources or political stability failed. (Adams, 1977:54)

Added to the historical reversion to pastoralism is the relatively recent sedentarization of many nomadic and seminomadic groups in both towns and villages. Some of these groups even represent the "founding populations" of many towns and villages (in the not so distant past) (see, for example, Barclay, 1964:10). Even longer established villages and towns had neither a stable population nor structure, and were considerably altered during the British occupational period. Similarly, the Egyptian and Mahdiya periods destroyed or altered tribal structure such that today the majority of villages are heterogeneous. Trimingham speculates that this could be the result of population migration or even remnants of the Mahdist army (Trimingham; 1949:19-21).

The combination of flexible subsistence and a late urbanization base was an important factor in the continued social and economic interaction between sedentary and nonsedentary populations in the Sudan. This interaction, whether on the basis of trade, slavery, lineage alliances, strategic resource alliances, or other, appears to have been in direct evidence as late as the beginning of this century, when neither social, economic, political, "urban", or population stability existed. MacMichael commented that any thought of an independent self-governing Sudan was not worth entertaining at the beginning of the twentieth century. This was due to the combination of famine and disease, internecine warfare, a declining population, slave raiding, and civil strife and revolt (1954:73).

Today the Republic of the Sudan (which formed the Anglo-Egyptian Condominium from 1899 until 1955) constitutes a political rather than a distinct geographic or ethnological area. Until 1924 there was no distinction between the areas of East and Western Sudan. At that time, a separation was drawn to the west of Lake Chad, and by 1965 the boundary was the lake itself (it being a geographic feature). Herskovits delineates the area of Eastern Sudan as reaching from the Nile to Lake Chad, and "lying west of the northernmost portion of the East African Cattle area. It comprehends the southern part of the Sudanese Republic, the Republic of Chad and northern part of the Central African Republic" (1962:72). He points out that there have been no adequate descriptions of cultures extant in the Eastern Sudan area, and that data that is available is fragmentary, and has, for the most part, been collected by "interested amateurs rather than . . . trained ethnographers" (1962:73). The "eastern" Sudan continues to be heterogeneous, and inadequately studied.

On a broader scale, this historically inherent problem of population heterogeneity has also hindered the qualification and treatment of this region as a "cultural area." Horowitz outlines this problem and notes that the nature of the contemporary eastern Sudan becomes more clear "when the focus is shifted from the single society or tribe, to the complex multi-tribal level, in which pastoralists, farmers, and townsmen, because of historico-ecologic factors, are linked in an intricate network of economic and political interdependence" (1967:389-90, 396).

On the contextual level, Abdel Ghaffar, in his discussion of the Rufa'a, provides an excellent example of the mechanics of heterogeneous population interdependence. (For a detailed description of this interdependence, see Abdel Ghaffar, 1973.) He points out that the relationship between nomad and sedentary is symbiotic rather than hostile, and that this symbiosis is facilitated, at least partially, by the "elite members" of these communities.[6] Because the elite act as value managers and mediators between their two communities, they have sole access to privileged information (Abdel Ghaffar, 1973:92). Abdel Ghaffar uses the Abu Ruf ruling family of the Rufa'a al-Hoi tribe as an example of a tribal elite group, whose positions of authority within the tribe are justified and legitimized by patrilineal descent ideology. Similarly, it is through these positions that "they have command over the important economic resources in the area and hence exert major influence on the fate of the community, being the main decision-making body" (1973:77).

The "community" in this case includes both nomadic and sedentary populations inhabiting that area that share the same Rural Council, Abu Hugar (Abdel Ghaffar, 1973:75). Generally speaking, the interdependence between sedentary and pastoral populations, as exemplified by the Rufa'a, remains prevalent in the Sudan today. It is evident in the continuing dependence on husbandry, the relatively recent tendency to sedentarize, the frequent temporary settlement of nomadic populations, the economic (market) interaction of ethnically distinct populations, and the continuing process of sedentarization of nomadic and seminomadic populations (MacMichael, 1967:38).[7] However, although the tendency to sedentarize has been a regular feature of the entire Nile valley, the continued dependence on husbandry will no doubt remain a valid economic facet of Sudanese society until the more expansive agricultural projects have not only proven their long-term economic viability, but also their success in achieving social stability. The latter is not only contingent upon the actual manifest productivity of these projects, however, but upon the development of a positive "work ethic" concept associated with agriculture and related activities.[8]

Of course, it could be contended that the doubling of the population, between 1954 and 1972, in the three largest cities (with smaller towns also growing rapidly), had a considerable effect on the percentage of the total population engaged in agriculture. The vast majority (85–90 percent) of these populations were listed as being sedentary farmers, most of whom grew subsistence crops in addition to at least one cash crop. The remainder of the population was represented either by nomadic herdsmen, or transhumant cattle herders who combined cultivation with seasonal herding (Nelson, 1973:50). However, the Sudanese figures of 14 percent for fully nomadic populations (in 1973) was a result of the difficulties of defining nomads, seminomads, etc. This was primarily due to the narrow definition of these terms. If, however, populations moving either seasonally or at regular intervals are included, this figure rises to 40 percent (including those groups falling into the category agro-pastoral) (Nelson, 1973:69; Abdel Ghaffar, 1976:2–4).

Barbour, in his geographic/demographic study of the northern and southern Sudan, showed cultivation as occupying an increasingly higher proportion of the population than animal rearing. Although the southern Sudan plays an important role in these statistics, there seems little doubt that sedentarization is on the increase, as can be seen in table 2.1, which indicates the general distribution of herders and farmers, based on the 1955–1956 census (reproduced from Barbour 1964:212–14; also see map 7).

The "herders" percentages for the Blue Nile, Equatoria, Kordofan, the Upper Nile, Bahr el Ghazal, Khartoum, and to some extent Darfur, represent primarily cattle pastoralists (who may also have some camels for transportation or food, and who (to some degree) qualify as agro-pastoralists). The "herders" percentages for Kassala, Northern Province, and to some extent Darfur, represent primarily camel nomads.

It must also be noted that not all subdivisions of a given tribal population, in a given region, share an identical subsistence base. The Rubatab, for example, are listed in the appendix as agriculturalists, but have at least one subdivision (the 'Awadia) that is largely nomadic (camel herders).[9]

MAP 7 - Sudan:
Distribution of Agriculturalists, Agro-Pastoralists, and Pastoralists

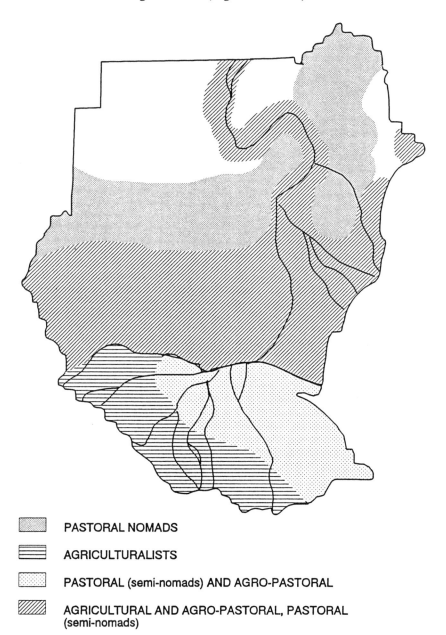

PASTORAL NOMADS

AGRICULTURALISTS

PASTORAL (semi-nomads) AND AGRO-PASTORAL

AGRICULTURAL AND AGRO-PASTORAL, PASTORAL
(semi-nomads)

TABLE 2.1: Farmers and Farm Laborers and Animal Owners and Herders
(in percentages)

Province	Animal Owners/Herders Percentage of all gainfully employed	Farmers/Farm Laborers Percentage of all gainfully employed
Blue Nile (E. Central)	9	74
Equatoria (South)	18	74
Kordofan (Central)	24	69
Darfur (W. Central)	27	67
Upper Nile (S. Central)	32	64
Northern (N. Central)	14	61
Bahr el Ghazal (S. West)	36	60
Kassala (N. East)	39	46
Khartoum (Central)	9	29
SUDAN	23	64

Some Examples of the Pastoral-Rural-Urban Interaction. The Three-Towns area represents the primary "urban" region of the Sudan, and includes Khartoum, Khartoum North (Bahri), and Omdurman. Although the Three-Towns area has long been inhabited, it is not known exactly when the "cities" were founded. Slatin mentions that the "great town" of Omdurman was but "a small village occupied by a few brigands" ten years before (vol. 3, 1896:164). The area's development as an urban region is thought to have begun during and after the Mahdiya period, in the late nineteenth century (see also ref. to Lobban, below; Rehfisch, 1964:35–47).

Generally speaking, the population of the Three-Towns is very heterogeneous; primarily the result of population migrations into the area. El-Awad Galal al Din states that the area evidenced a continuous influx of population from all over the Sudan, and that "all the nation's regions and tribes are represented among its inhabitants" (1980:606). Also contributing to the heterogeneity of the Three-Towns population is the turbulent political history of the Sudan and continuing population disruption through, for example, relocation, sedentarization, reversion to pastoralism. Lobban, while primarily discussing the process of "class formation," does provide an excellent example of population settlement and disruption in the Three-Towns area. He informs us that the two communities of Burri al Mahas and Tuti Island, both of which are in the Three-Towns agglomeration, were founded some centuries prior to the growth of the Three-Towns area. These communities were originally settled by Nubian Mahas migrants, who brought agriculture to an otherwise pastorally populated area. They also brought Islam to the central Sudan. Generally speaking, these communities were structurally similar until the end of the nineteenth century (Lobban, 1977:2). This changed with the British colonial period, when

> the residents of Burri al Mahas were forced to relocate completely and in so doing most lost their traditional agricultural lands and were transformed into skilled and unskilled workers, artisans, and to a certain extent, shopkeepers and clerical workers. For Tuti Island the trauma of relocation and land expropriation was strenuously resisted and did not take place thus maintaining a substantially different orientation to the land than that of the 'typical' worker of Burri al Mahas. (Lobban, 1977:3)

Burri al Lamaab is located on the banks of the Blue Nile (five miles from Khartoum). Barclay informs us that "until the Turko-Egyptian occupation in 1921 the vicinity of Buuri al Lamaab was frequented by semi-nomadic herders" (1964:10).[10] In addition, there were various (permanent) tribal settlements and villages. However, there was considerable unity in this community, in spite of the heterogeneous population of Arabs and Nubians (Barclay, 1964:10). Here again, we are dealing with a heterogeneous, originally pastoral tribal population, whose patterns of male and female circumcision, residence and marriage (e.g., jirtig ceremony, matrilocal residence until the birth of the first child) are identical to those described for the Omdurman area.

Umm Fila and Hallali are two rural villages located on the west bank of the Rahad River, and are separated by a seasonal tributary of the Rahad that also acts as a province boundary. Umm Fila thus lies in the Blue Nile Province, and Hallali in Kassala Province. Both villages engage in rainfall cultivation of subsistence and cash crops, in addition to herding cattle, sheep, and goats (Gruenbaum, 1979:7).

- *Umm Fila*: The population of this village (called Zabarma) originated in Mali (west Africa), and migrated to the Sudan in the late nineteenth century. They settled (after various relocations) in their present village about forty-five years ago. Gruenbaum notes that nearly all of the present population of the village was born there (1979:10). They are endogamous, and have close social ties (linked by kinship and intermarriage) with several other Zabarma communities in the area. They are Moslems, and recognize Islamic laws governing divorce, inheritance, and marriage, but they do not speak Arabic unless their activities bring them into contact with outsiders. Consequently, they are isolated by language and ethnic barriers from their immediate neighbors. Preferred parallel cousin marriage, as in most of the northern Sudan, is also the rule here, and polygamy is not unusual. The family here, as is the case in Hallali village, is the center of productive and reproductive activities. Generally speaking, the people of Umm Fila are more industrious and agriculturally oriented than are the people of Hallali. The latter have smaller fields, and rely more heavily on their livestock and wage labor for their livelihood. The general area inhabited by both villages has always, and continues to be utilized by nomads.

- *Hallali*: The population of this village (as is the case with their neighbors in Sherifa village (across the river) are of the Kenana Arab tribal group. The Hallali villagers maintain close ties with other Kenana, both settled and nomadic sections. Gruenbaum notes that they very often send their herds for dry season grazing to their nomadic relatives (1979:12). These people are also Moslems, but their language is Arabic. They are patrilineal, endogamous, and polygamous. As mentioned above, they are more heavily dependent upon their livestock than upon agriculture. Pastoral activities are accomplished by men and boys, with women engaged in agriculture. This is congruent with male avoidance of agricultural work, which has a low status value, as well as the less restricted role of women (Gruenbaum, 1979:35).

Infibulation in the Sudan

The northern Sudan (to include bordering populations located in Chad) seems to represent the most heterogeneous distribution of this practice. Unfortunately, the historical population diversity and political instability of this area compounds the difficulty of accurately determining even the more recent subsistence and social structural background of these diverse populations. The data in the appendix indicates that the majority of "traditional" infibulation-practicing populations in the Sudan area have, at a minimum, an agro-pastoral background, with even agriculturalists having maintained pastoral ties, almost to date. The data in the appendix also indicates that the practice seems to have been more traditionally prevalent in the north central and easternmost regions of northern Sudan, its evidence among Baggara populations reflecting a more recent adoption.

Three-Towns area: Because of its heterogeneity, it is extremely hazardous to generalize about the nature of the social structure and cultural traditions of the population in the Three-Towns area. There are, however, a small number of studies available indicating tribal affiliations, marriage customs, and the origins of various population groups in the Three-Towns area. Zenkovsky, for example, points outs that Omdurman is a conglomerate of Sudanese tribes, with primarily Ja'aliyyin and Mahas affiliation. She adds that, although these individual groups normally display variations in their customs and rituals, these have become standardized in the Omdurman area and have acquired "a unified system of customs and rituals for the ceremonies of birth, circumcision, marriage, and death. ... The tribes or populations coming in have pressure exerted upon them to conform to existing ritual and ceremonies" (1945:241–56).

In her discussion of marriage customs in Omdurman, Zenkovsky points out that girls are married at approximately twelve years of age in the Sudan (sometimes before), and that marriage in the Omdurman area includes the "jirtig" ceremony. Here, as with many northern tribes the ceremony lasts for forty days, during which the bride does not work, and is looked after by her mother. During this time, she resists the husband in all ways, nor does she speak to him.

> If the man is pleased with his wife, he must give her a present of money, cloth, or gold. If he wishes and has a house of his own, he may now remove her from her parents' compound. ... It is usual for the newly married pair to live in the compound of the girl's father, where they are given separate tukls or a room situated apart from the rest of the family. Often, if the man is in government service, he has to live elsewhere on duty and leaves his bride with her parents. (Zenkovsky, 1945:254)

This pattern, with minor variations, is common to many of the Sudanese tribes listed in the appendix. There is, in fact, some historical evidence of infibulation practiced in the general Khartoum area, and Brehm mentions that festivities were prevalent for both male and female circumcision (1847–1852; reissue, 1975:136). "As is the case for boys, the circumcision of girls is accompanied by a period of festivities. Days before the actual circumcision takes place, there is singing, dancing, drinking and general rejoicing until deep into the night. In so far as custom allows, the girl in question is also included in these festivities" (my translation) (Brehm, reissue 1975:136).

Umm Fila and Hallali: Women in both villages are secluded, but women among the Hallali appear to have more freedom of movement and mix more frequently and freely with the men than do the women of Umm Fila.[11] Marriage for girls in Umm Fila usually occurs at thirteen or fourteen years of age (although there is indication that girls were married earlier in the past), and in Hallali village between thirteen and fifteen years of age. In both cases males are between eighteen and twenty-four years of age at marriage. As Moslems, the Umm Fila like the Hallali villagers, circumcise their males. This is done between the ages of six and eight years. Both villages also circumcise their females, but the operations differ considerably. In Umm Fila, girls receive the "sunni" type (clitoral excision). In Hallali village, girls are infibulated (between five and seven years of age) (Gruenbaum, 1979:45–46).

The Horn Regions

This area (called northeastern Africa by Trimingham, 1952:1) has traditionally encompassed the political divisions of Eritrea, Ethiopia, Djibouti, and Somalia. These comprise the former Italian Eritrea, (Empire of Ethiopia), and the French, British, and Italian Somalilands (which traditionally were all part of the Ethiopian empire) (see map 8). Its territory borders the Red Sea in the north and east, Kenya and Somalia in the south, and Sudan to the west. Taken together, this region contains an extremely heterogeneous population (and is often referred to as an "ethnic museum," although some groups do have mutual histories [e.g., the Somali, Galla, and 'Afar-Saho]) (Lipsky, 1962:4; Trimingham, 1952:5, 8).

The pastoral populations distributed throughout this region are historically or genealogically related tribal affiliates in Eritrea, Ethiopia, Somalia, Sudan, and Kenya (e.g., the Somali and the Beja). The populations in the steppe and desert regions (toward the Red Sea and Indian Ocean) surrounding the Ethiopian plateau comprise primarily Moslem pastoral nomads, the major division of which are the Beja, 'Afar-Saho, Galla, and Somali (Trimingham, 1952:9). The majority of the populations inhabiting the plateau region of Ethiopia (the Tigre, Amhara, Agao, Sidama) are non-Moslem, sedentary agriculturalists (with animal husbandry). Agriculture is, however, also practiced in areas other than the plateau region (northwestern Somalia and Ethiopia). It occurs, in conjunction with husbandry for example, in the various religious settlements (tariqas) established around water holes (Somalia), and along the river banks of the Shebelle and Juba (southern Somalia) (Silberman, 1959:559; Trimingham, 1952:9–10) (see map 9).

MAP 8 - Distribution and Colonial Divisions (1935)—the Horn Area

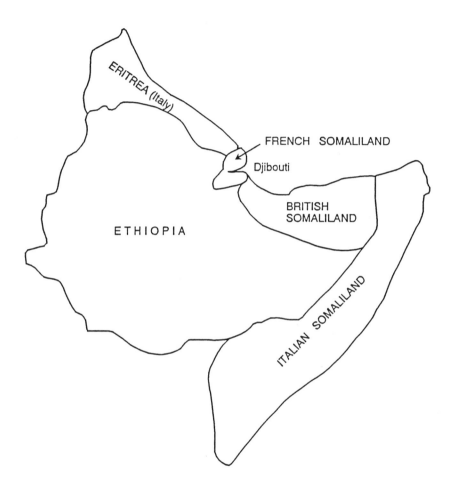

MAP 9 - The Horn: Agricultural, Agro-Pastoral, and Pastoral Distribution

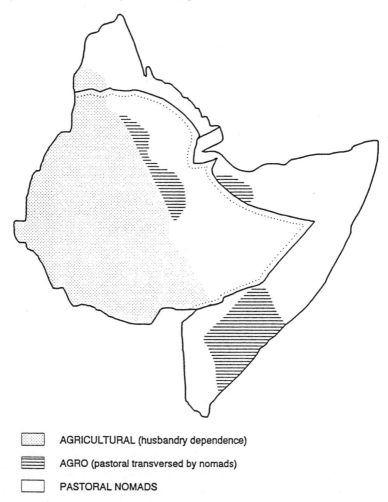

AGRICULTURAL (husbandry dependence)	
AGRO (pastoral transversed by nomads)	
PASTORAL NOMADS	

Ethiopia, Eritrea, and Djibout. Since no comprehensive census has ever been made in Ethiopia, the population size of that country can only be estimated (Nelson, 1980). On the basis of available statistical data the total population was estimated at 32.6 million in 1980, with a growth rate of approximately 2.5 percent. As is the case in Somalia (and other developing countries), much of the population is comprised of young people; approximately 45 percent are under the age of fifteen, and 2.6 percent sixty-five or older (Nelson, 1980:66ff). These estimates generally coincide with those published by Statistik des Auslandes (1982:12–13).[12]

Of the total population, 70 percent is estimated to inhabit the highlands, where the potential for settled agriculture is more favorable than at lower elevations.[13] This highland area is primarily inhabited by Amhara and Tigre populations, who have both political and cultural dominance in Ethiopia (Lipsky, 1962). Indeed, the majority of the population of Ethiopia remains rural, engaged either in agriculture or pastoralism (the pastoral population was estimated at approximately 5 million in 1979).[14]

Since the Eritrean boundary is political and not natural, many of the populations in this area are directly related to, or are geographical extensions of, groups located in Ethiopia and the Sudan. The plateau (or highlands) area of the central south (the smallest and richest region in Eritrea) is now populated primarily with sedentary agricultural coptic peoples. Generally, although agriculture is widely practiced, it supports only a part (perhaps half) of the population. Toward the north, where the surface area is largely light steppe (bordering on desert), the population is wholly pastoral. Of these, the Beni Amir are the largest tribal group, with some sixty thousand of the confederacy located there (and about thirty thousand in Sudan). They are Moslems. Another important tribal population, only partially located in Eritrea, are the Dankali people (Saho and Somali), who are also nomadic pastoralists, and Moslems.

Due to its strategic position on the Red Sea, Djibouti has historically regularly been overrun by invaders and traders. In addition to this, its lack of economic resources and sparse population indicates that its future will continue to be determined by forces external to it. The capital city, Djibouti, and the four interior provincial capitals, Obock, Tadjoura, Dikhil, and Ali Sabiah, provide the focal point for nomads herding in the country's interior. Other than the international character of Djibouti, the country's economic base is small, domestic agriculture being virtually nonexistent, and most food supplies being imported. Rainfall is about as prevalent as agriculture. Most of the population live in the city of Djibouti (total population in 1981 was three hundred thousand, of which almost half lived in Djibouti) (Djibouti Post Report, 1981:1). Those sedentary populations inhabiting Djibouti are comprised, in part, of nomadic immigrants and alien communities, of whom the majority are Somali immigrants.[15]

Somalia. Somalia is primarily a one-nationality state and, generally speaking, represents the only geographical area in this study with a homogeneous population. (The appendix outlines the physical geography of Somalia.) The northern arid area of Somalia houses primarily pastoral nomads. In the western section of the region, some cultivation (of sorghum) is practiced. Lewis (1962a:1) states that there is, however, no clear distinction between nomadic pastoralists and cultivators, many of whom practice both cultivation and husbandry. The area between the Shebelle and Juba rivers represents the primary agricultural possibility (although the Digil and Rahanwin agricultural tribes in this area do have camels and cattle, in addition to cultivating millet, durra, Indian corn, and other subsidiary crops and fruits) (Lewis, 1961a:13).

In 1952 the total population of Somalia was estimated at roughly 1.3 million (the majority of whom were pastoral nomadic to one degree or another) (Lewis, 1969:48-50). By 1965, this had increased to 3.7 million, and by 1982 the total population was estimated at approximately 5 million (Nelson, 1982:xv; Statistik des Auslandes 1984:16). Throughout, Somalia has remained predominantly rural, with one-fifth of the total population being sedentary/rural, and one-fifth urban (chiefly in Mogadishu), while nomads and seminomads comprise approximately three-fifths of the total population. Nelson (1982:xv) estimates that approximately 75 percent of this three-fifths (nomadic and seminomadic) is fully nomadic. He also points out that although nomads constituted nearly 59 percent of the total population in 1975, the growth rate for settled populations is considerably higher than that for nomadic groups, resulting in a steady decline in nomadic population numbers (1982:75). Potentially adding to this decline is the fact that there are more males than females among the nomadic population, and fewer males in the urban areas (unfortunately, the 1975 census did not provide the age and sex structure of the population) (Nelson, 1982:xvi, 75-76).16 We can conclude that today, as in the past, the majority of the population—especially in the north, remains pastoral (Silberman, 1959:559).[17]

The relevance of the pastoral-rural-urban interaction pattern to this study should by now be apparent. Nevertheless, the following may also bear some relationship to the general (historical) pastoral/sedentary interaction pattern in the Sudan, which has been only minimally studied. The reason for this may be the same as that posited by Cassanelli for

Somalia, the perception that towns are peripheral to the life-style of pastoralists (Cassanelli, 1980:1).

"Urban" centers in Somalia have traditionally been trading centers comprised largely of foreigners. They have also always been important points of contact between nomads and settled populations, as well as primary outlets for pastoral products (Cassanelli, 1982:72–73; Hess, 1966:6). Caravan routes, for example, and the participation of many pastoral populations in the long-distance transportation of goods, have long assisted the process of regularized contact between large sections of the nomadic interior and coastal towns (Abdirahman, 1977:171–76; Cassanelli, 1980:6). Towns (and other settlement areas) have also long functioned as places of refuge for nomads in times of drought. The Somali Peninsula has a serious drought once every twenty to twenty-five years, which usually results in serious livestock losses, and often in famine. Cassanelli summarizes the Somali response to drought as one of "decreasing dependents." This involves decreasing the number of animals and people the land has to support, which is accomplished by a movement of nomadic families into towns and villages where urban kinsmen or village (agricultural) allies reside, and can be relied upon for support and shelter of both people and herds during periods of drought (Cassanelli, 1980:5–6 and 1982:25ff., 52ff.).[18]

This urban-rural interaction has also been of considerable economic importance for sedentary populations, and Cassanelli provides examples of towns that were founded or sustained through the initiatives of pastoral populations (1982:74–75). Somali towns, unlike their Middle Eastern counterparts, are not the result of extensive agricultural societies, nor were they outposts of state systems. "While the towns of the Middle East represented the economically and politically dominant segments of an urban/rural complex, those of the Somali Peninsula were surrounded by a nomadic sector that was itself demographically and politically dominant through most of the pre-colonial period" (Cassanelli, 1980:1–4). The particularly harsh environment of the Horn requires nomads to have a wide range of resources at their disposal in order to survive (the reaction to serious drought [above] represents one example). Similarly, alliances must be made with riverine agriculturalists to ensure sufficient pasturage (or dispersion of livestock in times of need), and townsmen with market access for disposing of pastoral products and animals. Such alliances are accomplished via marriage, commercial contracts, or patron/client relationships. These widespread alliances continue to be a necessary part of the nomad's "range of supportive systems" in times of crisis (Cassanelli, 1980:5, 11-12).

This regularized interaction between nomads and settled is also evident in the pasturing and watering of animals in or near settlement sites during the dry season. In the Sudan, nomadic response to an exceptionally dry period may result in temporary settlement. That such settlement often becomes permanent is evident by rural, town, and urban population composition. Similarly, the social composition of many Somali towns reflects considerable rural elements and a continuing settled/nomadic interaction (although this does not entirely hold true for older, more cosmopolitan centers, e.g., Mogadishu, Marka, Zeila [Cerulli 1957, vol. 1:144]; but Grassivaro-Gallo [personal communciation, 1986] informed me that, for Mogadishu, this was still largely the case). I.M. Lewis has emphasized

> that in northern Somaliland town and rural community are not separate spheres of action. There is generally no discontinuity between rural and urban society for both town and interior form part of a common pattern of life dominated by pastoral values. Indeed, as trade-centres the typical northern towns are the focal points of the pastoral system. Territorially, like the home-wells, they give some definition to the dispersion of lineages in the pastures. But despite their greater stability as compared with that of the ephemeral grazing settlements in the pastures, towns generate little residential solidarity amongst their inhabitants. Yet their more heterogeneous constitution extends the bonds of clanship and contract and of economic co-operation in trade. . . . The continuing importance of clanship in towns is . . . apparent in the management of pastoral lineage affairs from the towns and even in the organization of . . . new political movements. (Lewis, 1961:124)[19]

Cassanelli (1980:13) points out the need for more extensive exploration of the historical relationship between town and country

> from the nomad's perspective. . . . Such an aproach . . . may . . . contribute to a better understanding of the growth of Somalia's coastal towns, both in size and in the complexity of their social and economic institutions. The appearance of new market places, or new groups of mediators, and of new geographical quarters may well reflect the changing composition of the pastoral populations in the interior. (Cassanelli, 1980:13-14)

Infibulation in the Horn Regions

Ethiopia, Eritrea, and Djibouti. As indicated in the population listing in the appendix, only the Somali related/influenced populations of Ethiopia practice infibulation. These include some Galla populations, the Dir, Esa, and Darod, and the southern Somali Sab and Dir populations resident in what is now Ethiopia. Infibulation is also normal among the 'Afar (Danakil) and the Saho, both of which primarily inhabit Eritrea (Southall, 1960:208). Although both the 'Afar and Saho are presumed to be related to the Somali, Lewis distinguishes between the Somali and the Afar, Saho, Galla and Beja social and political structure (Kesby, 1977:55; Lewis, 1961:10).

Djibouti is inhabited by two major cultural groups, the Somali Esa and the 'Afar, all or certainly most of which are Moslem, and infibulate their females (Thompson and Adloff, 1968:23ff.). The 'Afar and the Esa are similar in their tribal organization, Hamitic language, and profession of Islam; both herd camel, goats, sheep, and sometimes cattle, and both inhabit an extremely harsh physical environment, moving in small groups and families in search of pasture and water (the latter being so scarce that they regularly fight over water rights). According to Thompson and Adloff (1968:26), parallel cousin marriage is preferred by the 'Afar of "French Somaliland" (although this is in contradiction to Lewis [1969a] and Chedeville [1966]). In addition, they suggest that the combination of (1) marriage being sanctioned only during two months of the year; (2) normal husband absences (work or herding); and (3) the practice of infibulation, succeeds in keeping the birthrate quite low (Thompson and Adloff, 1968:26).

Widstrand references various French works describing infibulation in Djibouti, among Esa, Gadabursi, and Somali populations residing there (1964:99; see also Sanderson 1981:24). Among the nomadic populations in the entire area, the position of women is generally very low. All of them are illiterate, with activities restricted to childcare, and caring for small household herds. Here, as with the other examples, young girls are infibulated by the age of about seven years. After marriage, and the required matrilocal period of residence, the wife leaves her kin group to join that of her husband. Here again, under Moslem law, the female has virtually no rights in marriage, divorce or inheritance.

Somalia. According to Paulitschke (1893, vol. 1:174) all tribes of the Somali and 'Afar circumcise both males and females, while "the majority of the northern Oromo do not circumcise . . . circumcision occurs exclusively among those (populations) which have adopted Islam"

(1893, vol. 1:174) (my translation). Moreover, the Somali and 'Afar circumcised boys at the age of three, and

> the historical tradition for circumcising girls in this part of Africa involves truncating the clitoris. Among the Somali and the majority of 'Afar living on their borders and in Schoa and Harar, this practice is associated with infibulation. It is only rarely practiced by the Galla and not at all by pure Oromo populations. Girls are generally infibulated at 8 years of age, and sometimes younger. (my translation; (Paulitschke, 1893, vol. 1:174–75; he describes the operation in vol. 1, p. 175.)

Lewis, in writing about the northern Somali pastoralists, indicates that all women in all northern (and related) tribes, and all 'Afar women are infibulated (1962a:13; 1969:53, 135, 169; 1961:44; also see Southhall, 1960:208; and Deschamps, 1948:32). Similarly, Murdock (1959:322) states that all groups of the 'Afar and Somali "practice circumcision, clitoridectomy, and infibulation." In his category "Somali" (1959:320–21) he includes the major tribal groupings (and their affiliates) among both pastoralist and agricultural populations in the Horn area (i.e., the 'Afar [Danakil], Esa, Geri, Hawiya, Ishaak, Mijertein, Ogaden, Sab, Saho, West Somali [see map 12 for a distribution of these populations]).

Widstrand, in his research on infibulation, makes no mention of it occurring among southern Somali populations although he does make the rather cryptic remark that the tribes "south of the Somali do not practise infibulation although clitoridectomy is practised over large parts of East Africa" (Widstrand, 1964:108). It is difficult to know exactly what "Somali" includes in his article, although he consistently names northern Somali pastoral (and related [in Ethiopia/Eritrea/Djibouti]) populations when referencing Somalia (e.g., Esa, Gadabursi, Harar Province Somali, 'Afar, Saho, and those Galla living in close proximity to the Somali) (1964:100). In a brief discussion of reported infibulation among the pagan Konta (of the West Sidama group), and the Kaffa in southwestern Ethiopia; he indicates his doubts of its actual existence among these groups. "It does not occur among the Badditu or the Ometi who belong to the same West Sidama group as the Konta nor is it practiced among the Arbore, although Jovine reports so. . . . The Kafa probably do not practice infibulation" (Widstrand, 1964:100–01). I. Lewis (personal communication, June 1985) is of the opinion that most of the southern Somalia cultivating groups (Digil and Rahanwin) also practice infibulation.

Notes

1. Although the concern here is with a "culture trait" relative to specific population groups, I have considered it in terms of the geographic regions occupied by the various ethnic populations practicing infibulation. As a result of the migration of many of these populations, infibulation, although relatively widespread geographically (in terms of national boundaries), is often practiced only in specific regions of the nations concerned. It goes without saying that an analysis of infibulation cannot be accomplished without taking into account variables such as geographic distribution, ethnic interaction (acculturation and/or assimilation, etc.).

2. Where related populations practicing infibulation inhabit more than one country, they have been listed separately; their relationships, however, are specified in the text. Trimingham (1949, 1952, 1968, 1980) represents my primary source for Islam in the area of Sudan, Ethiopia, and to some extent Somalia. To my knowledge, his work continues to represent the best source material/analysis concerning the origins and historical presence of Islam in these areas.

3. According to D. Johnson (1969:12) pastoral nomadism can be qualified as "a livelihood form that is ecologically adjusted at a particular technological level of the utilization of marginal resources. These resources occur in areas too dry, too elevated, or too steep for agriculture to be available mode of livelihood, and the nomadic pastoralist thus makes use of resources that otherwise would be neglected."

4. For a more detailed discussion (and comparison) of nomadic/sedentary interaction than is here provided, see, for example, Salzman (1968: especially pp. 271–73, and 1978); Bates (1968), who points out that peasant/nomad interaction is not only on the basis of subsistence (and other) goods exchange, but is also related to competition for land use; and Edgerton (1965) for a discussion of the commonalities between pastoral and cultivating sections of the same tribe, as well as the differences between them (based on ecology and technology).

5. Although some post-1973 demographic literature (e.g., UN Country Programme Profile, 1981) designates different current administrative subdivisions (e.g., five northern regions, and one semi-autonomous southern region, each having two or more provinces), the more traditional provincial designations have been maintained throughout this text, since the majority of the literature utilized for this study employs these designations.

6. He qualifies "elites" as members of the community who occupy positions of authority, in terms of political and/or economic power.

7. Even though the Sudan has been qualified as being primarily agricultural, cattle continue to be kept wherever environmental conditions allow.

> At the southern limits of the Eastern Sudan sheep and goats predominate among the Banda, Fali, Laka, Mbum, Bongo, Jur, and Gisiga. Camels are the main domestic beast among the Daza and Kababish, where they are used for milk as well as for transport. Camels, sheep, goats, horses, and donkeys are found throughout the region, but the cow, for milk, meat, and sometimes for transport is supreme among the other groups .(Horowitz, 1967:386)

8. In the Sudan, agriculture has traditionally been an activity accomplished by "slaves" and not by direct farming activity on the part of the proprietor and his family.

9. This is also relevant where the practice of infibulation is concerned since a case might be made for a group(s) practicing infibulation by virtue of genealogical or proximity relationships when no other information exists (e.g., the Manasir and the Ga'aliin). This option was rejected, however, with the exception of the urban centers, which present a heterogeneous population originating from tribal sources, about which information does often exist.

10. Barclay (1964:96–97) provides statistical information regarding the number of members of the different tribes resident in Buuri al Lamaab in 1959. Of a total of 2,379, 1,693 were Arabs of the Ja'aliyyin/Juhayna/other categories; 290 were Nubians (Kanus, Mahas, Danagla, etc.); and 396 were from the southern provinces, west Africa, etc.

11. This is not an uncommon trait among nomadic populations—where labor patterns and general environment are not as conducive to strict public and private sphere creation as is the case among sedentary populations. See chapter 3 for a discussion of women and space.

12. In 1978/79 the Ethiopian government's Central Statistical Office (CSO) reported that 42 percent of the population of Addis Ababa (1.7 million) (the Statistik des Auslandes put the population at +/- 1.1 million in 1978) were under fifteen years of age, with 10 percent older than forty-five. Additionally, there was an even greater ratio of females to males than the general nation estimates of 100 females to 96.6 males (UN 1980 estimates) (Nelson, 1980). Nelson attributes this urban sex ratio to marriage and divorce patterns of rural populations (1980:66.ff). Divorce, common among these populations, often results in women moving to urban centers, whereas men remain in their rural environment (a factor no doubt closely related to property ownership and succession rights). Similarly, that men in rural areas marry relatively later than women may also result in more women migrating to urban areas to seek better opportunities.

13. Although Nelson points out that lower elevation areas are equally suitable for agriculture, they are sparsely populated primarily due to the presence of malaria-carrying mosquitoes at these levels, presenting a considerable health hazard (1980:68).

14. And according to the 1980 UN estimates, almost this many (4.7 million) also live in "urban" areas (classified by governmental guidelines as towns having at least two thousand inhabitants).

15. The four interior provincial capitals (Obock, Tadjoura, Dikhil, and Ali Sabieh) are focal points for the nomadic population herding in the interior.

16. Forni (although not using the most recent total population estimates [she puts the total at 3.5 million]) noted that, although there were no figures available to indicate what percentage of the total population were women, it is quite certain that there are fewer women than men among nomadic populations (although she is not clear as to the sources of this). Similarly, she also states that there is a significant difference in the fertility level of women in urban, rural, and nomadic environments: "this goes from 4.9% in the first to 2.2% in the second and hardly 1.7% in the last." Although the actual reasons are unclear, she indicates that the low fertility rate for nomadic women may be attributable to such factors as the harsh environment (fewer births), polygamy, separation of spouses, fertility control exercised by the women themselves (fertility is discussed in more detail in chapter 3) (1980: 20–21).

Another factor that may potentially affect pastoral population levels in the near future is the degree to which the large "youth" population base becomes sedentary through urban migration (e.g., Nelson, 1982:75–76).

17. Lewis (1962a) points out that, although there is a sharp distinction between nomads and cultivators, segments of one clan and lineage group may engage in both, simultaneously. Similarly, it is among these populations that social changes (increased dependence on agriculture, etc.) have occurred during the last few decades (Lewis, 1962a:1-4).

The index above (reproduced from *Statistik des Auslandes*, Somalia, 1984 [1984:30]), indicates that a large portion of the population in all districts is still primarily pastoral, with the exception of the south, where agriculture is primary and animal husbandry secondary.

TABLE 2.2: Population Distribution According to Settlement Patterns (1000's)

Region	Nomads	Farmers	Nonagricultural populations
Northwest	469	160	69
Northeast	295	64	27
Central Region	289	76	32
Schebelle	475	233	480
Juba	477	122	52
River valley region	179	156	67

18. Town and riverine settlement populations swell in times of drought (Cassanelli, 1980:5-6). See Cassanelli (1982:52ff.) for a chronology (this century) and discussion of major droughts and their consequences.

19. This description of town/nomadic interaction is also true for much of the Sudan.

3

Infibulation in the Social Nexus

Closed Cultural Systems

According to Horton, traditional cultures can be defined as closed when "there is no developed awareness of alternatives and anxiety about threats to the system." Specifically, the "closed" culture can be described as bound up in superstition and magic, where ideas are confined to occasions, thinking is unreflective, basic beliefs are not questioned, events and actions not falling in line with established categories are taboo, and where no concept of progress exists. Conversely, in scientifically oriented or "open" cultures, awareness, on all levels, is more "highly developed" (Horton, 1967:155).

However, while the perserverance of "closedness" may, in isolated cases, be due to a lack of exposure, Goody has pointed out that closed societies, such as those in Africa, have regularly been exposed to foreign (and other indigenous) cultures. He suggests that imperviousness to the effects of exposure only occurs in those societies where "ideas, religious or scientific, are written down in scholarly treatises or in Holy Writ" (Goody, 1977:43).

Theoretically, this can be extended to include societies that integrate the written word with an oral tradition. For example, in those social systems where Islam is perceived as incorporating a rule and regulation for daily life, and where its tenets are deemed sacrosanct, it is feasible that only a small proportion of the population will be confronted with conditions outside their immediate environment. Moreover, while the members of these societies may be sceptical or question traditional patterns and notions, they will have difficulty in developing "a line of sceptical thinking about, say, the nature of . . . man's relationship to God simply because a continuing critical tradition can hardly exist when sceptical thoughts are *not* written down, *not* communicated across time and space, *not* made available for men to contemplate in privacy as well as to hear in performance" (Goody, 1977:43). This is especially the case where the majority of a given population is illiterate, having access to primarily religious education, and then often only at the oral level. For such societies, exposure to "open" cultures falls on deaf ears; for as Goody has pointed out, in such cases, "it is 'oral' and 'literate' that need to be opposed rather than 'traditional' and 'modern'" (1977:43). In other words, awareness must be coupled with both availability *and* literacy in order that ideas and speech can be depersonalized, scrutinized, and divorced from occasion (Goody, 1977:44). "It is not so much scepticism itself that distinguishes post-scientific thought as the accumulated scepticism that writing makes possible; it is a question of establishing a cumulative tradition of critical discussion" (Goody, 1977:47).

Of course, literacy and availability of even a restricted percentage of the population will not always mitigate the effects of tradition. For example, in the urban northern Sudan, the continuance of old traditions has come into question in recent decades. Interestingly, the recent return to strict Islamic codes has been especially manifest among university students of both sexes! The explanation for this lies less in the lack of availability and access to information than in the fact that the student unions of all major universities in northern Sudan (with the exception of the University of Gezira) are completely controlled by Moslem Brothers (Ismail and Makki, 1990:9).

In a similar vein, Callaway and Creevey point out that the Senegalese government's enactment of secular rights, guaranteed to men and women alike, was done only reluctantly. Not only were the government leaders Moslems, but they were dependent on rural, conservative Moslem leaders who were opposed to any form of secularization (1989:100-01). In this case, although the urban setting may offer appropriate information exposure and availability (albeit to a delimited population), it remains the case that there is little formal education available at the rural level. The same can be said for the Sudan, where an estimated 80 percent of women, and 50 percent of men are illiterate (Ismail and Makki, 1990:25). Moreover, in both cases, there is a prevailing association, at the rural level, of education with a knowledge of the Koran. The purpose, especially in the case of women, is to enable them to inculcate the tenets of this belief in their children (Callaway and Creevey, 1989:107).

Although it could be argued that women in many African Moslem societies have gained increased opportunities for education and employment, it remains that this has been restricted to the upper and urban middle classes. It has had only a negligible effect on rural women. Moreover, the number of educated women, while on the increase, consitutes an elite and only a tiny percentage of the total female population (Lapidus, 1988:896).

In this overall context, the question of relevance for this study is whether it can be shown that the Islamic societies of northeastern Africa can be considered "closed." And, if so, what effect has this had, and does this continue to have, on the position of women in these societies, especially with respect to the practice of infibulation?

Islam: A Closed Cultural System

Islam, at its inception, and in its evolution, was clearly distinct from the development of the early Christian church and its subsequent evolution. Islam more closely resembled (early) Judaism in that the individual was a "total social personality: one of the 'people'" (Parsons, 1977:116–17). In Islamic tradition, the entire community (Umma) carried responsibility for maintaining the cultural tradition (Parsons, 1977:86).

In contradistinction, the early Christian church comprised religious groups that, while associated, were independent of *any* ascriptive (ethnic or territorial) community. The focus of these groups was strictly religious and differentiated from secular social organization. Association with the early Christian church was voluntary and individual; one could, for example, be both a Christian and a Roman.

Another important difference is that Islam did not develop an institutional church nor organized, formal clergy. This was in conjunction with Mohammed's banishment of a formalized system of control. It meant that the faithful were made (personally) responsible for following precise internalized rules and a code of behavior, to which end they were encouraged to learn and understand the (written) word (Mernissi, 1991:186). The Umma (community) thus comprised members whose solidarity was simultaneously based upon belief and a common allegiance. Their compliance was assured by granting them privileges withheld from those who were nonbelievers, that is, belief was coupled to civil rights, position, and privilege. Accordingly, religious law became

the basis, and the expression of community cohesion (Parsons, 1977:88).
The difficulty was that the law, which (in theory) applied equally to all
the faithful, had to do so in an increasingly pluralistic Islamic state. This
was further complicated by the fact that the law rested

> on the loosely integrated tradition of the *Qur'an*, the *Shari'a*, and the glosses.
> Although it was maintained by a group of experts, they never held an organized status
> in a corporate entity in the fashion, for example, of the canon lawyers in the Mediaeval
> Christian Church. . . . Furthermore, Islamic law remained legalistic. . . . The *Qur'an*
> and, even more, the *Shari'a* were aphoristic and unsystematized. . . . The Islamic
> tendency was to elaborate particular percepts and prohibitions on relatively *ad hoc*
> bases, adapting them to the various circumstances in which the faithful found
> themselves. Thus, Islamic law . . . characterized by ingenious casuistry rather than
> integration about clearly formulated legal principles . . . had hardly any philosophical
> grounding. (Parsons, 1977:88–89; see also Goody, 1977:43–47)

Moreover, the law became inviolable after the formal establishment of
the Shari'a (mid-nineteenth century). Independent judgment was prohibited, and only a "deeper and more literal understanding of the words
recorded was to be permitted" (Callaway and Creevey, 1989:88–90).
Unfortunately, the drive for the religiously based political unification of
a pluralistic state (gained primarily through military expansion) was
impaired by

> the anchorage of the Islamic masses in traditional agrarian or nomadic societies,
> organized about kinship and particularistic local solidarities that were never thor-
> oughly structured to match the religious universalism or even that attained by the
> highest political authorities and the law. Indeed, the particularism often penetrated
> the higher echelons. . . . Orthodox Islam adhered to a theological rigidity that could
> not legitimize any mediation with the diversity of human interests and motives.
> (Parsons, 1977:89)

This traditional fundamental lack of a philosophical grounding for
theology and law continues to inhibit the development of a distinction
between the secular and the religious. This is especially evident in
northeastern Africa (generally), where Islam has historically been a
popular religion. According to Lapidus, this is because encroaching
Arabs married into local families having matrilineal succession, allowing
their children to inherit local chieftainships (1988:524–26). Similarly, in
Somalia, Arab traders married Somali women, which created a concept
of (Arab) Moslem Somali lineage identity. In this way, the primarily
pastoral nomadic Somali culture became heavily infused with Islam and
the Arabic language (Lapidus, 1988:532).

Today, the north part of the Sudan and Somalia can be characterized as Arabic-speaking populations with a Moslem identity (Lapidus, 1988:852). It is primarily for this reason that Islamic religious movements have been able to become the basis of nationalist political parties, that is, it is only the religious leaders who can rally mass support (Lapidus, 1988:857).

Social Space in Islamic Societies

In contradistinction to many of his "followers," Mohammed did not distinguish between public and private spheres.[1] He created a space "in which the distance between private life and public life was nullified, where physical thresholds did not constitute obstacles . . . in which the living quarters opened easily onto the mosque, and which thus played a decisive role in the lives of women and their relationship to politics" (Mernissi, 1991:113). Unfortunately, neither traditional nor modern official Islam has opted to retain this concept of spatial overlap; a policy which has had serious consequences for the position of women.

According to Mernissi, this policy has its historical basis in the reponse to women's demand for the right to inherit and to bear arms. Originally, women were excluded from inheriting because they did not participate in the raiding parties, and hence were not in a position to share the booty. Moreover, women were themselves considered booty. The law of ghazawa (the right to raid an enemy and to strip him of his possessions)

> gave to the victor the right to . . . reduce the women and children of the loser to . . . prisoners of war. A woman prisoner could be sold by her captor as part of the booty. Her captor could also subject her to a conjugal relationship . . . or he could just use her as labor. Female slavery was a source of sexual gratification, of domestic labor, and of reproduction of that labor force. By demanding the right to bear arms, women were threatening a hugh reduction in the wealth that a man could gain by raids . . . . (Mernissi, 1991:132)

Their demands not only made women a potential political threat (should the nullification of the boundaries between mosque and home be made structural), but they were also a potential economic threat, especially since they themselves were part of a man's wealth (Mernissi, 1991:148). In response, the imams (religious leaders) declared that women were in the charge of men because "Allah hath made the one of them to excel the other, and because they spend their property (for the support of women)"

(Mernissi, 1991:154; see also Hjärpe, 1983:16). The result is that women in Islamic societies have not been accorded a sovereign will; nor do they have the full rights of formal citizenship in any part of the social nexus (public or private).

Thus, even though Islamic law does not prohibit women from engaging either in paid labor or public office, or seeking an education, it is made explicitly clear that their lives must be centered in the family, within which they have both rights and duties (Delaney, 1988:88–89; Callaway and Creevey, 1989:91). In contradistinction, men have the role of public wage earner, and hold a primarily supporting role in the family. However, men are also the heads of households and, as such, carry the responsibilty for, and have authority over the family. In the context of Islamic society "these inequities have the status of civil law" (Callaway and Creevey, 1989:93).

Although women are relegated to, and may very well rule the household (Ismail & Makki, 1990:10), the position they hold therein, like their authority, is tenuous and uncertain until they have produced one or more sons. Women belong, initially, to the spatial territory of their lineage and, later, to their husband's household. Both territories provide them their social reference point, space of action, and the right to protection (Malmberg, 1980:10). Neither provides them a share in ownership (even though a woman has de jure inheritance rights, the male members of her family invariably retain usufruct). In effect, women only have the right to use that portion of the household space allotted them by the head of household or, in the case of more wives, by the head wife. In all cases, however, the husband can evict a wife from his household by simply divorcing her. In this case she again becomes a ward of her family, where she also has the right of use of only a portion of that spatial territory.

Not only is the territorial space a woman is able to occupy owned by her father or her husband, but the former also has the right both to exercise authority over her, and to transfer this authority to her husband. In neither case does the woman hold the right to control her actions because that right does not legally exist (Coleman, 1990:67). Thus, the spatial territories that women occupy but do not own, nevertheless comprise the focal point for individual and family honor. This opens to public scrutiny their person, their actions, and their interactions, the honorability of which is reflected in the social honor accorded their family, husband and household.[2]

In this sense, there are no real public and private domains in Moslem societies. The range of activities that qualify the roles of women and men are governed by strict rules and regulations. By sanctioning the publicizing of activities that other societies relegate to the private sphere, Islam legally collectivizes individual acts within the private sphere. The effect is to depersonalize and deindividualize the members of society, subordinating them to the concept of community (Wolff, 1950:372). Paradoxically, however, while the boundaries between public and private space have been symbolically neutralized, they have been strictly delineated in the built environment, to include restrictions to physical access. Where possible, women are restricted in their movements, or secluded. Even their access to places of worship are minimal, at best.

This combination of public scrutiny of private space, and a segregated built environment has succeeded in propagating a subordinant position for women. Moreover, the religious sanction accorded this paradoxical concept of spatial integrity and transparent physical thresholds has underpinned male authority, which "can only exist and be consolidated if the public/private division is maintained as an almost sacred matter" (Mernissi, 1991:111). Women's authority is restricted to specific activity areas within the household, her female children, her male children (to a certain age), and other wives should she be the head wife. The highest authority to which a woman can aspire is found in her status as grandmother, in which case she has authority over individuals and activities within the household, is permitted to cross household thresholds, and has access to limited public sphere activities. The only other status and economic option available (and that only to some women) is as midwife.

It is in this context that we must consider the aspirations and social perceptions of women in Islamic northeast African societies. These societies, too, depend upon rigid adherence to role distinctions, that define and support their structure, and that are guaranteed by the authority of Islam. The central institution is the family, the structural integrity of which usually determines the cohesiveness of the system. At the level of family, these roles are guaranteed by parental authority. (For a clear and extensive consideration of social roles and structures, see especially Gerth and Wright Mills, 1954.)

Moreover, and of particular relevance to the present study, the overall social position of women in these societies has remained constant in spite of increasing urbanization and exposure to external elements. However, while the constancy of this position is certainly related to the identifi-cation of gender related roles, this does not give license, as some authors have assumed, to interpret the social position of women in closed societies in gender issue terms. It is important that we guard against drawing direct parallels, or evaluating the status position of these women on the basis of our own socionormative perspective.

Gender Identification and Differentiation in Open and Closed Cultural Systems

In the following, gender is qualified as the social image of masculinity and femininity: the former is associated with sexual assertiveness, career or public sector activities, and intelligence; the latter with sexual passiv-ity, motherhood, and low level intelligence. This perception, which was generated in "developed" nations, is associated with a strong movement to collectivize gender by viewing all members of society as being both *equal and the same*. The basic tenet of this movement is that maleness and femaleness are socially constructed. That is, gender socialization accentuates the differences between males and females, and impacts directly on the content and circumscription of social roles. But socialized behavior differences are only part of this distinction. "Elaborate belief systems about maleness and femaleness get encoded in social structure in myriad ways. The result is a complex system of constraints and opportunities that powerfully shapes the experiences that men and women can have, what they can know, and who they can become" (McAdam, 1992:1213).

Ideally, the purpose of the policy of "sameness" is to neutralize these rigid distinctions. In a sense, its very existence is made possible by the fact that "developed" societies have succeeded in privatizing the private sector (in contradistinction to closed societies). Because the private sphere no longer constitutes a domain that formally and directly influ-ences public sector survival, individuality can be both tolerated and even stimulated. Moreover, women can have a sovereign will, which they can (at least attempt to) exercise in the public sphere. They have formal de jure citizenship in the total social nexus (public and private). They can engage in paid labor, aspire to public office, and seek an education. As such, they are in a position to generate a discussion about the necessity to blur gender distinctions in the interests of equal opportunity.

While it remains the case that women in such "open" societies continue to fulfill a central role in the family, often simultaneous with their public sector activities, they now share ownership as well as responsibility for the household (together with their spouse). Nor is it any longer unusual for a woman to be the sole head of household. In short, they have acquired the full range of civil rights.

Of course, there is little doubt that the private sphere, in which context femaleness has usually been defined, continues to exert indirect influence over both the perception of women and their de facto occupational potential and social position in the public domain. This does not, however, detract from the fact that women in developed nations are able to both occupy and own a given territorial space, engage in competitive acquisition (of position or economic wealth) in the public sphere, and hold the legal right to control their own actions. This is the antithesis of that available to women in Islamic societies generally, and northeastern African societies in particular. In these societies, the roles of males and females dictate that the sexes be spatially and socially segregated (this is discussed in more detail below). However, this segregation does not have its basis in a gender issue warranting public debate. Nor can the distinction between "maleness and femaleness" be employed as a medium for explaining the social structure of these systems. It is rather more complex than that. Segregation of the sexes in these societies is based on the division of productive labor, ranging from reproduction and lineage identification to economic production. In this context, a woman is female by virtue of her capability to reproduce. Her femaleness becomes a formal issue, and indeed comes into question when she proves infertile.

In this context, it could certainly be contended that women fall victim to the vicissitudes of transactions within and between households, and to the authority of the male members of those households. However, it is also the case that the social identity of a woman changes as she ages.

> Within the cycle of domestic development the rights, obligations and social identity of a woman change . . . in the period from puberty to marriage she is quintessentially feminine. . . . Child-rearing gives her authority over a rising generation and requalifies her conjugal relationships . . . after the menopause, as their authority is further enhanced with age, women acquire 'more male' . . . attributes. (Robertson, 1991:102)

In short, we can just as easily contend that "generation qualifies gender" (Robertson, 1991:102; compare Boddy, 1989:177, 180).

In contrast to the situation in closed societies, the concept of gender distinction as used in "developed" nation politics, involves the issue of the identification, restriction, and/or ascription of social roles primarily in the *public sector*. Moreover, it is used, as such, to explain the overall potential (or lack thereof) women have in that sphere.

Nevertheless, in relevant literature, it is not unusual to find female circumcision correlated to the (Western) concept of gender distinction. For example, Boddy has correlated infibulation, gender distinction, and fertility. The latter qualifies and validates femaleness. Moreover, through circumcision, women "emphasize and embody in their daughters what they hold to be the essence of feminity; uncontaminated, morally appropriate fertility, the right and the physical potential to reproduce the lineage or found a lineage section" (Boddy, 1989:74).

While it is certainly the case that gender *identification* is important in learning socially acceptable roles in any society, the concept gender *distinction* was generated in conjunction both with women's entry into the labor force, and their right to equal opportunity. As such, the latter only has social relevance in systems where *all* individuals have (theoretically) equal economic and political freedom of movement, that is, open systems. Only in such social systems would issues arise that could, potentially, give credence to a discussion about gender distinctions (e.g., issues involving human resource utilization, questions of gender and science, education and the process of socialization).

Gender distinction is not a relevant issue in northeastern African societies. There, integration into womanhood is the acquisition of a specific social status. In this context, infibulation is not so much an affirmation or marker of feminine gender as an affirmation of reproductive license in the specific context of marriage. In this, it is symbolically and ritually associated with marriage. In a sense, a girl is 'married' by this initiation, despite the fact that she does as yet have a husband. (For a discussion of female initiation in this context see e.g., Gottlieb, 1988:57.)

Through this association with marriagability, infibulation also identifies women with the private (enclosed) sphere, which is protected from all outside elements of potential danger to the core institution on which the social structure is based, the family. Women are the essential element around which this institution pivots. Whether or not women in such societies are of social value to themselves and their social environment is based on whether or not they are able to produce sons. More importantly perhaps, women do not correlate their social identity and social responsibility with their genitals. Indeed, after the initial operation, the issue is closed (literally and figuratively speaking). Women do not even correlate subsequent physical discomfort, pain, and related gynecological and obstetric problems with having been circumcised. Such physical problems are perceived as being the common lot of women. That is, because these problems are, to one degree or other, prevalent among the majority of infibulated women, they are not viewed as unusual. Logically then, neither the act of infibulation nor related sequelae (unless requiring emergency treatment) are high priority issues for women in these societies. In short, infibulation is less perceived as a problem than as a badge of merit and identification. It accords girls the right to marriage and the protection and the status this union provides. *Individual social identity is based on being infibulated. Women's collective social identity is based on all women being infibulated.*

Invariably, however, women in "closed" social systems have been viewed by outsiders and activist insiders as oppressed, and without social and economic prospect. This view is, of course, not without validity, especially from the perspective of outsiders. Yet, we must not forget that in any social system, both the aspirations and perceptions of an individual actor or a population of actors will be determined by the traditions of that social system. The inherent nature of these traditions will also determine the degree to which actors have the opportunity to access and assimilate exposure to external stimuli. This means that the potential for social change, while not impossible, may be greatly inhibited in "closed" social systems. It is for this reason that the distinction between "closed" and "open" social systems is important when analyzing and evaluating the potential for, and rate of social change in Islamic northeast African societies.

Unfortunately, this distinction has rarely been taken into consideration by researchers engaged in studying (or attempting to eradicate) the practice of infibulation. They have fallen into the trap of evaluating the position of women in such societies on the basis of their own socionormative perspective. Worse, they have all too often gone so far as to *pass judgment* on women in such societies, on their rites and rituals, and on their relationship with men, all in the context of what they deem would constitute a social and legal problem in their own society.

Based on the foregoing, it should be clear that any adequate analysis of the potential for developing public policy designed to effect social change in Islamic northeastern Africa must consider the position of women in these societies. However, such an analysis must take into account the traditions and perceptions of indigenous populations. It is, after all, in this context that policies for effecting change will be developed and implemented.

The Status Position of Women in Infibulation Practicing Societies

Because the concept "status/position" is relative and can be misleading, a conscious attempt was made throughout this study to refer, in the first instance, to the de jure position of women and only in the second to their de facto position. Even this distinction proved problematic, however. For example, although Moslem women generally do not have individual rights to initiate divorce, Henin (1969b:245) observed that among northern Sudanese nomadic populations women have greater freedom to initiate divorce than do their sedentary counterparts. Consequently, the actual or variable legal and social position of women in the region under study must, for the moment, remain a matter for future research. As a result, I have adopted the more traditional view that women in the majority of Moslem countries, including those considered here, have limited legal rights. It is important to note, however, that the degree of Islamization is an important determinant in the overall position of women. Generally speaking, "the greater the hold of orthodox institutions the lower becomes the status of women" (Trimingham 1952:227).

Women in Islam: The Background

As Smith and Haddad have pointed out, any discussion involving the status of women in Moslem society might well begin with Eve, who, through some mysterious transmogrification in the course of the history of Islamic traditions, became totally responsible for the downfall and expulsion from Eden of both herself and Adam. Moreover, although there is more equality of both guilt and the consequences in the Koran, in the hadiths "additional burdens are said to be borne both by Eve and by the serpent. Adam, not Eve, is portrayed as overcome with shame" (1982:-135).

Similarly, although Adam was ashamed, it was Eve, indeed all womankind, who was cursed (for allegedly misleading him) with the pains of childbirth and monthly bleeding (Smith and Haddad, 1982:139–40). The current notion of the female as temptress is related to this concept of Eve, for although Adam and Eve together represent all of humanity, "the nature and role of the male of the species is understood to be fundamentally different from that of the female. The man wants and asks. The woman resists and tempts. . . . By her nature, then, woman is a temptress, not sharing in the feelings of guilt and remorse experienced by Adam when he has given way to her powers of beguilement" (Smith and Haddad, 1982:142). This is based upon Eve's having been created from the rib of her mate, who himself was created from mud. This has no small consequence for men, as a "man's zeal is . . . for mud and water, while the zeal of woman is for man" (Smith and Haddad, 1982:141).

By extension, since woman was created from man as a mate to man, her duties include fulfilling the male need for care, companionship, and sex, in addition to her more obvious procreative function. In short, it is virtually impossible to consider the position of women in Islamic society independent of their sexuality (Smith and Haddad, 1982:141–43). The relation of Islam to women lies in the degree to which all matters relating to women's status have either been directly interpreted from the Koran, or by subsequent legislation (derived from interpretations of the Koran and the traditions relative to Mohammed). Consequently, advocates of social change find themselves confronted not only with tradition, but by "religious law," which even today takes precedence over secular legislation in many Moslem countries. Aspects of the holy law (Sharia) directly relevant to women's low social status, and indirectly supporting the perpetuation of infibulation include:

- the legitimacy of marrying up to four wives, without any legal requirement (e.g., permission from the court or the consent of the current wife [wives] prior to contracting an additional marriage), although some Moslem countries have introduced restrictions on the contracting of additional marriages;

- divorce laws that (usually) unilaterally favor men, women only being able to obtain divorce under extreme conditions (e.g., on grounds of insanity, disease, desertion, etc.). Similarly, the man is legally under no obligation (after the woman has completed three menstrual cycles (or if pregnant, until delivery) to provide maintenance for his divorced wife;

- inheritance shares of family members, giving women half the share of men (and then often only symbolically). Similarly, should a woman's husband die, unless he has made specific provisions through gifts, etc., her share is determined by subscription to the estate from his children and male relatives, other wives, etc.;

- the injunctions of obedience of women to men;

- male guardianship of women, which (in some Moslem societies) traditionally allowed women to be married off at any age without their consent, and even against their will (although most Moslem countries have now set minimum ages for marriage);

- child custody after a certain age is awarded to the father even though he, more than likely, initiated the divorce (although these rules have also relaxed considerably during the course of this century);

- the de facto rights of men that even permeate courts of law when no specific reference in the Islamic text is available;

- and of course, purdah (seclusion) which dictates that, except for the hands and face (unless the veil is required), women must conceal the entire body.

(For a more detailed discussion of these aspects, see, for example, Roberts, 1980; Coulson, 1964; Schacht, 1964; Arberry, 1955; Smith and Haddad, 1982; Mernissi, 1991; Hjärpe, 1983; Callaway and Creevey, 1989.)

Of course the purpose here is not to present a treatise on Islamic law relative to women, nor to platform the argument that women have no rights at all in Moslem societies. Nevertheless, it *is* unfortunately the case that the majority of Islamic-based societies perpetuate a negative de jure position of women, often to the extent that they remain guilty until proven innocent. Although the Koran is usually blamed for the rather narrow legal potential allotted to women, and the wide berth usually given to men, it must be stressed that the Koran is not primarily a legislative document. Insofar as it prescribes appropriate types of behavior for men and women, it functions more as a declaration of Islamic ethic establishing moral norms rather than laws. (See, e.g., Hjärpe, 1983:12-14; Callaway and Creevey, 1989:88-90.) In the historical context, however, this has regularly opened the door to interpretive legislative free-lancing.

The de jure position of women is perpetuated and exacerbated by the conservative retention of legislation based on religious interpretation and related de facto manifestations, which through generations have become hard-core tradition. Most importantly this includes the exclusion of women from the public spheres of property and wealth accumulation (on which basis personal status, to a considerable extent, is determined), and their relegation to the family or private sphere (see section "Space and Seclusion," below, for a more detailed discussion of private and public spheres).

Codes of Modesty for Women and Family Honor

One reason often given for the existence of infibulation is that, because women are by nature "oversexed," they must be protected from themselves and from men (or the men protected from them). This concept of "dangerous" female sexuality seems to have been common throughout the Moslem world, if the view of Shaykh Nefzawi (sixteenth century) is any indication:

> Such is the nature of women; they are insatiable as far as their vulvas are concerned, and so long as their lust is satisfied they do not care whether it be with a buffoon, a negro, a valet, or even with a man that is despised and reprobated by society. . . . Women are demons, and were born as such. No one can trust them, as is known to all. If they love a man, it is only out of caprice. (Burton, 1982:203)

This view, to some extent, has its basis in the Koran which, presumably out of concern for the lust that uncovered women awaken in men, generally enjoins women to "guard and cover their hidden parts" from all except direct close relations (e.g., Suras 24:31, 24:59, 33:55, 4:34; see Dawood, 1974:216, 219, 295, 370). Interestingly, however, the Koran does not seem to view women as the only or major perpetrators of sexual license, for there are more references to men in the Koran relative to adultery and carnal activity (e.g., only Sura 24:6 specifically refers to unfaithfulness in women, while 25:6 and 23:1 refer specifically to men, and 24:1 and 17:32 refer to both men and women) (Dawood, 1974:213, 214, 220, 236). Relative to the carnal activities of men (with women or other men) see Suras 27:53, 18:28, 29:25, 24:27, 7:86, whereas only 4:13 relates to both men and women (Dawood, 1974:86, 94, 198, 216, 253, 368). Thus, there is some discrepancy between the Koran and how women are viewed in reality (even today), which still corresponds more closely with Shaykh Nefzawi's view (above). (Also see, e.g., Antoun, 1968:678-79; Canaan, 1931:174-75; Fuller, 1961:47.)

Since women are generally considered to be weaker and less responsible than men (who act as their guardians in all matters), it stands to reason that they will not be perceived as having the strength of character necessary to control their own sexuality. By extension, since the control of their sexuality (i.e., their 'ird [decency]) is directly associated with the honor and dignity (sharaf and karama) of the family, it is clearly in the interest of the males to preserve the 'ird of the female members of the family (Nordenstam, 1968:93–105; see also Schneider, 1970:2). As one villager commented to Antoun: "A woman is like a plough-animal; she has no honor" (1968:679). Males do have honor, however, and because women are sexually uncontrollable they represent a constant threat to the group and its honor. The modesty code thus functions to control women and, by doing so, "to counteract the threat. Only the full observance of the modesty code can . . . protect the fragile woman . . . and contain the lust that dwells within her" (Antoun, 1968:691).

The preservation of family sharaf and karama occurs by means of strict codes of modesty and chastity, the object of which is to protect women from pre- and extramarital sexual intercourse. This protection commences just prior to puberty, when the sexual status and "satr" of women begins (satr relates to modesty and chastity, its root means to veil or conceal). From this period, until menopause, "except for the face and the hands the whole female body is included in satr, which a woman must conceal even in her house from relatives. She cannot expose her satr before anybody including her father, brother or nephew, except her husband, and she cannot wear a dress that shows her satr" (Maududi, 1972:178). These rules of chastity, together with seclusion "become applicable . . . and remain in force . . . until she loses sexual attraction. . . . The Koran says, 'There is no harm if the old women, who have no hope of marriage lay aside their over-garments, provided that they do not mean to display their decoration'" (24:59) (Maududi, 1972:178).

Honor (sharaf) is thus related to the physical covering of women

> The conceptualization of honor seems to take as a model the fully-clothed women. Honor is complete when fully dressed (and thus protected) and incomplete when exposed (and open to violation). The height of immodesty, and thereby the greatest loss of honor, comes with the exposure of that which, above all, must remain protected and hidden, the pudenda. (Antoun, 1968:680)

By controlling women's sexuality and their virginity, a concomitant strict control is maintained over their (potential) fecundity, which is what it is probably all about in the first place (Boddy, 1982:687 and 1989:55,58; Delaney, 1988:86). Indeed, relative to circum-Mediterranean cultures (although it is not clear if this includes all Mediterranean cultures), Mernissi goes so far as to associate this relationship between controlled "sexuality/female, virginity/family honour" with the continued use of outdated and primitive technology at all levels of subsistence. As a result of this low level technology,

> Mediterranean culture is one in which the subordination of men to capricious and unpredictable natural forces is equalled only by the subordination of women to men, as though there were a strange link, albeit a veiled and distorted one, between women and nature, both being uncontrollable except by reversing the natural order of things. And, that is in fact the aim of the institution of virginity: to prevent women from producing children according to the rhythms of biology . . . pleasure . . . desire. (1982:183-84)

Schneider basically agrees that the harsh Mediterranean area ecology is related to the codes of honor and shame but stresses the importance of ecologically related community organizational problems (e.g., regulating access to natural resources for both human and animal populations) (Schneider, 1970:4-5).

This relationship between controlling women's sexuality, the environment, and resource management is of potential pertinence for this study in that infibulation is primarily found among populations inhabiting environments that are both unpredictable and harsh to the extreme. However, the degree to which any such relationship exists in reality is a subject for future research. Nevertheless, it is undoubtedly the case that environment is an important variable in the long-term perpetuation of certain traits. Of more immediate relevance for infibulation is the relationship between a basically marginal environment and the fragmentary nature of the family kin group. Extended family households are usually of temporary duration and "the more vulnerable and pressured a pastoral society, the smaller and more independent of each other are its basic economic units" (Schneider, 1970:6).

Schneider qualifies these units as the "nuclear family," which is "embedded in a joint patrilocal and sometimes polygynous household" (1970:7). These nuclear families generate "a social order based on networks of dyadic relations, which link nuclear family and lineage to external economic and political centers in the absence of effective state bureaucracies. Central to this social order are codes of honor and shame" (Schneider, 1970:17). According to Schneider (1970:17), honor aids in (1) creating and maintaining loyalties to a group; (2) defining its social boundaries; and (3) being a substitute for physical violence (e.g., can help convince others to exercise restraint). But, more importantly for this study,

> if the family or lineage is inherently unstable, or at least has no long-term, indivisible economic interest in common, what besides family name provides a focus for honor? The repository of family and lineage honor, the focus of common interest among the men of the family or lineage, is its women. A woman's status defines the status of all the men who are related to her in determinate ways. These men share the consequences of what happens to her, and share therefore the commitment to protect her virtue. She is part of their patrimony . . . it is among Mediterranean pastoralists that women play this role; and I think the role emerged spontaneously from the pastoral way of life. (Schneider, 1970:18)

Because of the importance placed on having large families in pastoral societies, and since the women will bear the sons who will maintain and expand the family economically and politically, it is the women who are the focus of attention, as important a resource as pastures and water (Schneider, 1970:18).

Any loss of control over women's sexuality and their virginity prior to marriage is (where possible) prevented by means of physical seclusion, strict codes of dress and behavior for women and, this study contends, the practice of infibulation (Nordenstam, 1968:95; Schneider, 1970:21; Delaney, 1988:86; Boddy, 1989:117). Infibulation is considered to both create and guarantee virginity. However, although it will not necessarily stop a female from having pre- or extramarital coitus, its combination with seclusion and a strict modesty code for females after the age of seven certainly represents a powerful physical and psychological deterrent to illicit sexual activities.

According to Mernissi, virginity, like honor,

> is the manifestation of a purely male preoccupation . . . the concepts of honour and virginity locate the prestige of a man between the legs of a woman. It is not by subjugating nature or by conquering mountains and rivers that a man secures his status, but by controlling the movements of women related to him by blood or by marriage, and by forbidding them any contact with male strangers. (1982:183)

Schneider agrees that men want to control the sexuality of women, but points out that

> women are for them a convenient focus, the most likely symbol around which to organize solidarity groups, in spite of powerful tendencies towards fragmentation. If female sexuality is evil and treacherous, then virgins are not only special; they are sacred, and their sanctity stands for much more than their mere utility as reproductive organisms. I suggest that the sanctity of virgins plays a critical role in holding together

the few corporate groups of males which occur in many traditional Mediterranean societies. (1970:22)

To this, Schneider adds the important note that prostitution, apart from its practical function, also "inflates the virginity ideal" (Schneider, 1970:23 footnote; also see Davis, 1937).

It would not be difficult to imagine an aberration of the traditional Moslem complex of family honor/female sexuality, and the related strict enforcement of modesty/chastity/virginity, into a physical closure of what might be interpreted as "exposed or unprotected" genitalia. Particularly susceptible would be those populations among which Arabic is not the indigeneous language, clitoral excision is associated with female puberty rites, and where seclusion in the resident unit is not feasible (e.g., among pastoral and agro-pastoral populations).

The potential for such a misinterpretation is evident when considering the pudendal aspects of the various terms referring to modesty. Antoun for example, points out that

> "Haya," a term that means bashfulness and pudency, also refers to the vulva of animals. Hishma refers to bashfulness or self restraint and ihtisham to modesty or respect, both related to the triliteral root form that means to cause to blush. But another form of the same root mahashim means pudenda. Many Quranic references to modesty and chastity are literally references to the protection of female genitalia (23:5, 24:31, 70:29). Farj, the term used, means pudenda or womb from the triliteral root faraja meaning to open or to part the legs. (1968:680)

Thus,

> there is an unequivocal suggestion here that femininity and the modesty that constitutes its principal and governing attribute inheres in the woman's physiology, her genital organs. But at the same time there is the suggestion, also clear cut, that her femininity and modesty are determined by her ethical behavior, her success in conducting herself in such a way as to avoid any person and any situation that might constitute a threat to her body. The double meaning is conveyed more easily by the fact that in a number of instances the same word refers to both the distinguishing physiological and the distinguishing ethical characteristics of the woman. (Antoun, 1968:680)

Interestingly, a sign of honor among women is their ignorance about the female body and its functions (Saadawi, 1980:45).

Although the norms of modesty also apply to men (especially where covering the body is concerned), they at least retain access to the outside world, whereas women, regardless of how they are dressed, have little or no access to either the outside world or to those areas of the residence where guests are received. This may, at least partially, be related to the view that women are ruled more by passion and emotion than by reason, resulting in the unpredictability of their actions (in short, they are not to be trusted in public). It may also be coupled to the greater ritual inferiority of women, who are the subjects of frequent ritual impurity (Antoun, 1968:677; Hjärpe, 1983:15; Mernissi, 1991:70). "Although the acts that create the condition of 'minor ritual impurity' (e.g., elimination, sleep) apply to both sexes equally, only three of the six acts that create the condition of 'major ritual impurity' (effusion of semen, afterbirthblood, sexual connection, menstruation, childbirth, and death) apply to men" (Antoun, 1968:674).

As indicated above, the existence and strength of the modesty code is to a great extent based upon the perpetuation of beliefs about women and men. Once these beliefs have been established, they are self-justifying and self-perpetuating and difficult to change (Antoun, 1968:690). They include the notions that women

> are physically weak and legally and economically inferior to men. Their honor, their property, and their lives are, therefore, susceptible to exploitation by the arbitrary whims of males. This is particularly true since men are by nature aggressive and women are by nature vulnerable. Women in effect have no honor, are protected. Men have honor, are protectors. As protected, women are essentially inviolate! Women must therefore be protected; the function of the modesty code is to offer this protection. (Antoun, 1968:690)

Such notions establish a rigid identity pattern for both males and females; men who simulate the attributes of women are regarded as such, and those women who approach male attributes are regarded more as men (e.g., post-menopausal women). The category of "women" thus also includes "decrepit men, poor peasants, workers, beggars, servants, i.e., all those who fall under the category of 'protected.'" Similarly, any man taking on the role of a woman, for whatever reason and whatever duration, by definition changes roles; in doing so he gains protection and loses honor (Antoun, 1968:690). "The modesty code determines the governing attributes of the male and female roles, and when these attributes are taken up by the opposite sex, the role that was defined by them is jeopardized" (Antoun, 1968:690).

The Role of Initiation

Northeast African societies are similar to the vast majority of preindustrial communities in that they attach paramount importance to the social organization of reproduction (Robertson, 1991:66–67). The social arrangement within which this occurs is the family. This arrangement is, in turn, based on marriage and the marriage contract (Stephens, 1963:8). Marriage endorses the "reproductive and productive progress of the union" (Robertson, 1991:58). In northeast African societies, this is further sustained and supported by the fact that marriage is considered a duty in Islam, and that all extramarital sexual intercourse is defined as adultery (Hjärpe, 1983:17).

In this context, infibulation is perceived as ensuring three things: that a girl is a virgin when she first marries (and therefore qualifies for marriage), that her sexuality has been controlled, and that it is unlikely that she will have extramarital affairs (Boddy, 1989:53; see also Gruenbaum, 1982:17). Consequently, it would not be incorrect to say that infibulation is associated with marriage. If a girl is not "purified" through circumcision, she may not marry, bear children, and "attain a position of respect in later years" (Boddy, 1989:55). In this sense, virginity is, as Boddy has pointed out, a "social construct," into which a girl must be initiated—by other women. Women "actively and ongoingly construct other women" (Boddy, 1989:58).

The operation itself is accomplished by a woman, and occurs behind closed doors with only women taking part. Men are completely excluded (Erlich, 1986:105). Moreover, it is the women who strongly defend the propagation of this practice, not surprisingly, since they "derive much of their social status and economic security from their roles as wives and mothers" (Gruenbaum, 1988:311). Interestingly, Holy has recently noted that, among the Berti of Sudan, it is the *men* who primarily support, indeed express preference for the Sunna form of circumcision (rather than infibulation) (1991:170).

While the foregoing could certainly be interpreted to mean that infibulation acts as a gender indicator, I would contend that it is more properly a de-individualization of females. As noted previously, individual social identity is based on being infibulated. Women's collective social identity is based on all women being infibulated, and it is the collective identity which is of paramount importance. In this context, the suppression of the individual [and] the disregard of . . . normal freedom of choice is important . . . at initiation, [the individual] must submit . . . is taken in hand by . . . elders . . . and forced to undergo an operation . . . submission is taken for granted, and it would be strange if at this time [s]he did not become aware of the power of traditional procedure, made manifest in the personalities [in the] social environment. (Firth, 1959:466)

In effect, the act of infibulating deindividualizes and depersonalizes women; it formally subordinates a young girl, as an individual, to the good and propogation of the family in the social system. Following Wolff, the deindividualization of the individual member of a society is here viewed as corresponding to subordination in systems where the "immediate concern of the society is not the interests of its elements; where the society rather transcends itself (as it were) by using its members as means for purposes and actions extraneous to them" (Wolff, 1950:372).

Accordingly, a traditional practice such as infibulation can only occur in a "closed" social system. In that context, it acts as a transition, or rite of passage, into the (female) adult collective. Moreover, and perhaps equally important, this transition is coupled to a reaffirmation, both of adult and parental authority, and the unity of the corporate social body. "The requirement that every adolescent must submit to some kind of ceremony, whether or not it involves ordeals and operations, and that every parent must support this event both materially and psychologically, requires a degree of social pressure which is perhaps most easily implemented by groups accustomed to acting as a unit" (Vizedom, 1976:30). Thus, the social identity of the individual is defined, circumscribed and guaranteed by the authority of the community, and initiated by the relevant group. In the case of females, it is the elder generation of women that initiates and carries out this ritual, and it is this privilege and authority that they decline to relinquish (Robertson, 1991:98). Rites of passage are thus "rites of access. . . . Implicit in the notion of access through ritual is the image of a person or persons granting it; in short, a rite of passage is also a ritual of confrontation with authority, often that of seniors" (Vizedom, 1976:45). It is through this ritual that young females are formally confronted with the authority of their female elders. It is also here that they become aware of their own potential to hold a similar position of authority, and that they begin to learn the necessary social protocol that must be followed in order to *achieve* this position. And achieve it they must, for even "the social status of a bride is low: she is a married woman with no children to her credit" (Boddy, 1989:180).

In addition to deindividualizing and depersonalizing women it may, of course, also be the case that infibulation demasculinizes them. Brain, for example, thinks that female initiation rites are meant to "reinforce the relative status of males and females" (Brain, 1977:197; see also Young, 1965). In a similar vein, Boddy contends that the removal of the external genitalia "accomplishes the social definition of a child's sex . . . the operations implicitly identify neophytes with their gender-appropriate spheres of interaction as adults . . . females are associated with enclosure, and enclosure ultimately with fertility; males are associated with the outside, with political and economic engagement of the world" (Boddy, 1989:58). However, while it is undoubtedly the case that such initiations serve gender (role) identification, "they are not concerned exclusively, or even primarily, with underlining sex differences" (Vizedom, 1976:35). Indeed, Van Gennep perceived initiations (for both girls and boys) as constituting a separation from the *asexual* world (1960:66). They are invariably associated with, or followed by some form of incorporation into the world of sexuality, and identification with a group of one sex or the other (Brain, 1977:193–94).

In this scenario, rather than intitially and restrictively distinguishing females from males (and from masculinity), infibulation could be interpreted as identifying and sexualizing females. For example, Erlich has suggested that there may be a correlation between infibulation, procreation, and the prevalence of the bi-sexual theme in ancient Egypt and (more recently) among other African populations (1986:211). Because women are central to the entire process of reproduction, they must be initiated into their procreative state. This occurs by identifying them as females (in this case, through infibulation).

Space and Seclusion

Space. As indicated previously, women's roles in Islamic northeast African societies are primarily ascribed, restricted to the private sphere (see note 1.), and defined in terms of their relationship to their own patrilineage and their husband (but rarely to his kin group). The only economic activities open to women (with the exception of urban areas) are midwifery, the manufacture and sale of small craft items, and the management control (but usually not the sale) of personal (dower) herds (although Rufa'a al-Hoi women are allowed to inherit animals that are then cared for solely by men [Abdel Ghaffar, 1976:87]).[3] These profits, herds, or other of her personal possessions invariably provide for many of the subsistence needs of her immediate family, in addition to contributing to a son's bridewealth payment, or a daughter's needs upon her marriage (Lewis, 1962:29). Among the Kababish, women seem to be in a slightly better position; bridewealth is paid to the bride's mother and her permission must be obtained to remove the wife from her natal home. Asad adds, however, that a large portion of the bridewealth animals are slaughtered for the wedding festivities, while others are returned to the groom as a token of goodwill (Asad, 1970:59-62).

Furthermore, all infibulation-practicing populations are polygamous, afford little or no rights of ownership or inheritance to women, have high marriage instability, relegate women to obedience to their fathers, brothers, and husbands (in that order). They also relegate subsistence responsibilities to women without commensurate (public sphere) status, prestige, or power (e.g., women care for flocks, perform all household duties, care for the children, and among pastoral populations, they are also responsible for dismantling, transporting, and reconstructing the residence unit during seasonal moves).

Where feasible, women in these societies also experience a rigid, and often extreme, delineation of the physical and social space they may occupy, all of which is sanctioned by religious law and tradition. This undoubtedly has its basis in the distinction between open (potentially dangerous) and enclosed (protected) space; and it is this distinction that underwrites the restriction of women's freedom of movement. Furthermore, it is in this context that the hijab (curtain/veil) was introduced.

While the hijab symbolically (if not literally) separates, and thereby protects women from the outside world, infibulation encloses, and thereby protects the area of reproduction from the unauthorized. From the outset, the hijab implied that the uncovered female body is vulnerable and defenseless, and acknowledged the street as "a space where *zina* (fornication) is permitted" (Mernissi, 1991:182). The hijab was also "a method of controlling sexuality and protecting a certain category of women at the expense of another" (Mernissi, 1991:182). Mernissi has pointed out that women in early Islamic society were divided into two categories: those who were free, and protected from violence and those who were slaves, and were not (1991:187). Any woman who did not belong to a tribe and have the protection of a well-armed husband was in danger of being captured, raped, or enslaved (Mernissi, 1991:182).

While infibulation has also been associated with controlling the sexuality of women, and protecting their purity until marriage, its actual enclosing function may have more to do with a monogenetic theory of procreation. According to this concept, a child originates in the seed of a man, which is planted in a woman for nurturing. This view, which was already common in preindustrial African societies, was also perpetuated (to the present) in those areas where Islam became the national religion. This view is supported by the Koran in the statement "Women are given to you as fields, go therein and sow your seed" (Delaney, 1988:85–86). In short, the female body nurtures the seed, but is not life-generating. This implies that, in order to guarantee paternity, one must be sure of whose "seed" is being sowed. Moreover, one must take control of the 'field' before fecundity becomes manifest. Infibulation can be construed as a closure of the field until the husband opens it for sowing. Thus, veiling and infibulation are synonymous with protection from exposure to outside dangers *and* from exposing oneself (Boddy, 1989:117).

With respect to the spatial distribution of males and females, both internal and external to the residence, an analogy can be drawn between what happens in Islamic northeast African societies and that described by Callaway for the Yoruba (in Ardener, 1981:180–81) of West Africa. In both cases, males and females have separate spatial domains (activity areas) to include eating and sleeping arrangements. Although a wife shares the residence with her husband, it is she and her children who regularly reside and sleep there (separate sleeping arrangments for spouses are usual for both pastoralists and urban dwellers—see below, and for example, Cloudsley, 1981:27). Her husband's action sphere is primarily external to the house, and it is even considered degrading for a man to involve himself with either 'household' activities or women generally. Thus, his time is primarily spent in the company of men, to the avoidance of women (e.g. Stenning, 1959:104–11, Cunnison, 1966:116). This separation of men and women also extends to eating habits. In none of the cases under consideration did men and women eat together. Both women and children eat after the men, the leavings of the latter forming their meal. Consequently, women and children are not as well fed as are men (e.g., Cloudsley, 1981:27, 119, Sanderson, 1981:103). Not only does the husband have no part in the household management, he also has little or nothing to do with the upbringing of his children (Minces, 1982:33). This effectively distances the husband on virtually all levels from the primary family unit, which is and remains his wife (wives) and her (their) children. However, although men have little directly to do with the household, they are greatly dependent upon the "private sphere" (residence unit) inhabited by their women. For example, when a women decides she wants to visit her kinsmen, and if her husband is left without a dependent kinswoman to care for him, "he will insist on going with her on any extended visit to his mother-in-law rather than remain alone in the tent" (Asad, 1970:45).

Similarly, while women may perform men's tasks should the need arise, men never perform women's work. This explains why women are often hesitant to part with their daughters, even after they are married; the labor force available to the mother decreases considerably with the marriage of each daughter.

But, although the women are formally relegated to the private sphere, so too are the men formally relegated to the public sphere. This separation occurs when the boy leaves the household to take up "social residence" with the men. It is at that time that formal social alienation from women begins, to be perpetuated by the strictest parameters relative to the social action sphere of men and women. This separation is perpetuated, especially in the case of pastoralists, by male absenteeism due to the differential watering and pasturing requirements of the herds and flocks. Goldschmidt, for example, has pointed out that the men in pastoralist populations spend a good deal of their time alone or in small groups, for it is the men who both own and are responsible for the main (wealth) herds and their pasturing (from which the women are excluded) (1968:299). The control of animals by the men

> creates a predilection for patri-orientation, in residence, filiation and heritage. It also tends to reduce the social role of women, though not their value as females. . . . The masculine orientation of the social system, together with aggressive independence, supports a pattern of sexuality in males which finds many recurrent expressions among pastoralists: the high incidence of polygyny, the overt sexuality of men, premarital sexual freedom, and jealous protection of wives. This emphasis on sexuality of males makes the acquisition of women a matter of prime importance, so that though women have low social status, they have a high social value. This is expressed in the institution of brideprice, polygyny, anxiety over adultery in the wives, and anxiety among the males regarding their own sexuality, and it leads to aggressive, rather than warm, relations between the sexes. (Goldschmidt, 1968:299–300)

Clearly, as long as the parameters of social space within which women may function include only the home and those areas directly or indirectly connected with it, no change will or can occur relative to the general position of women. This can change only when women are admitted to, and accepted in the public sphere. Similarly, should we wish to help this process along, we must understand the nature of the social interaction between men and women in Moslem society. In this context Khatib-Chahidi has pointed out that:

> Fundamental to an understanding of social interaction between the sexes is the Islamic ruling on the forbidden categories of person for marriage. Those men and women whose kinship, as defined by the jurists, represents an impediment to marriage are permitted to be on familiar terms with each other and share the same physical space; those not related in this way, should avoid each other's company. (In Ardener, 1981:112)

And since the public sphere makes it difficult to avoid unrelated persons, the easiest solution would be to exclude the potentially most "vulnerable" segment of the population from this sphere, i.e., the women, whose virginity and chastity it is necessary to preserve. But the social ideal of protecting women by enclosing or veiling them is not the same as saying that women are an "oppressed class." Paradoxically, even though women occupy a low status position and perceive men as they perceive themselves, i.e., dominant, neither sex perceives women as "dominated" or "oppressed."

In his consideration of the important role women fulfill in Moslem societies, Lapidus points out that women form a separate, albeit custodial society. They are the keepers of the family social status, they nurture and sustain the family and its members (Lapidus, 1988:892). Needless to say, women's custodial role has its basis in the paramount importance of the social organization of reproduction, and its control. Moreover, while their economic role is certainly significant, they do not have formal legal title to the fruits of their labor (Robertson, 1991:66-67, 72).

Of course, the degree to which women, in any society, fulfill the requirements of the rules they are culturally assigned greatly depends upon how women view themselves. In her study of a (Moslem) Sudanese village, Boddy found that women did indeed see themselves as social custodians or caretakers. They also saw themselves as the powerful essence of village society, which had to be "shielded against the ambivalence and disorderliness of the outside world" (Boddy, 1989:115). In return, they also bear primary responsibility for reproduction, and are the "first to be held accountable for its mishaps: sterility, miscarriage, stillbirth" (Boddy, 1989:113).

Interestingly, the same women equate themselves, and their socioeconomic value, with livestock. Like their goats, they are "pent up in tiny crowded rooms . . . tethered to men by the nuptial rope, forced to subsist on the poorest of foods" (Boddy, 1989:113). Similarly, like all domestic animals, they are valuable and, while expensive to acquire and maintain, if well cared for, provide for the family's physical well-being and social prosperity.

> Domestic animals consume fodder secured for them by human labor and convert it into meat and milk for the benefit of a man's family and village. Prodigiously fertile animals are extremely valuable and rarely slaughtered for meat. Likewise, women are consumers and transformers of food acquired by their husbands' labor, and reproducers. They are "kept" by men primarily for their reproductive abilities: if a woman does not demonstrate fertility by becoming pregnant soon after her wedding, she stands a good chance of being divorced. And when undervalued by her husband, a woman complains of being 'eaten', the ultimate fate of infertile livestock. (Boddy, 1989:113)

Boddy adds that the women's association of themselves with cattle is also related to their view of themselves as ignorant and unsophisticated. Few are literate (Boddy, 1989:114).

Of course, equating women with domestic animals is not unusual in Moslem societies. It, too, has its basis in religious tradition. In her study on the position of women in traditional Islam, Mernissi cites a tradition (Hadith), the effect of which was to generate a perception of women as being synonymous with dogs and asses, and equally disruptive (Mernissi, 1991:64). Mernissi points out that this Hadith, which has infiltrated many prestigious religious texts, underlines the polluting essence of women (and femaleness) (Mernissi, 1991:70). Moreover, aligning women with dogs and asses inevitably assigns them to the animal kingdom (which has no relationship with the divine) (Mernissi, 1991:69).

Nevertheless, equating women with domestic animals does nothing to undermine their social and reproductive importance, of which women are well cognizant. They are also cognizant of their indispensability in the generation and maintenance of family and, by extension, men's public and personal honor.

Seclusion. In almost every Islamic society, the seclusion of women is one of the most important norms of the modesty code, even though this ideal is regularly (of necessity) violated in practice (for example, Antoun,

1968:681). Generally speaking, where the formal seclusion of women is feasible, women will only be allowed outside the home for family or religious occasions, and then only under cover of the veil that allows them "to move in men's space without being seen" (Mernissi, 1982:189). However, clothing restrictions may also literally constrain the physical movement of women. For example, the "tobe," which is the traditional dress for women in the Sudan, is not conducive to freedom of movement. It must be constantly arranged and held in place with the arms.

One reason for excluding women from public space may relate to the fact that public space means exactly that; it belongs to the public and anything in it is free game. Hall has, for example, observed that "the Arab tendency to shove and push each other in public and to feel and pinch women in public conveyances would not be tolerated by westerners. It appeared to me that they must not have any concept of a private zone outside the body. This proved to be precisely the case" (Hall, 1969:157). Consequently, female mobility must either be restricted, controlled, or both. Fox (1977:805) has qualified three general means of regulating female mobility. These are

- "confinement," which restricts the spatial movement of women to the home, proscribing independent movement external to its confines;

- "protection," wherein women have access to the public sphere provided they are chaperoned by a kinsman, older female relative, or family friends; and

- "normative restriction," which involves value constructs relative to chastity, cleanliness, etc. These signify "both a standard for and goal of behavior.

Although she qualifies these three categories as manifesting themselves differently in different social systems (e.g., the latter as applying in a world where women have a high degree of independent mobility), they are not necessarily mutually exclusive.

> In the confinement and protection patterns, the major problem is to provide for the direct surveillance of the behavior of women . . . thus we should find a cultural elaboration of those features of social structure most directly connected with the problematic aspects of control. In purdah societies, for example, seclusion of women is intimately and complexly connected with family honor and the modesty code, with community standing and reputation, with the organization of the economy, and with age at marriage and marriage patterns. In brief, there is an elaborate infrastructure that undergirds and supports the confinement pattern of social control of women by making it not only feasible but even socially necessary to seclude women in such cultures. (Fox, 1977:806–07)

Of course, in social systems where such rules of strict seclusion to the residence unit are in evidence, they are usually more applicable in urban than in rural areas or among nomadic and seminomadic populations, where the nature of economic activities (e.g., working in the fields, herding, etc.) necessitates mobility external to the residence unit (see for example Constantinides, 1980:656-57; and Sciama, in Ardener, 1981:99). Although nomadic women have, as a rule, more public mobility, there are nevertheless two distinct worlds, that of the tent and that of the camp (Nelson, 1973:43). The former is the domain of the woman and her children, the latter of the men. Similarly, much of the woman's activity centers around the tent area for which she has the total responsibility. This includes dismantling, transporting, and re-erecting the tent during seasonal moves (e.g., Asad, 1970:44-45, Lewis, 1969a:129). Lewis also observed this separation of spheres for men and women among nomadic populations where women are

> excluded from direct participation in the Islamic life of the community; they worship, if they come at all, outside the mosques in which men pray, and this further consolidates the sexual cultural division which is such a marked feature of Somali life. Yet they are not veiled, except occasionally in towns, or subject in the nature of the nomadic life to any strict confinement which would justify the term "purdah." It is perhaps to some extent, because the exigencies of the nomadic life tend to throw men and women together, or at least husband and wife, such that there is a well-defined division of labour between them and so many exaggerated gestures by which men seek to demonstrate and maintain their ideal self-image as lords of creation unfettered by unmanly attachments to women. (Lewis, 1973:434)

Thus, the public sphere, actually and/or symbolically, represents the domain of men, who live most of their lives external to the (private sphere of the) residence unit and, by extension, the women associated with it (Lessner-Abdin, 1980:6-10).

Marriage Customs and Laws: An Overview

The Sudan

In his book "Matrimonial Laws of the Sudan," Farran explores various points of law and customary behavior relative to marriage in the Sudan. I have included some of these (relevant to this study) below. It should be noted, however, that custom and customary law usually always gives way to Moslem law in the Sudan Sharia Courts.[4]

Polygyny in the Sudan area has, since ancient times, been a normal (and implicit) practice associated with matrimony, and is still widely practiced by those who can afford it.[5] The number of wives, although restricted under Mohammedan law in the north, is unrestricted in the pagan south (and among the Baggara). Not all indigenous practices fall in line with Mohammedan law, however, for example, the "levirate" is prevalent among the tribal populations of the southern Sudan, and may have been indigeneous to pre-Moslem influenced populations in Dar Fur (Farran, 1963:5-6, 76, 77-78, 137-41).[6]

Under Mohammedan law (compared to Sudanese marriage laws) only a fairly narrow group of relations is barred from intermarriage. For example, marriage between blood relations (no matter how distant) is generally barred in pagan custom, whereas in the Moslem northern Sudan, cousin marriages are permissible, frequent, and even preferred (Farran, 1963:46, 73-74). LeBeuf informs us that parallel cousin marriage is especially prevalent among nomadic populations (1947:439).

Bridewealth payment is a general phenomenon, but of course is not paid to the bride, rather "to a large number of different categories of her relatives, so that a marriage concerns not merely the actual parties to it, but all their relations, for the husband's relations help him to assemble the bridewealth, while looking forward to sharing in that gained on the marriage of his sisters and the future daughters of the marriage" (Farran, 1963:76). Generally, ("in the traditions of the Sharia, followed by most Mohammedan Sudanese") the full bride price is not paid at once (Farran, 1963:288). A part of it is usually paid at the initial ceremony, with subseqent payments being made either when the groom has raised the amount needed, the first child (or first son) is born, or according to prescribed "stages" of matrimony, culminating with the establishment of a new household.

Although divorce rules vary from tribe to tribe, under Mohammedan law, the husband's power to divorce his wife is virtually unrestrained (Farran, 1963:53; Hjärpe, 1983:17). Among many pagan populations (e.g., Dinka, Shilluk, Fung, Nuba, etc.), it is not quite so simple, however, and the wife may also initiate divorce proceedings.

As to property, Farran informs us that Moslem law does not vest the bride's property in her husband at marriage—rather, it remains her own to do with as she will. Nevertheless, he points out that among some tribes in Darfur and Kordofan (and elsewhere), all of the wife's property is vested in the husband at marriage; but "in Southern pagan tribal customs the rule varies. In reality, little importance is usually attached to the matter, seemingly because a Southern bride is most unlikely to possess any property of value before her marriage" (Farran, 963:277–79).

This is not general to the Sudan, however, nor is it the case among nomadic and seminomadic tribesmen, where some animals and certainly the residence (tent and household goods) are brought into the marriage by the wife. Here, she retains her rights over them until her death, or until such time as she redistributes portions of her household items to her daughters (e.g., upon their marriage) (Cunnison, 1966:33–44 and 1976:69; Abdel Ghaffar, 1974:33; Barth, 1967:151; Parkyns, 1851:273; Asad, 1970:37; Yuzbashi, 1924:15). This does not seem to apply to sedentary populations, where the residence (a permanent structure) is the property of the husband. Nevertheless, even among many sedentary populations, the custom of initial matrilocal residence (up to and sometimes after the birth of the first child) remains valid (e.g., Hayder, 1979:66). Prins indicates that this is a widespread custom among all Swahili-speaking peoples (1961:104).

Northern Somalia

Girls among the Somali (as in the Sudan) usually marry at fourteen or fifteen. Barclay claims that forty years ago, in the Sudan, they were married at the age of ten or eleven, and Lewis indicates that infant betrothal may have been common in the past among the Somali (Barclay, 1964:243; Lewis, 1962a:12; Hayder, 1979:115).

The Somali are strongly Islamic, patrilineal, polygynous, exogamous, and patrilocal (after an initial period of matrilocal residence [which can last from a few months to a few years] the wife will go to live with her husband) (Lewis, 1962a:16, 1969:110, 1973:428–29; Deschamps, 1948:31; Burton, 1894:95; James, 1888:212).[7] According to Lewis (1962a:8), most marriages among the Somali are polygynous, with the majority of men between forty and sixty having polygynous families.[8] These polygynous units are autonomous and fluid in both composition and residence. Their basic herding and residence units fall into two categories: the camel camp (containing only young men and camels); and the nomadic hamlet, which contains sheep, goats, and the primary social unit, consisting of the oldest male, the patriarch, his wives, children, attached close kin and stock . . . so divided that each wife with her children has flocks of sheep and goats in her care and a few subsistence camels, normally the husband's concern, while the surplus camels, all that are immediately dispensable, in fact, are sent out to the best grazing in the care of the young men often far from the home stock-camp. (Lewis, 1969:88)[9]

Even though the basic social unit of a hamlet is the nuclear or polygynous family, the women, their immediate offspring, and their flocks, of necessity, form a unit capable of splitting and fusing as the ecological occasion dictates.

The polygynous family is known as raasas or haasas, the plural forms of raas and haas, the nuclear family. The expression haas particularly connotes weakness and refers to the demanding water requirements of the flocks and to the vulnerability of a mother and her young children whose leader, the father, is not always with them. For a man has to share his time out amongst his co-wives who are often not in the same hamlet, and especially in the dry seasons is forced to spend much time away from his children at the wells where his camels water. (Lewis, 1962a:8)

The composition of the hamlets is thus continuously changing; a man's several wives may be resident in the same hamlet, or "they may move as widely separated units amongst whom the husband shares his time and affection" (Lewis, 1962a:5), with men attaching

their families now to one group of close kin, and now to another. . . . Thus the composition of hamlets fluctuates partly in accordance with domestic affairs, individual convenience and preference, and lineage-group politics. The female kin of a man's wives come to visit and temporarily attach themselves to his hamlet. A widowed mother, or father, moves amongst the hamlets of married sons. (Lewis, 1961:59)

One direct result of the fluid and segmentary character of these social relationships is unstable marriage (Lewis, 1962a:23). But unstable marriages are also attributed to female sterility, and the fact that women are retained as members of their natal family, even after marriage (Lewis, 1962a:34, 1973:428). Lewis notes that in Somalia, for example, the strength of patrilineal affiliation "binds a woman more strongly to her own kin than marriage binds her to her husband's kin" (Lewis, 1962a:1). Although a woman goes to live with her husband after marriage, she never completely identifies with his kin.

A married woman's position is thus similar to that of a protected relative living among non-agnates . . . throughout any marriage a woman retains firm ties, affective as well as jural, with her own siblings and agnates who she visits regularly and who also visit her. To a considerable degree, if not entirely, a married woman retains the legal and political status of her birth. The actual division of responsibility in law between lineage of birth and lineage of marriage varies to some extent from clan-family to clan-family. In contrast to the position in some other societies, in Somaliland it is possible to discuss the distribution of legal responsibility quantitatively in terms of a married woman's bloodwealth. (Lewis, 1962a:31)

An example of the latter can be found among the Isaaq clans, where bloodwealth for a murdered married woman is shared by her own and her husband's kin. The same is true of the contribution to the bloodwealth that must be paid should the wife be guilty of murder (Lewis, 1962a:31).

After her marriage, it is the wife who carries the primarily responsibility for subsistence. Even though the husband is the legal owner of his wife's (wives') flocks, it is the wife who manages and controls them, and it is these flocks upon which each uterine family is primarily dependent for subsistence (each of a man's wives has her own hut, tends her own flocks, and is responsible for herself and her offspring) (Lewis, 1962a:10).[10]

The flock(s) (sheep and goats, as camels are normally reserved for male ownership and management, with the exception of the burden camels in the hamlet) is usually a part of the wife's dowry upon marriage. In effect, it is a return of part of the bride-price, its value being determined the bride's family. Additionally, the dowry includes the necessary domestic equipment, and the material from which the residence "hut" is to be constructed, all of which are also "managed and controlled" by the wife. Gradually, however, a large part of her flock(s), and parts of her hut, will be used as bridewealth for her sons and to prepare the bridal hut(s) for her daughter(s) (Lewis, 1962a:15–16, 29, 39). As a result, should her husband pre-decease her, she becomes totally dependent upon her children, unless his (her deceased husband's) brother (or brother's son) is available to marry her (levirate marriage).[11] Conversely, should the wife die, her kin group must provide a substitute (normally a sister) (Lewis, 1969:110, 1973:429; Paulitschke, 1893, vol.1:205).

Should she be divorced, she will often forfeit her personal dower (due her from her husband upon divorce, or from his estate upon his death), in addition to which the husband will also often keep her hut. Thus, her legal rights to all or part of her husband's estate (upon divorce or his death) are even less than her rights upon the death of her own father. Marriage provides her with "little more than usufruct rights in her husband's home, similar to those which she enjoyed in her father's home before her marriage" (Lewis, 1962a:39).

The position of women among the Somali (as is generally true among Horn populations) is very low. They cannot own property or inherit, and their children belong to their husband and his lineage (Paulitschke, 1893, vol.1:190). In the event of a divorce, the custody of the children is divided between the parents according to sex (boys to the father, girls with the mother). However, the wife retains custody of her sons until they are six years of age (her daughters stay with her until they marry). Nevertheless, even these rights are lost immediately if she remarries (Lewis, 1969:138). Consequently, even her limited de jure rights over her children are conditional.

Exogamy and Lineage Endogamy

At the outset, I should like to point out that for the purposes of this study (and the following brief discussion), preferential parallel cousin marriage does *not* refer only to patrilateral unions, and exogamy also *includes all* cross-cousin marital unions.

The historical presence and integration of Islam into northeastern Africa makes it difficult to extricate inherently Islamic patterns from indigenous practices. For example, stable marriage patterns have, in the past, often been associated with exogamous unions where the wife is formally cut off from her natal group, becoming a member of and the responsibility of her husband's kin group. This is not the case in Somalia, for example, where marriage is both exogamous and unstable. This may, at least partially, be explained by an indigenous preference for exogamous unions, coupled to (Islamic influenced) continuous paternal responsibility for the wife, even after her marriage (Lewis, 1980a:57).

Similarly, insufficient ethnographic data deters any adequate enumeration, definition, or comparative analysis of preferred marriage unions for the entire area under consideration (but especially for the Moslem Sudan). Added to this difficulty is the fact that a man's wives may represent different types of marital unions. In Somalia, for example, first marriage elopement is relatively common and, throughout the area under consideration, second or subsequent marriages invariably involve greater freedom of choice (Lewis, 1962:12). Nevertheless, in the hopes of establishing potential indicators of the degree of Islamization, the variables preferred parallel cousin marriage and exogamy (see chap. 4) were included in the study. These variables were also used to determine (tentatively) whether there exists a general homogeneity of marriage patterns for infibulation-practicing populations.

While a strong negative correlation between exogamous unions and infibulation was indicated (see chap. 4), neither was infibulation positively associated with preferential parallel cousin marriage. However, Boddy (1989) has suggested that parallel cousin marriage in northern Sudan is quite consistent with the idiom of closure (which includes the practice of infibulation); "marriage between parallel cousins can be considered less 'open,' less parlous than one between cross-cousins" (Boddy, 1989:83). By extension, marriage between cross-cousins generates an "asymmetrical and unbalanced relationship between the families." The wife's brother retains moral responsibility for her even after her marriage, is her legal custodian, comes to her aid if she has a dispute with her husband, and maintains her if she is divorced (Boddy, 1989:83). Woe to the woman with no brothers.

Oldfield-Hayes and Lobban also found preferential parallel cousin marriage to be the pattern in the Sudan. However, in both cases, reference is made primarily to the "Three-towns" area of Khartoum, Khartoum North, and Omdurman (Lobban, 1977:1, 8ff.).

Interestingly, patrilateral parallel cousin marriage (father's brother's daughter) is not generally permitted among the majority of those populations practicing infibulation *outside* the area of northern Sudan (with a few exceptions) (Lewis, 1962:26). Moreover, in some cases, it even represents a relatively recent adoption in the northern Sudan. (See the appendix and table 4.1 in chap. 4 for examples of exogamy among northern infibulation-practicing populations.)

Although marriage union types vary, historically speaking it can be generalized that among the northern Somali, possible marital unions include (but not in order of frequency or preference) elopement, marriage with a woman from a man's mother's primary section or clan, e.g., matrilateral cross-cousin unions (mother's brother's daughter), sororate and levirate, and intratribal and intertribal, (as long as the intermarrying units do not directly descend from uterine brothers). Lewis summarizes that "marriage rarely takes place inside those units which are most closely integrated in the reciprocal duties of day-to-day life, and whose solidarity is particularly affirmed in the mutual contribution, and division, of compensation paid to or received from outside groups" (Lewis, 1969:111). However, as "the greater inclusiveness of the higher segments is reached, culminating in the extension of the tribe, the degree of exogamy decreases and intermarriage between primary sections is as common as, perhaps indeed more common, by reason of greater accessibility, than marriage between tribes" (Lewis, 1969:111).

Similarly, because dia-paying members (dia refers to politically solidaristic groups) are invariably close agnates, marriage between them is forbidden. However, extended

> agnation is cut across and reinforced by affinal ties. . . . Thus people are at once agnates (in the extended sense) and affines. But when they act politically as corporate groups they do so through agnation. Exogamous lineages refer their refusal to marry internally to their relatively small numbers and correspondingly strong agnatic identity. . . . Conversely, marriage is relied upon to bridge the gaps in loose agnatic kinship by the creation of affinal ties. Thus, though rare today, it was in the past formerly apparently quite common to settle a dispute between lineages not only with the payment of blood-wealth but also by giving a nubile girl without bride-wealth to create affinal links of amity. (Lewis, 1961:140–41) (See Lewis for a more detailed discussion of the complexity of northern Somali affinal and political alliances than can here be provided [1961:especially 127–60; 1962:26ff.; 1969:111].)

Although appearances have it that exogamous unions are preferred in the Horn region (including, for this study, Somalia, Ethiopia, Eritrea and Djibouti), and parallel cousin unions are preferred in the northern Sudan, Lewis points out that the incidence of patrilateral parallel cousin marriage in the Moslem Sudan "is not necessarily very high, and may even be surpassed by other patterns of cousin marriage, as, for example, with father's sister's daughter, and mother's brother's daughter. . . . Elsewhere . . . as with the northern pastoral Somali nomads . . . the practice has made no obvious inroads at all" (Lewis, ed. 1980:52). If this is true, then there is a potentially greater similarity than disparity between the actual marriage patterns of all infibulation populations. Unfortunately, this must remain a relatively moot issue until more data is available.

One related element that has not only made inroads into the entire geographic region under consideration, but which also often represents a crucial issue between traditional beliefs and practices, is the Moslem "concept" of marriage (Lewis, ed. 1980:52–53). For Moslems, marriage is a voluntary contract betweeen individuals, and although this presents no problems when superimposed upon other patrilineal systems, it does become problematic where a matrilineal system, or where dual affiliation prevails (e.g., the mother is not Moslem). This can result in conflicts relative to affiliation, succession, marriage payments, and residence after marriage (Lewis, ed. 1980:53–54). Where the Moslem marriage ceremony and the mahr (marriage gift to the bride, payable upon the divorce or death of her husband) have been concluded, but no other marriage payments have been made, this does "establish a full marital union between the couple and gives the husband complete control over his wife's fertility (during their union)," but it does not "create an affinal relationship between the lineages of the spouses; nor . . . entitle the husband to claim a sororatic replacement in the event of his wife's death, or allow his kin to automatically inherit his widow" (Lewis, ed. 1980:55). Of course, even though leviratic marriage, widow inheritance, and sororatic replacement are disapproved of by Islamic law, they do continue to occur among the Somali where, even today "corporate kin groups . . . play an important part in social relations, and where marriage establishes an affinal relationship between groups" (Lewis, ed. 1980:56).

In spite of the primary relevance of the foregoing to Horn region populations, the crucial need to establish affinal relationships between groups in order to coordinate the pasturing and watering of herds is prevalent throughout the geographic area under consideration. Neither the Moslem marriage contract (between individual spouses), nor the Moslem preferential parallel cousin marriage pattern creates widespread affinal alliances between groups; although such marriage patterns no doubt do facilitate and reinforce agnatic bonds by creating solidarity with the father's brother, and by extension, his brother's sons (Barth, in Sweet, 1970, vol. 1:136; but see also Murphy, 1959). In addition, given the extreme ecological instability of the areas inhabited by pastoralists in northern Somalia and northern Sudan, the effective establishment of wide affinal alliances would seem imperative to survival (Lewis, 1962:23 and 1980:248).

A discussion of the potential relationship between exogamy and infibulation can be found in chapter 5.

Male Absenteeism, Sexual Abstinence, Sleeping Arrangements, and Infibulation

Male Absenteeism

Male absenteeism here refers to the physical absence of the husband due to differential herding requirements, separate sleeping arrangements (e.g., husband external to the residence, wife and children within the residence), and polygyny, where the husband must share his time equally with all of his wives who, especially in a pastoral environment, may not even be in the same geographic location. Even agro-pastoralists often maintain one wife and family in the nomadic sector, and another in the settled sector.

In addition to absenting the male from the residence for long periods of time, differential herding requirements may also result in the variable fission and fusion of agnates, affines, and more distantly related individuals and their dependents during hamlet formation (as can be seen in the examples provided below).

Although there is no extensive hamlet census material available for the general area under consideration, Lewis, in his study of marriage and residence among the northern Somali does provide us with some examples of grazing clusters and associated hamlet composition. The encampments involved in his census range from single lineage inhabitants to mixed lineage hamlets. Lewis qualifies an encampment as being a "loose cluster of hamlets (having) no sense of residential unity apart from the lineage ties of its members" (Lewis, 1962a:45). He describes the membership composition of six settlement hamlets. Information selected from these descriptions indicates the range of relationships (Lewis, 1962a:45–48 and chapter 6).

- Hamlet 3. This hamlet contained three huts, two of which were occupied by brothers, and the other of which was occupied by another man of the same lineage. The wives of these three men were unrelated.

- Hamlet 5. This hamlet had five huts. Hut 1 was occupied by a man and his wife. Hut 2 was occupied by his wife's widowed mother. Hut 3 was occupied by his son and his wife, and Hut 4 by the mother of the son's wife (whose husband had recently died). Hut 5 was occupied by another man of the same lineage as the man occupying Hut 1, together with his wife, who was a member of the same lineage as the woman occupying Hut 4.

- Hamlet 7. This hamlet contained four huts, two of which were occupied by two men of the same lineage, together with their wives and families. Huts three and four were occupied by two other men from other lineages, together with their wives and families. The man occupying Hut 3 was related to the wife of the man occupying Hut 1. The woman occupying Hut 4 was also related to the woman occupying Hut 1.

- Hamlet 11. This hamlet was occupied by men from the same lineage occupying 4 huts. The elder man of the hamlet had three wives, two of whom were in the hamlet, and each of whom occupied one hut. Hut 3 was occupied by the son of this man and his wife. Hut 4 was occupied by a male relative and his wife. The women were only related through their husbands.

- Hamlet 13. This hamlet also had four huts, occupied by families from the same lineage. The elder of the hamlet and his younger brother occupied two of the huts. Related to these brothers are the other men occupying the other two huts. Here again, none of the wives were related except through their husbands.

- Hamlet 20. This hamlet had two huts, occupied, respectively, by a man and his wife, and his widowed mother.

Thus, in the formation of a given hamlet, women may or may not be directly related either to one another, or to those male members, other than their husbands, occupying huts in the same hamlet (although these male are then usually related to their husbands).

Lactation, Sleeping Arrangements, and Sexual Abstinence

The various factors involving male absenteeism, by extension, also involve sexual abstinence (between husband and wife). But prior to a discussion of this relationship, I should point out that sexual abstinence is also related to lactation. The Koran dictates a formal postpartum sexual taboo lasting no longer than forty days. And, although this is theoretically subscribed to, a simultaneous prolonged lactation period (and often a two to three year birth interval) is the norm (however the latter seems more true for rural regions, whereas in urban areas this period is +/- twenty months) (W.H.O., 1981:119-22, 156-58; Henin, 1969:194-95; Crowfoot, 1918:129-30).

Relative to the Somali, Messing mentions that a two-year postpartum abstinence was formerly adhered to, but the forty day Islamic rule is currently more prevalent. He also points out however, that abstinence is practiced with a lactating or pregnant wife (lactation usually lasts for two years, but "the ideal spacing is two to three years between each child") (Messing, 1973:432, 439–40).

Given the general length of this lactation period and the fact that birth intervals are crucial to the survival of infants (where extended breast-feeding is the norm), we might safely presume at least infrequent sexual relations with a lactating mother. In northeastern Africa, for example, where the child does not even leave the maternal hut until at least a year has elapsed, we can also presume separate sleeping arrangements for husband and wife (Lewis, 1969a:134). In this context, Whiting (in a cross-cultural study) contends that in areas where undernourishment is common, only prolonged abstinence or a formal prolonged postpartum taboo will permit a woman to avoid pregnancy while lactating (Whiting, 1969:435).

Saucier, however, points out that although protein deficiency certainly contributes to child-spacing, the work situation is an equally important determinant, especially where the women perform much of the labor and must simultaneously care for their children (1972:243). Moreover, his statistical testing did not strongly support Whiting's contention of a direct relationship between polygyny, separate sleeping quarters, and a pro-longed postpartum taboo (1972:245). He did however find that a long postpartum taboo is "associated least frequently with monogamy and increasingly frequently with family forms characterized by increasing isolation of the wife from her husband and the rest of the household" (1972:246). Also, there is "an increasing psychological distance between husband and wife . . . as a parallel to physical and sexual distance" (1972:246).

Sexual distance and male absenteeism can especially affect fertility among nomadic couples, which is not high to begin with (Henin, 1969:196). Henin suggests that one reason for the low fertility levels among pastoral populations involves an interesting misconception: "that the most fertile period is the three days immediately after menstruation. The couple make a point of meeting during this period" (Henin, 1969:196).

Dorjahn similarly associates lower fertility with abstinence, polygamy (due to a lowered coitus rate per wife per year), a high divorce rate, and conjectures that the coitus rate "per husband per year is higher for polygynous than for monogamous men . . . and thus that the sperm rate per emission is lower for polygynously married men" (1958:857).

This may not apply to the Somali, however, since men sometimes deliberately restrain their sexual desires; the Somali view sexual intercourse as "a gift to be used sparingly" (Lewis, 1961:30–31). Furthermore, since the men usually sleep external to the hut in conjunction with caring for the livestock (women and children sleep inside), some prior arrangement must presumably be made between a man and his wife should they desire to cohabit (Lewis 1969:165).

Of course, low fertility in nomadic societies may also relate to the fact that, when the only means of transporting infants is to carry them, women have to find some way to space children (Whiting, 1969:424ff.). Its agrees, adding that controlling reproduction is not used to keep family size low, that is, it is not used as a means for controlling population growth, but for

> spacing births, or killing sickly children, or eliminating one or more of multiple births . . . is . . . necessary to the health and welfare of as many offspring as possible in the tenuous material circumstances. Reproductive planning for social production is not the same as controlling population for resource management. It is, in fact, quite the opposite. Reproductive planning mechanisms are quality control, having little to do with numbers at all, for by resulting in maximally productive members, the population in fact increases slowly. . . . The recognition of the potential of labour necessitated this reproductive planning. (Its, 1975:251, 253; see also Young, 1965:118–19)

Eberstadt also points out the association between abstinence and insuring infant survival rather than limiting family size, and concludes that abstinence will inevitably decline with social change, if such change involves a concomitant decline in male absence and polygny (Eberstadt, 1981:109–10).

As mentioned above, sleeping arrangements involving separate residences or separate sleeping areas for a husband and wife may also facilitate abstinence. Lewis has observed that the Somali have separate sleeping arrangements for a husband and his wife and children, and Tubiana observed similar behavior among the Zaghawa, where the father sleeps with his "dog . . . spear and sword, in a circular, roofless dwelling, beside the animals' enclosure; the mother sleeps with her children in the building containing the granaries" (1977:74; also see Whiting, 1969:418).

Whiting also found that, where polygynous marriages are the rule, men will not generally sleep with those wives who have a nursing infant (1969:418). His sample indicated that in approximately two-thirds of the cases, an infant slept with its mother (and did so exclusively in nearly half the sample) (1969:423). He noted that, in polygynous societies, the rule seems to be mother/infant together with father separate, while in monogamous societies it is either mother/father together with infant separate, or mother/infant/father together in the same bed (see also Molnos, 1973, vol. 3:7–15; Stephens, 1963:67–68).

Burton and Whiting go one step further in associating the potential for identity conflict with mother/infant sleeping arrangements. They suggest that the primary means for resolving these identity conflicts lies in ceremonial rituals (e.g., circumcision ceremonies for boys who initially sleep exclusively with their mother) (Burton and Whiting, 1961:90).

Cohen, on the other hand, disagrees that a conflict of identity is the cause of ceremonial rituals such as circumcision; rather, they function "to interfere or weaken a child's identification with his parents" (1964:532–34).

Although "identity conflicts" may, in the case of this study, explain the presence of ceremony for boys in infibulation-practicing societies, this is clearly not applicable for females, since girls are left with little doubt as to their social position and identity. Similarly, since they spend the majority of their lives primarily in the company of other women, and not generally in the public sphere with men, and from early on are made well aware of the social and physical parameters of their existence, the chances of them having an identity crisis would seem negligible. Weakening the female child's identification with the parents would, however, be relevant if early marriage were the rule, and residence (ultimately) patrilocal. In the case of infibulation, identification with the parents is effectively broken at the time of the operation, which transforms the girl into a marriageable woman.

Fertility Levels and Patterns, Mortality and Birthrates, Sex Ratio Distribution, and Infibulation

Fertility Levels

One consequence (or function) of infibulation that has been given is that it curtails the fertility of women (e.g. Oldfield-Hayes, 1975: 619, 628, 631; Levin, 1980:199–202; Rushwan, 1983:83). Cook also notes that infibulation "makes a significant contribution to infertility" and cites references that attribute approximately "between 20 and 25 per cent of all cases of infertility in the Sudan: to Pharaonic circumcision (1979:62). It is contended that this is because infibulation often results in sterility, decreased pre-, extra-, and marital coitus, a high neo-natal mortality rate, a possible high death rate due to the operation of infibulation, and so forth.

Although no directly relevant data is available, and census information is largely approximate, given the above contentions (which must, by definition, be based on the same census data), we would at least expect the demographic data to show:

- a decline in the birthrate among infibulated populations;
- a high mortality rate for female children between the ages of four and eleven (when the majority are infibulated), or at least;
- a high mortality rate for women at birth of first child, i.e., between the ages of fifteen and twenty-two; as well as for firstborn infants.

In so far as statistical demographic data is available, *none of these appear to be the case*. Of course, if only nomadic and seminomadic populations are considered, it is certainly true that their density and number are usually always lower than that of sedentary or urban populations. Salzman (1968:267) has pointed out that when resources and climactic conditions are unpredictable and scarce, there is usually a low population density.

Although many short- and long-term medical consequences can be found in more recent literature, there is as yet insufficient statistical data available to determine even an approximate percentage of infibulated women who suffer physical and/or psychological damage, much less the nature and extent of that damage. This is as true today as it has been historically. Indeed, the following extract from James is one of the earliest, and clearly least serious, records of the medical consequences of infibulation that I have come across; and even here I am not certain that infibulation is the culprit. If we can presume that infibulation was indeed the cause of the woman's condition, even in James' time it seems to have represented the exception rather than the rule. He recalls the story of two Somali women who arrived seeking help from a white doctor.

> The first was married, and had been with child during the last three years, without the infant showing any disposition to leave the limited confines of its earliest formation. Thus she had become an object of reproach among her sex, who said that if they all took three years in begetting sons or daughters, establishing a family would become a slow and weary process,

to which the doctor replied,

"Three years being the period of gestation for an elephant, and an elephant being the Somali metaphor for a strong man, she could silence all who cast reproach upon her by assuring them that when her child was born it would be the finest elephant in the land." (James, 1888:72)

Rather more coherent evidence relative to the myriad of complications arising from infibulation, as well as indications of the distribution and degree to which it is diminishing can be found in, for example, Taba, 1980:21-24; Hosken, 1978:150-56; Cook, 1979:41-137; Verzin, 1975:163-69; El-Dareer, 1983:131-143; and Rushwan, 1983:45-54, and especially 67-86). There is little doubt that infibulation-related infections could potentially cause sterility, and probably even death in women, but this is a long way from saying that it is the major factor of "infertility" and, by extension, a major aid in population control.[12]

Eberstadt has pointed out that there is a general overall decline in fertility in less developed countries (1981:40). Moreover, those areas practicing infibulation are by no means the most infertile of these. He attributes this decline to such factors as age structure change, higher proportion of females unmarried, and females having fewer children after marriage (1981:47). Similarly, a consideration of mortality rates must also take into account many more factors than infibulation alone. Generally poor health conditions, a high prevalence of innumerable disabling and/or life-threatening diseases (especially to children), and poor nutrition, are all prevalent in rural areas (Gruenbaum, 1982:8; W.H.O., 1981:43).

But let us view infibulation in the light of available statistical data relative to mortality, birth, fertility levels and patterns for the Sudan and (where possible) northeastern Africa.

Mortality Rate and Sex Ratios

Statistical data from the 1956 census in Sudan indicated an average mortality rate for females to be not substantially higher than that for males, nor are the overall population ratios of males to females indicative of high female mortality rates. Allgemeine Statistik des Auslandes for Sudan in 1966 (for 1964) are similar to the results of 1982 (for 1980) (see also Barbour, 1964 especially pp. 211, 212, and 213). The figures from Statistik des Auslandes for Sudan 1964 are listed in table 3.1.

TABLE 3.1: Census Data for Sudan for 1964

Age	Total 1000's	Males 1000's	Females 1000's
under 5	2513	1273	1240
5-15	3651	1847	1804
15-25	2576	1306	1270
25-35	1767	899	868
35-45	1189	606	583
45-55	766	386	380
55-65	451	220	231
65+	267	125	142
Totals	13180	6662	6518
under 15	6164	3120	3044
15-65	6749	3417	3332
65+	267	125	142

For life expectancy at birth in Sudan see the Appendix and W.H.O., 1981:54. Statistik des Auslandes for Ethiopia, 1982 (for 1970, 1975, and 1980) also indicate roughly half the total population as being female (table 3.2).

TABLE 3.2: Total Male/Female Population (listed in percentages and by age group), for Ethiopia for 1970, 1975, and 1980

Age	1970		1975		1980	
	Males	Females	Males	Females	Males	Females
under 15	45.3	22.9	43.1	21.9	44.5	23.2
15-45	42.7	21.3	43.6	22.3	40.7	19.7
45-60	8.1	4.3	8.9	4.4	8.5	4.4
60+	3.9	2.4	4.4	2.0	5.3	3.0

Unfortunately, the figures for Somalia only indicate total population per region according to male and female, but not age group. Nevertheless, these total figures are equally interesting (see table 3.3; from Statistik des Auslandes, 1984 [from 1975] the figures represent totals, in thousands).

TABLE 3.3: Totals per Region (in thousands), of the Male/Female Population in Somali for 1975

Region	Total	Males	Females
Northwestern	697.6	365.2	332.4
Northeastern	370.0	192.3	177.7
Central	380.8	202.8	178.0
Schebeli	1116.2	582.1	534.0
Juba	440.0	235.5	204.6
Meso-river	402.7	211.2	191.5

Here, although the total figures indicate a somewhat higher percentage of males in the population, southern districts (among whom infibulation has not traditionally been widespread) actually show a slightly higher percentile discrepancy between males and females than do the northern, pastoral districts, which do practice infibulation.

As to infant mortality, it was noted in the "Ad Hoc survey in greater Khartoum in Relation to Fertility Patterns" that many infant deaths go unreported, but that child mortality is greater in the south (where infibulation does not occur) than in the north (W.H.O., 1981:51-53; see also Barbour, 1964:213).

An important category for mortality control would be the ages five to puberty (+/- fifteen), during which time infibulation occurs. Barbour calculated the demographic structure on the basis of males and females within various age categories. For the category five to puberty the southern provinces have higher totals than the northern areas; but Barbour suggests that this is due to environment, health conditions, poor nutrition, etc. Although masculinity ratios were generally high, Barbour points out that this is primarily related to the early age of marriage for women, which results in their being classed as "over puberty." But, even taking this adjustment into account, the percentage of males to females in the northern provinces for this age group (as of 1956) was relatively equal. Were infibulation deadly one would expect this to be reflected, at least to some degree, in these figures.

Birthrate

Like infant/child mortality, the southern provinces also seem to have a higher crude birthrate than the north. Using the 1956 census material for the Sudan, Barbour estimated the crude birthrates and infant mortality rates indicated in table 3.4 (1964:212–13).

Although the southern provinces (noncircumcising populations) have considerably higher figures for both infant mortality and the crude birthrate, the W.H.O. Ad Hoc survey report points out (1981:28) that this birthrate is not necessarily indicative of high fertility (even though the crude birth rate is dependent on fertility levels, it is also dependent upon the proportion of women in a population who are of childbearing age). The report also indicates that fertility is affected by education (see also El-Awad 1980:612). That is, fertility will first tend to fall among the more highly educated women (W.H.O., 1981:98)

TABLE 3.4: Crude Birth Rate and Infant Mortality Rates for the Sudan (from 1956 census data)

Province	Crude Birth Rate Per 1000	Infant Mortality Rate Per 1000
Northern Regions		
Khartoum	40.7	71.4
Darfur	41.8	75.6
Kassala	42.6	82.0
Northern	43.0	66.7
Blue Nile	45.7	72.2
Kordofan	50.0	76.0
Southern Regions		
Equatoria	54.1	132.9
Upper Nile	69.3	143.9
Bahr el Ghaza	184.6	111.8
Sudan	51.7	93.6

However, although the report cites no figures, and makes no direct references to infibulation, it does point out that a greater proportion of illiterate women were reported as childless, than was true for females with an elementary education. This was probably the result of the higher incidence of sterility or subfecundity among the illiterate females for a variety of factors. It is more likely for example, that circumcision was followed by an infection that resulted in sterility among the illiterate females than among those with an elementary education. (W.H.O., 1981:101; see also Eberstadt, 1981:108)

We might summarize that, although infibulation undoubtedly has dele-terious effects on the health of women, the extent or degree to which this affects the overall fertility of infibulated females cannot at present be determined. This is further substantiated below.

Fertility Levels and Marriage Patterns

Henin's reports on fertility and marriage in the Sudan indicate that marriage and divorce trends have a greater effect on fertility and popula-tion control than, for example, infibulation. According to Henin (1969a:97) the overall average crude birth rate for the African continent is estimated at forty-seven per thousand (the highest of all the continents, Asia having forty-one per thousand). In his Sudan sample, there were approximately forty-six per thousand for the sedentary, and thirty-seven per thousand for the nomadic populations.

He points out that fertility is higher in some countries than in others, and in some regions of countries than in others. Rate of fertility is (conjectured to be) related to (1) age at marriage and proportions marry-ing; (2) polygamy; (3) frequency of divorce and early widowhood; (4) husband absenteeism; (5) prolonged lactation; (6) malnutrition, ill health, venereal disease, a life of hard labor.

Henin stresses that, while he considered all of these factors, taken together, as being associated with low fertility, they are "the result of other circumstances, namely of people's environmental conditions and, generally, their mode of life" (1969a:99). His findings for the Sudan (discussed below) indicated higher birthrates and child/woman ratios among settled agricultural populations than for either nomadic or urban populations (all of whom practice infibulation to one degree of other).

His studies in the Sudan include (a) sedentary agricultural populations in Gezira and Managil; (b) populations intermediate between (a) and (c) (i.e., Muglad village, headquarters of the Messeryia Humr); and (c) pastoral nomads and seminomads (Baggara and Blue Nile nomads). Those populations which I have termed "intermediate" are semisettled and practice some rain cultivation. "They also own a few cattle, which they either send with their relatives who become nomadic, or alternatively some members of the family join the nomadic section of the tribe for a time. . . . No investment of any kind has been made in the area, and whatever cultivation takes place in the area is carried out by very primitive techniques" (Henin, 1968:158).

In his study on marriage patterns among both settled and nomadic populations in the Sudan, Henin found that "frequency of divorce and polygamy play an important part in determining the effective reproductive period" (1969b:239). Similarly, lower sex ratios and low proportions of males married existed among nomads than settled. Moreover, even though "the later age at marriage is responsible for the lower proportions married at the younger ages, the important factor at the older ages is the higher proportions divorced" (1969b:240).

This higher divorce rate is also confirmed by W.H.O. (1981:26). Henin also points out that the nomads had higher proportions of single men than did sedentary groups (also a function of later age at marriage). The age at first marriage is substantially higher for females in nomadic populations (16.9–17.5 for sedentary groups vs. 19.1–19.9 for nomadic groups) (Henin, 1969b:241; W.H.O., 1981:102). This is substantiated by the higher age-specific fertility distribution. The highest rates were in the age groups twenty-five through twenty-nine, and thirty through thirty-four (Henin, 1968:154–57).

Additionally, a higher proportion of nomadic females are divorced. They marry, on the average, more often than do settled women. This is important in that "while frequent male remarriage may possibly result in higher fertility for the community as a whole, high female remarriage rates could act in the opposite direction . . . reducing the period during which the woman is exposed to the risk of pregnancy" (Henin, 1969b:242–43, 245). One factor clearly associated with the high frequency of marriage is divorce. Interestingly, greater freedom is enjoyed by nomadic women; 46 percent of the divorces were initiated by the wife, with 38 percent being initiated by the husband. Of the total however, 28 percent "were reported to result from the fact that the woman gave birth to no children, or stopped having children, or became too old" (Henin, 1969b:245). Although this may certainly indicate greater freedom for females, and a concomitant higher status, it is not clear from Henin's material on what basis these females initiated divorce, whether it was of their own free will, or at the behest of their husbands or families.

With advanced age, marriage instability increased among the nomadic population (marriage duration is also shorter than among the settled groups studied). Polygamy was more prevalent among nomadic groups than settled (Henin, 1969:184; 1969b:247) and, "fertility decreases as family instability increases. Thus if divorce is more frequent in the polygamously married segment of a given population a fertility differential would result" (Henin, 1969:184; see also Dorjahn, 1958: especially 846 and 849). Although it is certainly true that one of the most common contributions to divorce is infertility (e.g., Lewis, 1962a:35), Paulitschke found fertility to be generally high among northeast African women. Of course he also observed that there were "many sterile women among the Somali as well as among the Oromo and 'Afar" (my translation) (1893, vol. 1:172). He contends that this is the result of "Islamic customs," but omits to inform us which customs. It should be kept in mind here that the Oromo (Galla) generally (unless Somali associated) are not known to have infibulated their females.

The impact of settlement on marriage habits appears to be considerable. There is a drop in the age at first marriage for both males and females, greater marriage stability, and lower incidence of polygamy. All of these factors are affected by (1) the availablility of males; (2) the availability of better economic opportunities (higher and more stable income); and (3) lower bride-price (because a dearth of cattle which are the primary form of wealth for many nomads may delay marriage). Moreover, a decrease in the importance of cattle lowers bride-price and reduces the delay for marriage. Marriage expenses are also generally lower among the settled population. Finally, settlement makes possible greater adherence to the laws of Islam (e.g., early marriage for ensured fertility) (Henin, 1969b:250-55). All of these sedentary related changes are, by extension, conducive to higher fertility.

Relative to fertility levels of both nomadic and settled populations in the Sudan, Henin points out that although valid birth and death records do not actually exist, there is some evidence to indicate fertility differentials. Of primary importance here are those differentials between the northern settled and nomadic populations. This is especially important in light of government policy aimed at the settlement of nomadic and seminomadic populations. If the results of such settlement are a pronounced rise in the birth rate, "the demographic repercussions of this movement should not go unforeseen" (Henin, 1968:147).

Henin's study showed a sizable difference in the number of children in nomadic and sedentary populations (40 percent of the nomadic test population were under fifteen years of age, and over 50 percent of the sedentary test population fell into this age group). "Since the proportion of children in a population is determined primarily by the level of fertility, these differences in age structure may be taken as prima facie evidence of the fertility differentials" (Henin, 1968:150). Henin found, after taking fluctuations into account, that fertility is not only generally higher for sedentary populations, but appears to be increasing. This was not the case for the nomadic population sample (Henin, 1968:152-53, 161). Similarly, the mean number of (total) live births for women currently at fifty years and over, and for that group between fifteen and twenty-nine was considerably higher for the sedentary than the nomadic population (90 percent higher for the "intermediate" (see above) group and almost 2 1/2 times greater for Gezira) (Henin, 1968:157). Also, the proportion of childless women was higher among the nomadic sample (and the "intermediate" population) than the sedentary groups (Henin, 1969:171-74). The higher fertility of the "intermediate" group may be explained by their settlement, while the "low income per head may have prevented a rise in fertility to levels comparable with those prevailing in the Gezira and Managil" (Henin, 1968:158).

Higher fertility after sedentarization may also be related to decreased mobility (especially of nomadic women) during pregnancy and lactation, in addition to a generally more stable, and higher caloric intake. Frisch, for example, points out that if a

> minimum of stored fat is necessary for normal menstrual function, one would expect that women who live on marginal diets would have irregular cycles, and be less fertile, as has been observed, and that poorly nourished lactating women would not resume menstrual cycles as early after parturition as well-nourished women, as has also been observed. (1974:950)

It is interesting to note here that the protein content of the milk of poorly nourished lactating women is not reduced until after the first six months of lactation, and "from 6 to 24 months of lactation the protein content of milk remains relatively constant. . . . Within very wide limits it seems reasonable to conclude that lactation can be subsidized from maternal tissues as long as reserves are available" (Filer, 1977:153). Thus, given

(1) the generally undernourished condition of much of the population in the area under consideration; and (2) the average duration of lactation (increasing the potential for postpartum amenorrhea (decreasing fertility), it is not difficult to imagine that female fertility levels will be low. Moreover, the duration of lactational amenorrhea would, if Frisch is accurate, be effected by subsequent diet, e.g., dependent upon the various food taboos and restrictions following by women (see, for example, W.H.O/EMRO, 1979:15-41). Also important is the fact that women (and children) are generally not as well fed as men (men are fed first), which is exacerbated by the Islamic obligation of hospitality that dictates that none must be turned away. An unexpected guest may thus well consume a goodly portion of the share destined for the women and children.

However, care must be taken when correlating lactational amenorrhea (and related low fertility) only with nutritional levels. MacCormack cautions that although lactational amenorrhea is associated with "reduced probability of conception, we are not sure how to explain fully the variables involved" (MacCormack, 1982:9; see also Harrell, 1981:796-823). Disease and malnutrition can also be primary factors contributing to infertility, sometimes even resulting in sterility (Dorjahn, 1958:851). Henin found a fairly high frequency of diseases, including venereal disease, in his sample (Henin, 1969:188-89). Unfortunately, because the sample was not actually representative, it was difficult to estimate the extent of either sterility or venereal disease, or to determine the degree to which the two are related. Nor do we have information relative to the prevalence of venereal disease prior to this century. We do, however, know that malaria has a long history in the general area, as does the absence of medical services. Both are especially relevant to nomadic and seminomadic women, whose whole way of life necessitates presence near water and grazing sources, which is where malaria is endemic (Henin, 1969:189-90). Similarly, the amount and nature of the work undertaken daily by nomadic women, even during pregnancy, is considerably more strenuous than that of sedentary women. Nomadic women are also regularly on the move; not even pregnancy prevents them from having to take part in seasonal migrations. Added to this is the problem of obstetric assistance while on a seasonal move (Henin, 1969:190-91). "The absence of obstetric assistance might result in partial or complete sterility long before the usual termination of the childbearing period. More complications are added by the fact that women continue their journey almost immediately after delivery" (Henin, 1969:192). He summarizes that "malnutrition, together with the amount and type of work which the nomadic women do, their continuous movements, venereal disease, malaria and the poor sanitary conditions which characterize nomadic life almost certainly affect the age at first maternity, the length of the reproductive span, the age at which the last child is born and birth intervals" (Henin 1969:192).

We might conclude from the above that there is as yet little evidence to indicate that infibulation has any direct consequence for fertility, child, infant, or "mother" mortality. Indeed, high and low fertility appears to be more related to (respectively) a sedentary and a nomadic life-style, than to the practice of infibulation.

More importantly, however, any association between infibulation and low fertility or population control must also take general health conditions and life-style into consideration.

Notes

1. *Private sphere*, as used in this study, specifically refers to (a) that spatial area defined as the residence, its interior and immediate exterior space; and (b) activity areas directly associated with the residence unit. This latter qualification is with specific reference to women in pastoral populations. In this case women cannot, because of the nature of their duties, be restricted and secluded in the residence unit (whatever its nature). Their duties in the maintenance and management of this unit necessitate a certain mobility exterior to the residence.
   Public sphere refers to all areas external to the residence unit or the residence unit of related individuals. Public domain activities include wage employment (outside the home) and the acquisition of wealth, involvement in public affairs, religious ceremonies and related activities, political activities, to include holding office, membership in active organizations (e.g., unions) (Crow and Thorpe, 1988:61–62). In short, the full range of civil rights and duties normally associated with citizenship status.
2. The public face of both sexes is determined by conduct in the private sphere, that is, by control over women (specifically, over their fecundity); by the birth of children, preferably sons; by the capacity of the wife to nurture the family and do honor to the house of her own and her husband's lineage.
3. In Moslem societies, generally, the potential for accumulating wealth (of all kinds) lies strictly within the province of males. Women are, in a very real sense, part and parcel of the wealth source. This is indirectly the case where the number of wives a man has determines his status within the community, and directly so in that women are negotiated for in terms of property (moveable or other). Women also provide a necessary source of labor (Robertson, 1991:56). Women are totally dependent on their kinship relations (their own and that of their husband), both in the de jura and the de facto sense. The wife is dependent on her own kinsmen, her husband, and after his death her son and/or her own kinsmen for her livelihood. Since her rights

of inheritance are strictly limited, she may find herself with nothing upon the death of her husband (although this is not true for every case). At this point her alternatives are once again between kin relations (her son's, brother's, or father's house). Should she be young enough, her only alternative (unless the levirate functions) is to return to her father's house, for it is from there that she must remarry. The strictness with which her movements are controlled are in direct relationship to her sexuality, translated in terms of family honor. Only her husband, sons, brothers, or father can provide the necessary moral shelter for her reputation.

4. This rule relative to Moslem law has no doubt increased since Sudanese Independence. However, as the concern here is with (historically) defining and differentiating (in so far as possible) Moslem from traditional (indigenous) practice, Farran's study retains its validity. Moreover, Farran (1963:254) points out that since much of the tribal population of the Sudan was converted to Islam long ago, "it may be argued, that their pre-Islamic customs have ceased to prevail and the rules of Mohammedan law have taken their place . . . as the custom of the tribe in question. On this view, Mohammedan law has been rightly applied not (as such), but (as custom)."

5. According to Stephens (1963:67–68), polygynous societies and the individuals raised in them can be characterized as (1) taboo ridden and highly supersitious; (2) having spatially scattered families, with mother-child households, where men are either occupying their own house or rotating among wives; and (3) separating or excluding boys from the household at puberty.

6. The levirate refers to the practice of requiring or permitting a man to marry the widow of his brother, or another close relative. Similarly, the sororate refers to the practice of requiring or permitting a man to marry his wife's sister, after the wife's death.

7. Relative to cousin marriage, Paulitschke informs us that the 'Afar and Somali forbid marriage between close relatives; and that, although such marriages are very unusual among the Galla, they do sometimes occur (1893, vol. 1:196). James, however, reported that although all Somals refused to marry their father's brother's daughters, they were known to marry their "aunt's daughters" (1888:212).

8. Lewis (1962a:8), in his sample of seventy-seven men (between +/- thirty and sixty years of age) found that 44.2 percent (thirty-four) had one wife, 36.4 prcent (twenty-eight) had two wives, 13 percent (ten) had three wives, and 6.5 percent (five) had four wives (the legal maximum). Thus, 55.9 percent (forty-three) had more than one wife. Although he does not indicate the ages of those with only one wife, we may reasonably expect them to be more in the thirty-forty years-old range, since "polygyny tends to increase with age and status; older men have generally more wives than young men and usually also more livestock" (Lewis, 1962a:8).

9. This no doubt facilitates the relocation of dependents in times of crisis. In such a situation, the wife, offspring, and livestock can retain their autonomy, since the tent, and all the household baggage is formally her property. This allows her to maintain at least a symbolic seclusion, as well as unit identity during those periods when she is separated from her husband and his immediate agnates. Membership in a dia-paying group also provides the necessary protection for a woman and her immediate household during her husbands absence. She could, by virtue of his "lineage" dia membership be attached for a given period to any group within that dia-paying system. Lewis qualifies the pastoral hamlet as unstable, and more frequently comprising "close agnates within the dia-paying group with their fami-

lies" than "a domestic group of a man with his wife or wives, with his father and brothers and their families, or only the latter" (1961:61).

10. Although the husband is the legal owner of the flocks, he may not interfere with their management, or sell or kill a sheep without his wife's permission. Lewis points out that men will convert any profits into camels; and since women "cannot own camels this removes wealth to a sphere where its control by the head of the family is less directly subject to the pressures of his wives" (1962a:30).

11. Lewis (1961a:70n) states that the Somali do not practice the "true" levirate (although the 'Afar [Danakil] do), where a man will marry the wife of a deceased kinsman, and rear subsequent children to the name of the deceased rather than his own.

12. Another point often made is that infibulation complicates labor; and although this is undoubtedly the case, Cloudsley points out that women in the Sudan (and probably throughout the region) labor better than do European women. This is related to regularized squatting and sitting positions, which allow the thighs to help support the abdominal muscles (as well as abdominal organs and the enlarged uterus) (Cloudsley 1981:112). These positions also

> flex the lubar spine forward, so that the back muscles of this region become alternatively stretched and shortened, reducing the possibility of muscle spasm in this area, which is common in Europeans . . . the European woman often keeps almost the same posture in her lumbar region when standing as in sitting . . . furthermore, the laxer abdominal muscles of the Sudanese may save the pelvic floor from being over-stretched, as the former bears the burden of the increased abdominal content. Prolapse is not common in the Sudan. (Cloudsley, 1981:90, 104)

Cloudsley formulates her hypothesis that

> Sudanese women have a greater lumbar curve, more supple joints and weaker abdominal muscles than Europeans. Consequently, in the second stage of labour, when the uterus contracts strongly and antiflexes, it can expel the fetus in a straight line along the birth canal, which is not distorted by the strong contractions of the abdominal muscles. Birth is therefore effected more by uterine contractions alone than with the help of the abdominal muscles, as it is in European women, and so is often easier (despite the weaker abdominal muscles of the Sudanese). The Moslem Sudanese tradition of remaining forty days in a horizontal position during the puerperium may be significant, as the rehabilitation of stretched abdominal muscles is slow. The uterine musculature of Sudanese women has been observed to be stronger than that of Europeans. This is probably correlated with their comparatively weak abdominal muscles. (Cloudsley, 1981:105)

4

Methodological Approach and Research Strategy

The Problem of Sources

The lack of concise explanation of ceremonies or ritual activity in general compounds the confusion surrounding the study of infibulation. Even the historical and ethnographic data utilized by this study are:

(a) rarely primarily concerned with infibulation (or any other type of circumcision);

(b) often contradictory due to specific colonial interests or absence of extensive field research;

(c) not exhaustive or comprehensive in either historical or ethnographic terms.

Relevant information was extracted from all available sources concerning those geographic areas where infibulation was reported to occur. These included colonial government sponsored studies and reports, medical/demographic (indigenous government and other institutionally sponsored) studies, travel journals, ethnographic studies, and general historical and/or geographic treatises, all dating from the nineteenth through the twentieth centuries (and earlier, where material was available and/or accessible).

More recent studies of female circumcision were also utilized, but most were not heavily relied upon. Not only is the primary concern of many of these studies the elimination of all types of female circumcision, but their sources are often unclear, and the reliability of the statistics upon which their arguments are based is questionable. Although I only minimally cited such studies in the actual text, many of them are listed in the bibliography. The bibliography includes all directly and indirectly related reference materials. Excluded are those references that, although pertinent, I was not able to locate physically, with the exception of those few references that, although not available to me, were regularly cited by other sources.

Although the actual total population number and the distribution of infibulation may be considerably greater and more widespread than is indicated below, the infibulation-practicing groups included in the sample represent only those generic populations (and their subdivisions) about which sufficient independent corroborating information exists to indicate that infibulation is, or has been practiced.

Many of these data "availability and reliability" problems can certainly be related to the nature of the available information (e.g. travel journals). Indeed, even those studies emanating from the relatively controlled and organized colonial period proved not completely reliable. Reputable scholars from that period were also too often relegated to assembling demographic studies and histories from incomplete, minimal, or inaccurate data. Of course, data-related problems can also be traced to the research methods employed. Carlstein cites examples of research method-related problems in his discussion of time-resource investigation. Specifically, he points out the "poverty of research methods" relative to their theoretical foundations (1982, vol. 1:chap. 9). His concern is with the fact that theoretical propositions are often made on the basis of inadequate methodological precision, wherein, although the resulting analyses may prove extremely valuable, the "data they have had to rely on are simply not up to the standard required by the hypotheses that are being tested, except perhaps in a handful of cases" (Carlstein, 1982:358-59).

Although the present study suffers from a similar data disparity, a major research objective has been to qualify and evaluate both the available data and those theories that have been posited to explain the existence of the practice of infibulation.

The Sample

The sources outlined above formed the basis of both the geographic and demographic delineation of the occurrence of infibulation. The appendix represents a listing of those populations about whom information (either current or historic) was available. The general geographic location of both infibulating and noninfibulating populations (with the exception of those listed in the appendix) can be found on maps 10, 11, 12. This listing is by no means exhaustive, comprising, with few exceptions, infibulating and noninfibulating populations, which inhabit regions where infibulation is known to occur, and for which at least minimal data were available.

The total listing (approximately 105 populations) includes both generic populations and their subdivisions (e.g., the Baggara, Beja, and Somali represent generic or major populations, whereas the Humr, Ben Amer, and Esa represent subdivisions, respectively). Both categories appear in the appendix and in the tables in this chapter. Both the study sample (twenty-six populations) and the control sample (twenty populations) were extracted from this general listing. Where both generic populations and (some of) their subdivisions are listed (see tables, this chapter), the information was obtained from different sources. Generally speaking, many of the older sources tended to aggregate populations, delineating only, for example, the "Beja," "Baggara," etc. (although this was not always the case), whereas other, often later sources, treated some of the better known subdivisions of some of these major populations (although examples of both cases can be found throughout the text, see especially the appendix). Although there is insufficient information relative to all of the subdivisions of generic populations, there *is* sufficient information to indicate that not all subdivisions of all major populations share an identical or even a similar socioeconomic structure. As a consequence, when one or more sources attributed certain characteristics to a generic population, I was hesitant to attribute these same characteristics to subdivisions of that population unless they too were specifically referenced. Ideally, of course, only subdivisions of major populations should have been included. This proved not feasible for two major reasons: (1) it is (currently and historically) difficult to determine the relationship of minor (and sometimes major) tribal groups to a given generic population; and (2) there is insufficient information about many of the subdivisions of most of these major populations (e.g., the Nubians, Beja, Baggara, Somali). In the interests of making available as much information as possible, major (generic) populations have, where necessary, also been listed in the tables (this chapter). The Nubians, Beja, Baggara, and Somali represent the only major (generic) populations for which tribal subdivisions have also been listed (major populations are listed in capital letters). The remaining major populations (five) represent single entries.

The sample employed in this study is the subset of the +/- 105 populations mentioned above, about which sufficient information is available to provide a relatively secure base for statistical analysis. With few exceptions (listed below), all of these populations can be found in the geographic region under consideration. The resulting population listing, although small, is at least reasonably verifiable. As such, it can be used to formulate some preliminary conclusions, useful in initiating hypotheses for field testing.

Sample Selection and Statistical Analysis

The Study and Control Samples

The sample utilized by this study (see table 4.1) does not represent a complete statistical sample. The application of sampling techniques proved impossible, given the exploratory nature of this study and the general paucity of both geographic and demographic information relative to the entire region of northeast Africa, including the Sudan. Nevertheless, the sample can be considered representative of both infibulation-practicing and noninfibulating, but otherwise comparable populations.

Of the 105 total populations considered in the appendix, a minimum of two independent sources confirmed the presence of the practice of infibulation in a total of twenty-six groups. Excluded from the subsequent Chi-square and HOMALS application to the data were those population groups for which the practice of infibulation could be confirmed only by a single source.

The study sample thus comprises all those populations for which there was adequate data to indicate the presence of the practice of infibulation (a total of twenty-six populations). The control sample, which includes a total of twenty populations, is also a subset of the complete sample in the appendix. Although control sample membership was limited to twenty primarily as a result of information availability, in order to facilitate comparative analysis it was also restricted to those populations not practicing infibulation, but which:

1. are located in or near the same geographic regions as the study sample (with some exceptions);

2. exhibit subsistence patterns similar to those populations who currently practice infibulation: to include agriculture, agro-pastoralism, semi- and nomadic cattle/camel complex pastoralism (in the control sample, eleven groups can be categorized nomadic/seminomadic, seven as agro-pastoral, and two as agricultural);

3. manifest at least one of those attributes initially found to be common to all infibulation-practicing populations, variables IX, XII, XV, and/or XVIII (see table 4.3). The latter variable was present for twenty-four members of the total study sample, its presence/absence unknown for the remaining two members. In the control sample, only one group manifested the minimum number of attributes, five had two attributes present, eight had three, and six had all four attributes manifest.

All of the populations listed in table 4.1, with the exception of the Tuareg, Rendille, Al Murrah, Rwala, and Fulani, inhabit the same general region as the infibulation-practicing populations, but do not, themselves, practice infibulation. All of these exceptions exhibit characteristics similar to those populations that do practice infibulation. Both the Tuareg and Fulani come from regions where the practice of infibulation has been reported, but could not be substantiated. The Al Murrah and Rwala have attributes, and occupy an environmental setting, almost completely identical to the majority of infibulating populations, in addition to which they are traditional bedouin, Moslems, and originate in Saudi Arabia, a region that has had a considerable and lengthy influence on all of Islamic northeastern Africa (see chapter 1 and the appendix).

Of the twenty total populations comprising the control sample, ten practice excision (four of which are located in the Sudan and borderland areas and six in the Horn region), and ten do not practice any form of female circumcision (four in the Sudan and borderland areas, one in the Horn region, one in Kenya, and four external to the general geographic location of these populations).

A total of forty-six populations (study and control sample) were then subjected to Chi-square testing and the HOMALS application.

The Attributes Considered

Because an ethnographic survey of the composite geographic area under consideration was not possible (nor currently exists), this study was exploratory on every level. A primary problem in analyzing the function of infibulation is its current occurrence among populations at all subsistence levels. Consequently, of preeminent concern was a determination of the historical subsistence mode(s) of infibulation-practicing populations. Available information indicated that, even though the populations currently practicing infibulation are distributed all along the urban-pastoral continuum, the majority historically fall into the pastoralist/agro-pastoralist categories (see chapter 2). Consequently, only those attributes were retained for which there was evidence to indicate their historical presence among those pastoral and agro-pastoral populations (both infibulating and noninfibulating), located within the geographic confines where infibulation is practiced. Although severely restricted by data limitations, a compilation of twenty-one attributes proved feasible (listed in table 4.1). Even in those cases where a given population could be subdivided into individual member groups, it should be stressed that the degree of relevance of these attributes within the individual member groups is unknown.

Those attributes considered include:

I. Agricultural. Generally speaking, those populations practicing agriculture in all of the geographic areas under consideration do so in conjunction with husbandry, which even today retains equal or secondary importance to agriculture (but is rarely merely subsidiary). This category also includes those populations qualifying as agro-pastoral (see chapter 2).

II. Nomadic camel/cattle (to include sheep/goat) complex. This category includes all primarily nomadic populations (see chapter 2), either camel or cattle complex, or a combination of both, as well as sheep and goat complex (whether subsidiary to camel/cattle, or primary). These populations, in some few instances, also practice minimal cultivation.

III. Seminomadic cattle/camel (to include sheep/goat) complex. This category includes both cattle and cattle/camel complex (to include sheep and goats), with minimal cultivation.

IV. Camel/cattle owners—men. This category defines the gender of the primary owners of camel/cattle as males. Although in some cases women are alloted rights to herding animals, they are rarely the actual owners; they retain usufruct to the by-products, but not alienability rights. Similarly, in some instances women also take part in the herding of "wealth" animals (camel and cattle), although more generally this is the province of males, who also have alienability rights over these herds.

V. Sheep/goat herding—women. Unless sheep and goats represent the primary form of wealth, they are herded and cared for by women and used primarily for the household. They thus fall under the control of the women as subsistence rather than wealth source herds. In cases where sheep and goats are secondary to camel/ cattle, it is the women who have usufruct rights and who are totally responsible for these herds. However, even when this is the case, they rarely retain alienability rights over the herds, with the exception of perhaps passing them on to their children, to their sons for bridewealth, or to their daughters upon their marriage.

VI. and VII. Respectively, bride-price paid primarily in livestock, and bride price high. These categories represent the traditional forms and levels of bride price payment; today, bridewealth is not always paid in the form of animals. The concern here is to determine the importance of herd animals in the various populations under consideration, especially those now manifestly sedentary. Theoretically, when bridewealth is paid in animals, it seems safe to assume that wealth is also perceived in terms of livestock.

VIII. Male absenteeism. This variable was primarily considered relative to herding populations. Where males are the primary, or only herders of camels/cattle, they will regularly be absent from the residence unit and immediate family (wife/children). This type of herding is usually in conjunction with secondary sheep/goat herding, the province of women. Important here is that pasturing requirements differ for camels, cattle, sheep, and goats. Similarly, in cases where pastoralism coincides with polygamy, regularized male absence can be extensive, depending upon the number of wives and their geographic location, matrilocal residence requirements, including bride-service, and so forth. Additionally, those populations adapted to extended male absenteeism due to herding requirements will potentially more readily adopt "urban" male absenteeism, involving, for example, long-term male migration in search of employment, government-related employment, etc.

IX. Generally low position of women (in legal and social rank terms). Reference here made primarily to the de jure position of women. Their de facto position is taken into account only secondarily, or when their de jure position is either unclear, or a considerable discrepancy exists between their de jure rights and de facto practice.

X. Excision practiced. Excision refers to clitoridectomy only.

XI. Infibulation practiced. Infibulation generally practiced.

XII. Islamic. As many of the populations concerned in this study have converted to Islam since the last century (while others have been influenced by Arab traders and Islam over a number of centuries), it is difficult to specifically qualify the extent to which Islam has permeated the entire social system. This variable thus includes all forms of Islamic conversion, from minimal to complete.

XIII. Preferred parallel cousin marriage. Includes those populations that currently prefer parallel cousin marriages. Where information was available, recent adoption of preferred parallel cousin unions as well as the specific form they take can be found in the appendix.

XIV. Exogamy (all other unions, to include cross-cousin unions). Comprises all unions other than parallel cousin unions. Unfortunately, traditional exogamic practices (all forms) proved difficult to verify historically, since populations converting to Islam often make a quite rapid shift to preferred parallel cousin unions. The existence, or lack of pre-Islamic exogamy among Sudanese populations is thus virtually impossible to determine. Since endogamy at the lowest level (preferred parallel cousin unions) occurs primarily among strongly Islamic populations in northern Africa (Murdock, 1959:28), and since the majority of northeast African infibulating groups are endogamous, marriage preferences were considered for potential correlations.

XV. Polygamy. None of the populations considered in this study were polyandrous. Similarly, few of the total number of populations had traditions of prescriptive monogamy.

XVI. Women (married) remain the responsibility of their kin group, and are not assimilated into the husband's kin group. Even after marriage, women remain both members, and the responsibility of their own kin group. This continues throughout their lives, as they are never formally assimilated into the husband's kin group.

XVII. Levirate practiced. General information relative to this practice among the specific population groups in the Sudan was not available (with the exception of the Rufa'a). Consequently, Farran's position, which is that it exists primarily among southern Sudanese populations, was adopted for this study (Farran, 1963:5-6, 77-78, 137-41).

XVIII. Virilocal residence only after the birth of the first (or subsequent) child(ren). Included here are all cases of initial uxorilocal residence, whether this involves only the wife, or both spouses. Generally speaking, where both spouses are in residence uxorilocally, the bridegroom, in addition to paying the bride-price, must provide a specific amount of bride service. *Where 'y*'appears in table 4.1, it indicates that only the wife remains in uxorilocal residence, and then usually only until after the birth of the first child.* Although this period is sometimes protracted to include subsequent children, this practice is usually restricted to secondary wives.

XIX. Wife is manager and/or owner of the residence unit. In most cases (but not all), although the husband has de jure rights over the residence and its contents, it is the wife who has de facto rights to the residence and its contents. In all cases, it is she who manages the residence.

XX. Unstable marriages. Unstable marriages here refer to the ease with which divorce is possible, and the frequency with which it occurs, although it must be mentioned that in the majority of the cases studied, it is the husband who retains primary de jure divorce rights, not the wife. Generally speaking, stable marriages (de jure or de facto) were found to be the exception rather than the rule.

XXI. Jirtig. The "jirtig" ceremony occurs (to my knowledge) only in the Sudan, among northern Sudanese populations, and by no means among all of these. It is included as a variable here primarily because it is found concomitant with traditional infibulation-practicing populations in the northern Sudan. It is not, however, found among populations who have recently adopted the practice (e.g., the various Baggara tribes). A determination of its actual significance among northern Sudanese populations would require extensive field research, since, to my knowledge, no formal study has to date been published concerning this practice.

Attribute Anomalies

Since this study is concerned with traditional infibulation-practicing populations and their traditional socioeconomic structure, a population was classified in tables 4.1 and 4.2 according to both historical and current subsistence patterns. That is to say, when a population was originally nomadic (with all, or some sections only recently becoming sedentary, (i.e., during the last 1 to 1.5 centuries), it was qualified as being both agricultural and camel/cattle nomadic (or seminomadic). This applies to both infibulation- and noninfibulation-practicing populations.

Because the data is historical rather than synchronous, variability was inevitable. This resulted in certain insufficiently defined attributes. In the case of variables I, II, and III, this was exacerbated by an ongoing variability inherent in the overall subsistence patterns prevalent in the geographic area concerned. Reasons for variability include such factors as ecological instability, slavery, migrations, etc.

Consequently, one finds that a "current" rather than "historical" determination of subsistence patterns of populations practicing infibulation indicates a wide variety of populations that are engaged in an equally wide variety of subsistence patterns. On the other hand, a strictly "historical" approach indicates that the majority "traditionally" have been pastoral (nomadic or seminomadic); the remainder are more agro-pastoral than agricultural (e.g., populations falling into this category often rely on nomadic or seminomadic relations to care for their herds). The traditional practice of the agricultural Nubians to pay a high bride-price in the form of livestock (although currently bride-price is often paid in cash or goods) is indicative of a pastoral background.

That the area inhabited by infibulation-practicing "sedentary" populations in the Sudan and northeastern Africa is (and has historically been) regularly traversed by nomadic and seminomadic groups (see maps 2, 3, 5) is also influential in maintaining pastoral/sedentary relationships. In addition, many subsections of infibulation-practicing populations have become sedentarized only within the last century while other subsections continue to be nomadic or seminomadic.

Table 4.1 lists all the populations according to the known subsistence patterns prevalent within the entire population. It identifies the initial twenty-two variables and their distribution among the total population sample. Thus, for example, the Rufa'a are listed as both agricultural and camel/cattle nomadic, whereas the Shaiqiyya are listed as all three (although currently they are primarily urban employed or agricultural). This issue is more fully discussed in chapter 2.

(Although much of the information presented in this table is provided in the appendix and/or can be found throughout the text, the reader is also referred to the bibliography, which lists all of the sources used to compile this table.)

Lack of space and available information precluded an adequate consideration of the often radical sociopolitical and economic changes and the effects of extreme environmental fluctuations on this general region during recent decades.

TABLE 4.1 - A—A Listing of the Variables Considered

	I	II	III	IV	V	VI	VII
SUDAN							
1 NUBIANS	y			-	-	y	y
2 Danagla	y			-	-	?	?
3 Mahas	y			-	-	?	?
4 BEJA		y	y	y	y	y	y
5 Ababda		y		y	y	y	y
6 Beni Amer		y	y	y	y	y	y
7 Bisharin		y	y	y	y	y	y
8 Hadendoa		y		y	?	y	y
9 Rubatab	y	y		y	?	?	?
10 Shaiqiyya	y	y	y	-	-	n	y
11 BAGGARA		y		y	y	y	y
12 Mahamid		y	y	y	?	y	y
13 Salamat		y	y	y	?	y	y
14 Messyria	y		y	y	?	?	?
15 Humr	y		y	y	?	?	?
16 Kababish		y		y	y	y	va
17 Rufa'a	y	y		y	y	y	y
18 Shukriyya		y	y	?	?	?	?
19 Hasania		y	y	y	?	?	?
20 Kenana	y	y	y	y	?	?	?
21 Bedayat		y		y	?	y	y
22 Berti	y			-	-	yn	y
23 Dagu	y		y	?	?	?	?
24 FUR	y			y	-	y	n
25 Meidob	y		y	y	mf	n	n
26 NUBA	y		y	y	?	y	va
27 Zaghawa		y	y	y	y	y	y
28 Ingassana	y		y	y	-	n	va

I	agricultural	-	n.a.
II	camel/cattle - nomads	n	no yn yes&no
III	camel/cattle - semi-nomads	y	yes
IV	camel/cattle owners - men	mf	male and female
V	sheep/goat herding - women	va	varies
VI	brideprice livestock	sl	slaves
VII	brideprice high	pa	Pagan
		pi	Pagan/Islamic

TABLE 4.1 - B—A Listing of the Variables Considered

	VIII	IX	X	XI	XII	XIII	XIV
SUDAN							
1 NUBIANS	-	y		y	y	y	y
2 Danagla	-	y		y	y	y	
3 Mahas	-	y		y	y	y	
4 BEJA	y	y		y	y	y	
5 Ababda	y	y		y	y	?	
6 Beni Amer	y	y		y	y	y	
7 Bisharin	y	y		y	y	?	
8 Hadendoa	y	y		y	y	?	
9 Rubatab	-	y		y	y	y	
10 Shaiqiyya	?	y		y	y	y	
11 BAGGARA	y	y		y	y	y	
12 Mahamid	y	y		y	y		y
13 Salamat	?	y		y	y		y
14 Messyria	?	y		y	y	?	
15 Humr	?	y		y	y	y	
16 Kababish	y	y		y	y	y	
17 Rufa'a	y	y		y	y	y	
18 Shukriyya	?	y		y	y	y	
19 Hasania	?	y		y	y	?	
20 Kenana	?	y		y	y	y	
21 Bedayat	?	?	n		pi		y
22 Berti	-	y	n		y	y	
23 Dagu	?	y	y		y	?	
24 FUR	-	n	n		y		y
25 Meidob	?	n	y		pi	y	y
26 NUBA	?	y	n		pa		y
27 Zaghawa	mf	y	y		pi		y
28 Ingassana	n	n	n		pa		y

VIII	male absenteeism	-	n.a.
IX	low position women	n	no yn yes&no
X	excision practiced	y	yes
XI	infibulation	mf	male and female
XII	Islamic	va	varies
XIII	preferred parallel cousin marriage	sl	slaves
XIV	exogamy	pa	Pagan
		pi	Pagan/Islamic

TABLE 4.1 - C—A Listing of the Variables Considered

	XV	XVI	XVII	XVIII	XIX	XX	XXI
SUDAN							
1 NUBIANS	y	y		y	y	?	y
2 Danagla	y	?		y	?	y	y
3 Mahas	y	?		y	?	?	y
4 BEJA	y	y	y	y	y	y	y
5 Ababda	y	y		y	y	y	y
6 Beni Amer	y	y		y	y	y	y
7 Bisharin	y	y		y	y	y	y
8 Hadendoa	y	?		y	?	y	y
9 Rubatab	y	?		y	?	?	y
10 Shaiqiyya	y	y		y	y	n	y
11 BAGGARA	y	y		y	y	y	n
12 Mahamid	y	?		y	?	?	n
13 Salamat	y	?		y	?	?	n
14 Messyria	y	y		y	y	y	n
15 Humr	y	y		y	y	y	n
16 Kababish	y	y		y	y	y	n
17 Rufa'a	y	y	y/n	y	y	y	y
18 Shukriyya	y	?		y	?	?	n
19 Hasania	y	?		y	?	?	y
20 Kenana	y	?		?	?	?	?
21 Bedayat	y	?	y	y	?	?	?
22 Berti	y	y/n		y	y	y	n
23 Dagu	y	?		y	?	?	?
24 FUR	n	n		y	y	n	n
25 Meidob	?	?		?	?	y	n
26 NUBA	y	?		y	?	?	n
27 Zaghawa	y/n	?	y	y	?	?	n
28 Ingassana	y/n	n	y	y*	y	n	n

XV polygamy		-	n.a.
XVI married women resp. kin-group		n	no yn yes&no
XVII levirate practiced		y	yes
XVIII initial matrilocal resident		mf	male and female
XIX woman man / owners / res. unit		va	varies
XX unstable marriages		sl	slaves
XXI jirtig		pa	Pagan
		pi	Pagan/Islamic

TABLE 4.1 - D—A Listing of the Variables Considered

	I	II	III	IV	V	VI	VII
N.E AFRICA AND OTHER							
29 Dasenetsch			y	y	-	y	y
30 GALLA	y	y	y	y	-	y	va
31 Afar/Danakil		y		y	y	y	y
32 Bilen/Bogos	y		y	?	?	?	?
33 Saho			y	?	?	?	?
34 SOMALI		y		y	y	y	y
35 Somali/Ogaden	y		y	y	y	y	y
36 Esa/Dir		y	y	y	y	y	y
37 SAB	y		y	y	?	?	?
38 Boran (Ethiopia)			y	y	-	y	va
39 KAFFA	y		y	mf	mf	y	va
40 Tuareg (Sahara)		y	y	mf	sl	y	va
41 Rendille (Kenya)		y	y	y	y	y	y
42 Gabra (Kenya)		y		y	n	y	n
43 Turkana (Kenya)		y	y	mf	mf	y	va
44 AlMurrah (Saudi A.)		y		y	n	y	y
45 Rwala Saudi A.)		y		y	n	y	y
46 Fulani (Nigeria)		y	y	y	-	none	n

I	agricultural	-	n.a
II	camel/cattle - nomads	n	no yn yes&no
III	camel/cattle - semi-nomads	y	yes
IV	camel/cattle owners - men	mf	male and female
V	sheep/goat herding - women	va	varies
VI	brideprice livestock	sl	slaves
VII	brideprice high	pa	Pagan
		pi	Pagan/Islamic

TABLE 4.1 - E—A Listing of the Variables Considered

	VIII	IX	X	XI	XII	XIII	XIV
N.E AFRICA AND OTHER							
29 Dasenetsch	n	n	y		pa		y
30 GALLA	?	y	y		pi		y
31 Afar/Danakil	y	y		y	y		y
32 Bilen/Bogos	?	y		y	pi	?	
33 Saho	?	y		y	y	?	
34 SOMALI	y	y		y	y		y
35 Somali/Ogaden	y	y	y		y		y
36 Esa/Dir	y	y		y	y		y
37 SAB	y	y		y	y	y	
38 Boran (Ethiopia)	n	n	n		pa		y
39 KAFFA	n	y	y		pi		y
40 Tuareg (Sahara)	n	n	n		y	y	
41 Rendille (Kenya)	y	y	y		pa		y
42 Gabra (Kenya)	y	y	y		pa		y
43 Turkana (Kenya)	mf	y	n		y		y
44 AlMurrah (Saudi A.)	y	y	n		y	y	
45 Rwala Saudi A.)	y	y	n		y	y	
46 Fulani (Nigeria)	n	n	n		y	y	

VIII	male absenteeism	-	n.a
IX	low position women	n	no yn yes&no
X	excision practiced	y	yes
XI	infibulation	mf	male and female
XII	Islamic	va	varies
XIII	preferred parallel cousin marriage	sl	slaves
XIV	exogamy	pa	Pagan
		pi	Pagan/Islamic

TABLE 4.1 - F—A Listing of the Variables Considered

	XV	XVI	XVII	XVIII	XIX	XX	XXI
N.E AFRICA AND OTHER							
29 Dasenetsch	y	n	y	y	y	n	
30 GALLA	y/n	y	y	n	y	n	
31 Afar/Danakil	y	y	y	y	y	y	
32 Bilen/Bogos	y	?	y	y	?	?	
33 Saho	y	y	?	?	?	?	
34 SOMALI	y	y	y	y	y	y	
35 Somali/Ogaden	y	y	y	?	y	y	
36 Esa/Dir	y	y	y	y	y	y	
37 SAB	y	y	?	y	y	y	
38 Boran (Ethiopia)	y/n	n	y	y	y	n	
39 KAFFA	y	n	y	?	y	?	
40 Tuareg (Sahara)	y/n	-	n	y	?	y	
41 Rendille (Kenya)	y	?	?	n	y	n	
42 Gabra (Kenya)	y/n	n	y	y	y	n	
43 Turkana (Kenya)	y	n	n	y	y	n	
44 AlMurrah (Saudi A.)	y	y	n	y*	y	y	
45 Rwala Saudi A.)	y	y	n	y*	y	y	
46 Fulani (Nigeria)	y	y	y	y*	y	y	

XV polygamy		-	n.a
XVI married women resp. kin-group		n	no yn yes&no
XVII levirate practiced		y	yes
XVIII initial matrilocal resident		mf	male and female
XIX woman man /owners/ resident unit		va	varies
XX unstable marriages		sl	slaves
XXI jirtig		pa	Pagan
		pi	Pagan/Islamic

Statistical Analysis

It must be stressed at the outset that the statistical analyses outlined below were used only as analytical tools to extract those attributes preferentially associated with the phenomenon of infibulation. They do not constitute an absolute validation of statistical correlations. Moreover, statistical testing, although useful for synchronous analyses, cannot address the process of historical development. Thus, the application of statistical analysis to the current distribution of the practice of infibulation would result in correlations that are not indicative of the traditional (i.e., historical) distribution, functions or causes of this practice. An example of this problem is addressed in the discussion relative to Islam and exogamy in chapters 3 and 5.

The historical and unreliable nature of the data base utilized in this study rendered any classical statistical analysis impossible. Consequently, although the traditional chi-square technique was applied to determine which individual variables were related to the practice of infibulation, the more general HOMALS technique provided the actual analytical basis.

The primary goal of the statistical analysis was to determine whether infibulation-practicing and noninfibulating populations form respective homogeneous groups on the basis of specific common attributes, that is, they share a common trait pattern. It was desired to determine the validity of the hypothesis that infibulation-practicing populations are significantly distinct from those that do not practice infibulation.

The Chi-square Test

The chi-square test was used to determine those variables that were significantly associated with the practice of infibulation. The categories considered included the presence or absence of individual variables, as well as a "missing" category where neither presence nor absence could be confirmed. The chi-square test results (see tables 4.2 and 4.3) indicated a significant association (99 percent confidence level) of the following variables with the practice of infibulation:

V	Sheep/goat herding by women
VII	Bride-price high
VIII	Male absenteeism
IX	Generally low position of women
X	Excision (not) practiced

XII	Islamic
XIII	Preferred parallel cousine marriage
XIV	(No) exogamy
XVI	Women (married) remain responsibility of own kin-group
XX	Unstable marriages
XXI	Jirtig

Although this test was useful in determining both the relationship of each individual variable to the practice of infibulation and the direction of that relationship, it could not indicate which configuration of variables is potentially associated with the practice of infibulation. Specifically, the chi-square test cannot determine the relationship between a combination of variables and the practice of infibulation, nor can it determine whether infibulation-practicing populations share a trait complex that is significantly different from that found in noninfibulation-practicing populations. To this end, the data was re-analysed, using the HOMALS-technique.

The HOMALS-technique

Generally speaking, social science data do not lend themselves to the use of the classical statistical techniques applied to the natural sciences. Some reasons for this difficulty of application involve the rigorous quantification requirements, which are usually only realizable in the natural sciences. The requisite of an underlying normal or reasonably symmetric data distribution is rarely met by social science data samples, which all too often involve skewed or multiple peaked distribution. While the use of classical techniques presumes a linear relationship between characteristics, the validity of such an assumption in the social sciences is questionable (Nuijten-Edelbroek, 1980:1-3).

One frequently adopted solution to the problem of analyzing social science data involves the use of contingency tables. The chi-square statistic for nominal variables is an example of such an application, although an underlying normal distribution is tacitly assumed. Two major disadvantages of using this type of technique are the difficulty of maintaining a composite overview when numerous variables are involved, and an assessment of the way in which several variables are associated (short of constructing complex multidimensional contingency tables) (Kers, 1986:7). Another solution involves the nonlinear analytic techniques developed in recent years. One of these, the HOMALS-technique, has been utilized in this study (Gifi, 1981).

TABLE 4.2 - Frequency Distribution of the Variables

VARIABLES	YES	NO	MISSING
I	20	26	0
II	26	20	0
III	30	16	0
IV	34	8	4
V	13	18	15
VI	29	5	12
VII	22	12	12
VIII	18	14	14
IX	38	7	1
XII	40	6	0
XIII	20	18	8
XIV	20	26	0
XV	44	1	1
XVI	21	9	16
XVII	16	27	3
XVIII	39	2	5
XIX	29	0	17
XX	22	9	15
XXI	12	31	3

I	AGRIC	VIII	MALAB	XVI	WOKIN
II	NOMAD	IX	LOWWO	XVII	LEVIR
III	SEMNO	XII	ISLAM	XVIII	INMAR
IV	CAMEN	XIII	PLCOU	XIX	WIRES
V	SHEWO	XIV	EXOGA	XX	UNMAR
VI	BRILI	XV	POLYG	XXI	JIRTI
VII	BRIHI				

TABLE 4.3 - Infibulation Data - A

* = associated with infibulation

X^2 test results   (df. for all variables = 1)

I AGRICULTURE						
		yes	no	total	X^2	sign.
infibulation	yes	11	15	26	0.033	0.855
	no	9	11	20		
	total	20	26	46		

II NOMADIC						
		yes	no	total	X^2	sign.
infibulation	yes	17	9	26	1.911	0.167
	no	9	11	20		
	total	26	20	46		

III SEMI-NOMADIC						
		yes	no	total	X^2	sign.
infibulation	yes	16	10	26	0.357	0.550
	no	14	6	20		
	total	30	16	46		

IV CAMEL/CATTLE OWNERS - MEN						
		yes	no	total	X^2	sign.
infibulation	yes	19	4	23	0.090	0.764
	no	15	4	19		
	total	34	8	42		

TABLE 4.3 - Infibulation Data - B

* = associated with infibulation

X^2 test results   (df. for all variables = 1)

V SHEEP/GOAT HERDING - WOMEN						
		yes	no	total	X^2	sign.
infibulation	yes	10	4	14	9.120	0.003	*
	no	3	14	17			
	total	13	18	31			

VI BRIDEPRICE LIVESTOCK						
		yes	no	total	X^2	sign.
infibulation	yes	14	1	15	1.383	0.240
	no	15	4	19		
	total	29	5	34		

VII BRIDEPRICE HIGH						
		yes	no	total	X^2	sign.
infibulation	yes	14	1	15	9.632	0.002	*
	no	8	11	19			
	total	22	12	34			

VIII MALE ABSENTEEISM						
		yes	no	total	X^2	sign.
infibulation	yes	13	4	17	6.026	0.014	*
	no	5	10	15			
	total	18	14	32			

TABLE 4.3 - Infibulation Data - C

* = associated with infibulation

X^2 test results   (df. for all variables = 1)

IX LOW POSITION WOMEN							
		yes	no	total	X^2	sign.	
infibulation	yes	26	0	26	11.343	0.001	*
	no	12	7	19			
	total	38	7	45			

X EXCISION PRACTICED							
		yes	no	total	X^2	sign.	
infibulation	yes	0	26	26	16.611	0.000	*
	no	10	10	20			
	total	10	36	46			

XII ISLAMIC							
		yes	no	total	X^2	sign.	
infibulation	yes	26	0	26	8.970	0.003	*
	no	14	6	20			
	total	40	6	46			

XIII PREFERRED PARALLEL COUSIN MARRIAGE							
		yes	no	total	X^2	sign.	
infibulation	yes	14	5	19	6.756	0.009	*
	no	6	13	19			
	total	20	18	38			

TABLE 4.3 - Infibulation Data - D

* = associated with infibulation

x^2 test results (df. for all variables = 1)

XIV EXOGAMY							
		yes	no	total	x^2	sign.	
infibulation	yes	6	20	26	10.128	0.001	*
	no	14	6	20			
	total	20	26	46			

XV POLYGAMY							
		yes	no	total	x^2	sign.	
infibulation	yes	26	0	26	1.400	0.237	
	no	18	1	19			
	total	44	1	45			

XVI MARRIED WOMEN RESPONSIBILITY KINSHIP GROUP							
		yes	no	total	x^2	sign.	
infibulation	yes	16	0	16	14.694	0.000	*
	no	5	9	14			
	total	21	9	30			

XVII LEVIRATE PRACTICED							
		yes	no	total	x^2	sign.	
infibulation	yes	6	18	24	3.465	0.063	
	no	10	9	19			
	total	16	27	43			

TABLE 4.3 - Infibulation Data - E

* = associated with infibulation

x^2 test results   (df. for all variables = 1)

XVIII INITIAL MATRILOCAL RESIDENT						
		yes	no	total	x^2	sign.
	yes	24	0	24	2.968	0.085
infibulation	no	15	2	17		
	total	39	2	41		

XIX WOMAN MAN / OWNERS / RESIDENT UNIT						
		yes	no	total	x^2	sign.
	yes	15	0	15	no stastistics -	
infibulation	no	14	0	14	insufficient	
	total	29	0	29	cases/categories	

XX UNSTABLE MARRIAGES							
		yes	no	total	x^2	sign.	
	yes	15	1	16	8.330	0.004	*
infibulation	no	7	8	15			
	total	22	9	31			

XXI JIRTIG							
		yes	no	total	x^2	sign.	
	yes	12	13	25	11.985	0.001	*
infibulation	no	0	18	18			
	total	12	31	43			

Frequency Distribution of the Variables

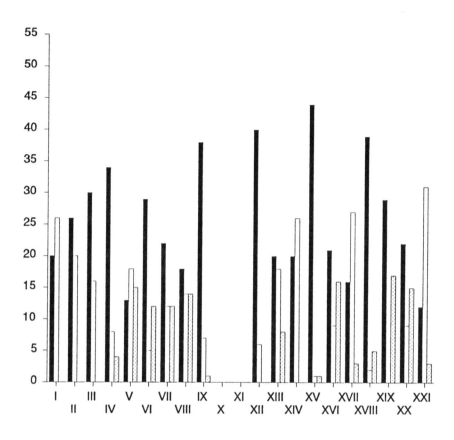

legend

■ YES

☐ NO

▦ MISSING

HOMALS (HOMogeneity Analysis with Alternating Least Squares) does not treat a variable as an integrated given. Rather, a variable is conceived as being composed of multiple units, qualified as "categories" of the variable. These categories are subsequently taken as the starting point of analysis, rather than using the variables themselves. For example, variables X and XI (respectively excision and infibulation practiced) were recombined into one new variable having three categories (see below). By treating the research data as categorical, many of the problems normally encountered in using classical techniques are circumvented. Even missing data present no real problems for HOMALS. There is no deletion of the "non-missing" information for those objects and/or variables having missing information (Gifi, 1983:3-4).

The goal of this technique is to determine not only the existence of certain patterns or combinations of categories in the data, but also to look for combinations of objects, that is, objects having a common configuration of categories. HOMALS scores both the objects and the categories with respect to the "dimensionality" of the quantification, which is chosen by the user. It allots one point in a multidimensional space for each object and category score on the basis of contiguity and separation (Gifi, 1983:3). This means that those objects or categories that appear to be similar are grouped together in a multidimensional space (contiguity); those which have nothing in common are located as far apart in space as possible (separation).

HOMALS Evaluation of All Variables in the Data Set

The study sample and the control sample were delineated by the values of variables X and XI. For the HOMALS analysis, these variables were recombined into a new variable having three categories:

1 =   Infibulation practiced - INFIB
2 =   Excision practiced - EXCIS
3 =   Neither infibulation nor excision practiced - NONE

This variable functioned only to "label" the objects with the categories of the variables, but was not included in the HOMALS analysis as a formal variable. This was deemed necessary to determine the existence of any similarity between the pattern formation of populations (objects), determined on the basis of an analysis of the other variables, and any patterns found prevalent in infibulating and/or noninfibulating populations. This recombination reduced the total number of variables included in the initial analysis to nineteen.

Table 4.4 lists these nineteen remaining variables and the eigenvalues and discrimination measures. Since the HOMALS technique constructs the axes directions such that the eigenvalue in dimension 3 should, and in this case did, drop sharply, minimal information loss is incurred by deleting this dimension from further consideration.

Several of the variables (see plot 1) are below the eigenvalue of dimensions 1 and 2, which indicates that they only minimally discriminate between the populations (objects). This was to be expected since the majority of the populations scored similarly for variables XV (polygamy), XVIII (matrilocal residence after marriage), and XIX (women as owners/managers of the residence). Thus, none of these variables discriminate very much between the objects. Because variables III (camel/cattle seminomads) and XXI (jirtig) are also below or equal to the eigenvalues of dimensions 1 and 2, they, too, do not overly discriminate between the populations in the data samples. A final total of fourteen variables was retained for further analysis; those noted above were excluded.

HOMALS Evaluation of the Remaining Variables in the Data Samples

Prior to determining which of these fourteen remaining variables were primarily associated with the practice of infibulation, it was necessary to determine whether infibulating and non-infibulating populations form homogeneous groups on the basis of specific common traits. The HOMALS population plot (plot 2) clearly indicates that infibulating and noninfibulating populations are separated in the two-dimensional HOMALS plot of the labeled object scores (Kers, 1985:14). That infibulating and noninfibulating populations differ from one another in some way was thus substantiated. In plot 2, a straight line has been drawn to designate the division between infibulating and noninfibulating populations. Noninfibulating populations are represented to the left of the line, with infibulating populations to the right of it. By extension, the chance of finding an infibulating population increases as one moves from left to right on the plot. This implies that infibulating and noninfibulating populations are separated from each other by variables having high discrimination measures on the first dimension. Conversely, infibulating and non-infibulating populations are spread almost equally (are mixed)

TABLE 4.4 - Discrimination Measures

VARIABLES	DIMENSION 1	DIMENSION 2	DIMENSION 3
I	0.041	0.458 *	0.093
II	0.194	0.314 *	0.253
III	0.048	0.011	0.659 *
IV	0.031	0.392 *	0.185
V	0.378 *	0.347 *	0.074
VI	0.092	0.336 *	0.068
VII	0.500 *	0.135	0.048
VIII	0.388 *	0.338 *	0.131
IX	0.513 *	0.029	0.021
XII	0.414 *	0.122	0.014
XIII	0.312 *	0.539 *	0.002
XIV	0.477 *	0.377 *	0.033
XV	0.115	0.007	0.062
XVI	0.626 *	0.015	0.104
XVII	0.135	0.304 *	0.009
XVIII	0.043	0.140	0.024
XIX	0.003	0.017	0.000
XX	0.531 *	0.037	0.017
XXI	0.276	0.100	0.280
'EIGEN' VALUES	0.269	0.212	0.108

I	AGRIC	VIII	MALAB	XVI	WOKIN
II	NOMAD	IX	LOWWO	XVII	LEVIR
III	SEMNO	XII	ISLAM	XVIII	INMAR
IV	CAMEN	XIII	PLCOU	XIX	WIRES
V	SHEWO	XIV	EXOGA	XX	UNMAR
VI	BRILI	XV	POLYG	XXI	JIRTI
VII	BRIHI				

Graphic Belonging to Table 4.4 - A

DISCRIMINATION MEASURES

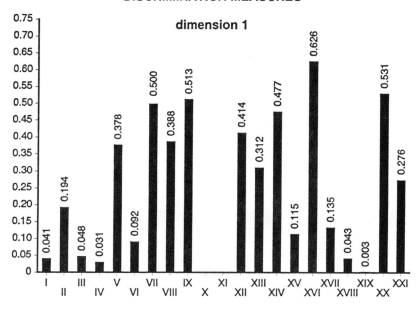

DISCRIMINATION MEASURES

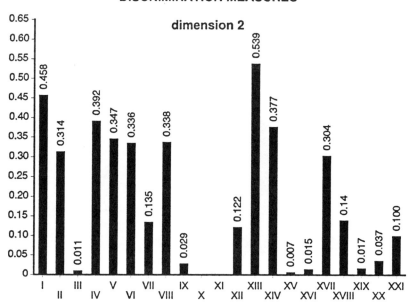

Graphic Belonging to Table 4.4 - B

DISCRIMINATION MEASURES

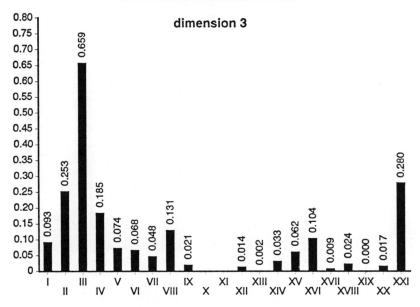

dimension 3

Graphic Belonging to Table 4.4 - C

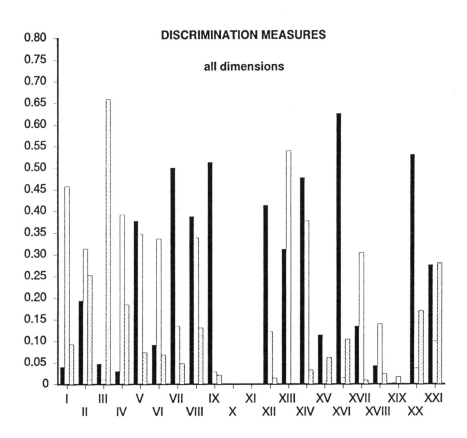

legend

■ dimension 1
☐ dimension 2
▨ dimension 3

**TABLE 4.5 - Variables with High Discrimination Measures
on the Several Dimensions**

on the first dimension:

XVI	women (married) remain the responsibility of their kin-group and are not assimilated into the husband's kin-group	0.626
XX	unstable marriages	0.531
IX	generally low position of women	0.513
VII	brideprices high	0.500
XIV	exogamy	0.477
XII	Islamic	0.414
VIII	male absenteeism	0.388
V	sheep/goat herding - women	0.378
XIII	preferred parallel cousin marriage	0.312

on the second dimension:

XIII	preferred parallel cousin marriage	0.539
I	agricultural	0.458
IV	camel/cattle owners - men	0.392
XIV	exogamy	0.377
V	sheep/goat herding - women	0.347
VIII	male absenteeism	0.338
VI	brideprice paid primarily in livestock	0.336
II	nomadic cattle/camel (to include sheep/goat) complex	0.314
XVII	levirate practiced	0.304

on the third dimension:

III	semi-nomadic camel/cattle (to include sheep/goat) complex	0.659

Graphic Belonging to Table 4.5

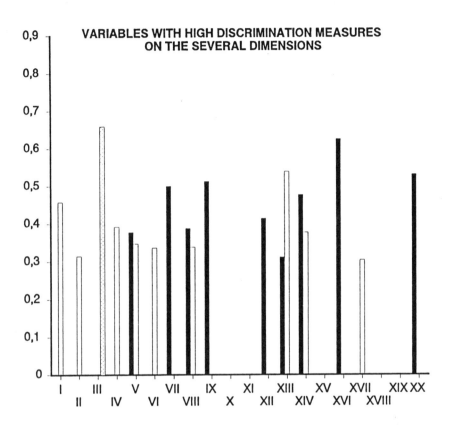

VARIABLES WITH HIGH DISCRIMINATION MEASURES
ON THE SEVERAL DIMENSIONS

legend

■ first dimension

☐ second dimension

▨ third dimension

TABLE 4.6 - Labels of the Populations and Categories
Used in the HOMALS Plots

ABABD	Ababda	KABAB	Kababish
ALMUR	AlMurrah (Saudi Arabia)	KAFFA	KAFFA
BAGGA	BAGGARA	KENAN	Kenana
BEDAY	Bedayat	MAHAM	Mahamid
BEJA	BEJA	MAHAS	Mahas
BENIA	Beni Amer	MEIDO	Meidob
BERTI	Berti	MESSY	Messyria
BILEN	Bilen/Bogos	NUBA	NUBA
BISHA	Bisharin	NUBIA	Nubians
BORAN	Boran (Ethiopia)	OGADE	Somali/Ogaden
DAGU	Dagu	RENDI	Rendille (Kenya)
DANAG	Danagla	RUBAT	Rubatab
DANAK	Afar/Danakil	RUFAA	Rufa'a
DASEN	Dasenetsch	RWALA	Rwala (Saudi Arabia)
ESADI	Esa/Dir	SAB	SAB
FULAN	Fulani (Nigeria)	SAHO	Saho
FUR	FUR	SALAM	Salamat
GABRA	Gabra (Kenya)	SHAIQ	Shaiqiyya
GALLA	GALLA	SHUKR	Shukriyya
HADEN	Hadendoa	SOMAL	SOMALI
HASAN	Hasania	TUARE	Tuareg (Sahara)
HUMR	Humr	TURKA	Turkana (Kenya)
INGAS	Ingassana	ZAGHA	Zaghawa

TABLE 4.7 - Labels of the Categories Used in the HOMALS Plots

AGRIC   agricultural
-AGRI   not agricultural

NOMAD nomadic
-NOMA not nomadic

SEMNO semi-nomadic
(no category in plot)

CAMEN camel/cattle owners - men
-CAME no camel/catttle complex

SHEWO sheep/goat herding -
       women
-SHEW no sheep/goat herding by
       women

BRILI   brideprice livestock
-BRIL   brideprice not livestock

BRIHI   brideprice high
-BRIH   brideprice not high

MALAB male absenteeisme
-MALA no male absence

LOWWO low position of women
-LOWW no low position of women

ISLAM islamic
-ISLA not islamic

PLCOU preferred parallel cousin
       marriage
-PLCO parallel cousin marriage not
       preferred

EXOGA exogamy
-EXOG no exogamy

POLYG polygamy
(no category in plot)

WOKIN married women responsi-
       bility kinship group
-WOKI women do not remain
       member of kinship group

LEVIR levirate practiced
-LEVI no levirate practiced

INMAR initial matrilocal resident
(no category in plot)

WIRES wife manager resident unit
(no category in plot)

UNMAR unstable marriages
-UNMAR stable marriages

JIRTI jirtig practiced
(no category in plot)

INFIB infibulation practiced

EXCIS excision practiced

NONE neither infibulation nor
      excision practiced

PLOT 1 - HOMALS Discrimination Measures (all variables)

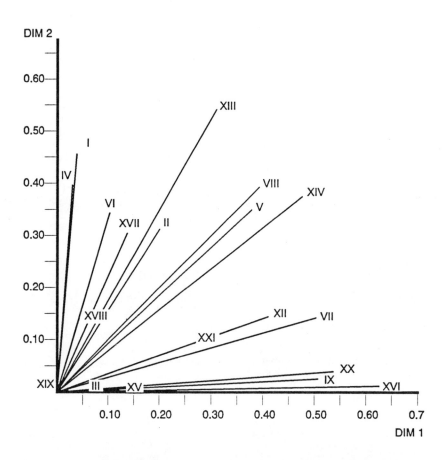

VARS		DIM 1	DIM 2	DIM 3	VARS		DIM 1	DIM 2	DIM 3
I	AGRIC	0.041	0.458	0.093	XIII	PLCOU	0.312	0.539	0.002
II	NOMAD	0.194	0.314	0.253	XIV	EXOGA	0.477	0.377	0.033
III	SEMNO	0.048	0.011	0.659	XV	POLYG	0.115	0.007	0.062
IV	CAMEN	0.031	0.392	0.185	XVI	WOKIN	0.626	0.015	0.104
V	SHEWO	0.378	0.347	0.074	XVII	LEVIR	0.135	0.304	0.009
VI	BRILI	0.092	0.336	0.068	XVIII	INMAR	0.043	0.140	0.024
VII	BRIHI	0.500	0.135	0.048	XIX	WIRES	0.003	0.017	0.000
VIII	MALAB	0.388	0.338	0.131	XX	UNMAR	0.531	0.037	0.017
IX	LOWWO	0.513	0.029	0.021	XXI	JIRTI	0.276	0.100	0.280
XII	ISLAM	0.414	0.122	0.014					

over the second dimension, implying that the second dimension does not discriminate betweeen infibulating and noninfibulating populations (Kers, 1985:14). Additionally, plots 2, 5, and 6 indicate that infibulating populations form a more homogeneous group than do noninfibulating populations.

PLOT 2 - HOMALS Infibulating/Noninfibulating Population Plot

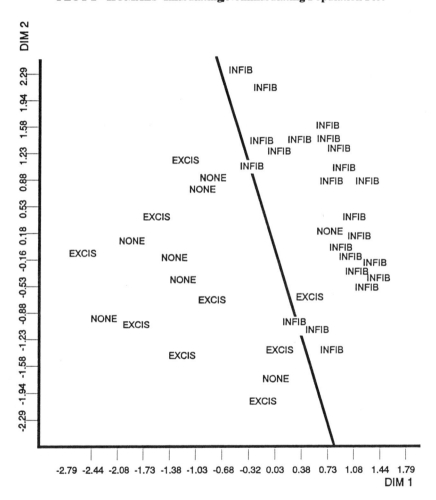

When the remaining fourteen variables (see above) were submitted to HOMALS testing, the eigenvalues of the two HOMALS dimensions

were slightly raised (see plot 4; plot 3 contains the categories of the fourteen variables). This implies that the dimensions defined by the new combination of variables are better able to discriminate between the two groups. A comparison of the discrimination measures of the variables with the eigenvalues of the two dimensions indicates that *variables V, VII, VIII, IX, XII, XIV, XVI, XX have a high discrimination measure on the first dimension, with Variables I, II, IV, VI, XIII, XIV, XVII on the second dimension.*

Since a clear separation between infibulating and noninfibulating populations should be on the basis of those variables having high discrimination measures on the first HOMALS dimension, the differences between the two groups may be considered on the basis of the discrimination measures of the variables (and the positions of the objects and categories) on the first dimension (Kers, 1986:22). Tables 4.8 and 4.9 illustrate the scores of the objects and categories on the first dimension.

Ordering the variables hierarchically, that is, according to the value of their discrimination measures on the first dimension (to include only those with a discrimination measure higher than the eigenvalue) results in the following arrangement:

- XVI	WOKIN	.678
- VIII	MALAB	.529
- XX	UNMAR	.515
- IX	LOWWO	.501
- V	SHEWO	.488
- VII	BRIHI	.483
- XII	ISLAM	.393
- XIV	EXOGA	.374

Infibulation-practicing populations are thus primarily characterized by these traits, while non-infibulation practicing populations are primarily characterized by the opposite traits. The category scores in table 4.9 and plot 4 indicate that the primary traits that characterize infibulating populations include:

(XVI)	Women (married) remain the responsibility of their kin-goup and are not assimilated into the husband's kin group (WOKIN)
(VIII)	Male absenteeism (MALAB)
(XX)	Unstable marriages (UNMAR)
(IX)	Generally low position of women (LOWWO)
(V)	Sheep/goat herding by women (SHEWO)
(VII)	Bride-price high (BRIHI)
(XII)	Islam (ISLAM)
(XIV)	No exogamy; (-EXOG)

TABLE 4.8 - The Position (scores) of the Objects on HOMALS Dimension 1

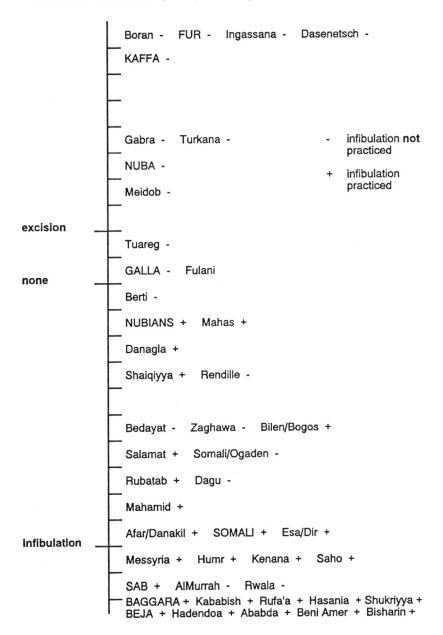

Boran -   FUR -   Ingassana -   Dasenetsch -

KAFFA -

Gabra -   Turkana -   -   infibulation **not** practiced

NUBA -   +   infibulation practiced

Meidob -

excision

Tuareg -

GALLA -   Fulani

none

Berti -

NUBIANS +   Mahas +

Danagla +

Shaiqiyya +   Rendille -

Bedayat -   Zaghawa -   Bilen/Bogos +

Salamat +   Somali/Ogaden -

Rubatab +   Dagu -

Mahamid +

Afar/Danakil +   SOMALI +   Esa/Dir +

Infibulation

Messyria +   Humr +   Kenana +   Saho +

SAB +   AlMurrah -   Rwala -

BAGGARA + Kababish + Rufa'a + Hasania + Shukriyya +
BEJA + Hadendoa + Ababda + Beni Amer + Bisharin +

TABLE 4.9 - The Position (scores) of the Categories on HOMALS Dimension 1

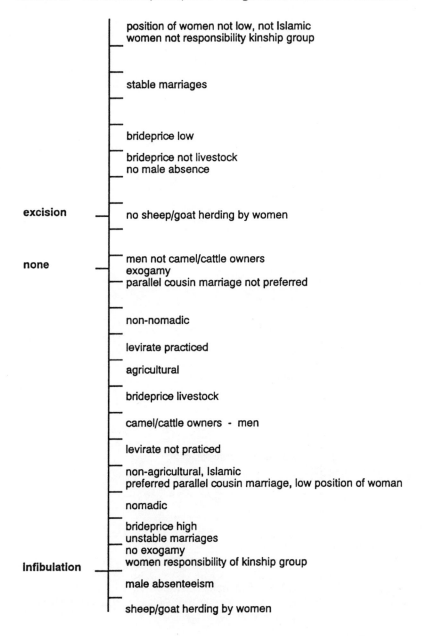

position of women not low, not Islamic
women not responsibility kinship group

stable marriages

brideprice low

brideprice not livestock
no male absence

excision   no sheep/goat herding by women

none   men not camel/cattle owners
exogamy
parallel cousin marriage not preferred

non-nomadic

levirate practiced

agricultural

brideprice livestock

camel/cattle owners - men

levirate not praticed

non-agricultural, Islamic
preferred parallel cousin marriage, low position of woman

nomadic

brideprice high
unstable marriages
no exogamy
women responsibility of kinship group

Infibulation   male absenteeism

sheep/goat herding by women

PLOT 3 - HOMALS Variable Category Plot

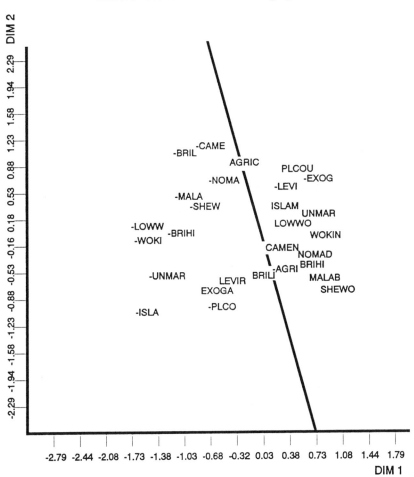

while the secondary traits that characterize these populations (although these variables have a discrimination measure below the eigenvalue of the first dimension) include:

(II)	Nomadic (NOMAD)
(XIII)	Preferred parallel cousin marriage (PLCOU)
(I)	Nonagricultural (-AGRI)
(XVII)	No levirate (-LEVI)
(IV)	Camel/cattle owners - men (CAMEN)
(VI)	Bride-price livestock (BRILI)

PLOT 4 - HOMALS Discrimination Measures

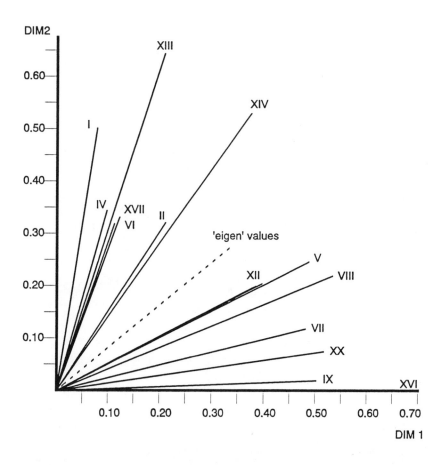

VARS		DIM 1	DIM 2	VARS		DIM 1	DIM 2
I	AGRIC	0.078	0.500	XIII	PLCOU	0.209	0.645
II	NOMAD	0.218	0.322	XIV	EXOGA	0.374	0.529
III	SEMNO			XV	POLYG		
IV	CAMEN	0.098	0.320	XVI	WOKIN	0.678	0.002
V	SHEWO	0.488	0.245	XVII	LEVIR	0.095	0.333
VI	BRILI	0.116	0.320	XVIII	INMAR		
VII	BRIHI	0.483	0.120	XIX	WIRES		
VIII	MALAB	0.529	0.215	XX	UNMAR	0.515	0.078
IX	LOWWO	0.501	0.020	XXI	JIRTI		
XII	ISLAM	0.393	0.199	'eigen' values		0.341	0.275

PLOT 5 - Infibulation Data Plot

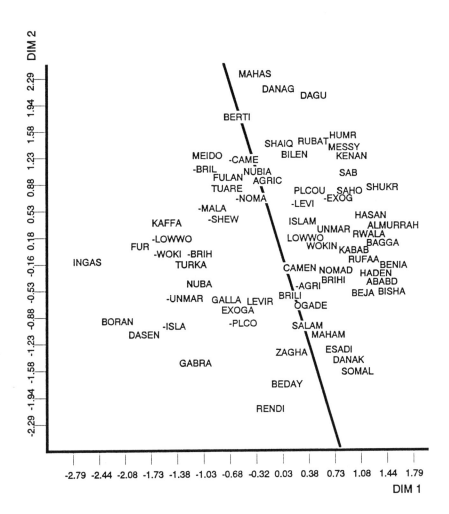

PLOT 6 - HOMALS Population Data

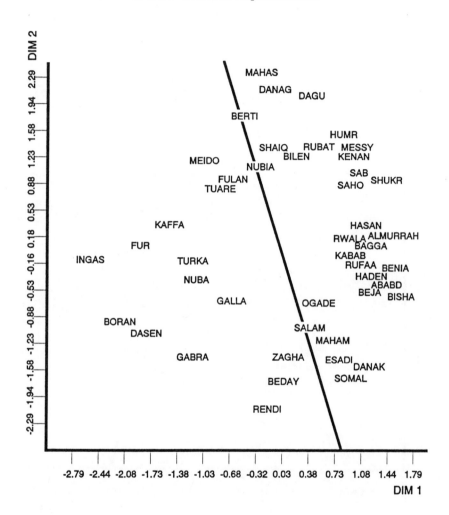

Object anomalies

In the object plots (2, 5, 6), and in table 4.8, there are three non-infibulating populations within the "core" of infibulating populations (to the right of the plot). These are the AlMurrah and Rwala of Saudi Arabia, who presumably do not practice female circumcision, and the Dagu, who practice excision. The first two share all of the above primary or first dimension characteristics with the exception of variable V (sheep/goat herding women). Until relatively recently, the first two of these populations were primarily camel nomads and neither population had sheep or goats.

The first two populations also exhibit all of the secondary traits characteristic of infibulating populations with the exception or modification of XIII (parallel cousin preferred marriage). The Dagu are primarily sedentary, although they do also practice animal husbandry. They farm their animals out to Arab pastoralists in exchange for grazing rights. Like the AlMurrah and Rwala, they are Moslems, but are non-Arab. These three exceptions, together with the variables differentiating them from infibulation-practicing populations have been considered in chapter 5. In the same chapter, the eight primary characteristics that were found to be associated with infibulation are considered within the social context of their occurrence, together with other factors potentially related to this practice.

5

Infibulation and the Composite Variables

The exploratory and preliminary nature of the current study dictated, in the first instance, a compilation of all available information. To that end, the HOMALS technique (see chapter 4) afforded an efficient means of isolating and hierarchically organizing the available data. Unfortunately, it is certainly the case that, with the exception of variable V (sheep and goats herded by, and the responsibility of, the wife), many of the variables tested (see tables in chapter 4) can independently, and in limited combinations, be found in noninfibulating, and even non-Islamic social systems in other parts of Africa. Moreover, again with the exception of variable V, all of the individual primary variables can, to some extent, be found distributed among most Moslem pastoral populations. This is an unfortunate consequence of the paucity of available data, which rendered impossible a determination of clear definitional parameters for each individual variable.

Nevertheless, the interest of these variables for this study lies in the fact that all of them have, compositely, been found in those infibulation-practicing populations about which we have sufficient information. Only a subsequent testing of the occurrence of these variables against a larger pastoral population sample will determine the degree of their functional importance to the practice of infibulation. In this context, field/library research testable hypotheses include:

- a determination of the significance of the jirtig ceremony. This practice was found to be concomitant with traditional northern Sudanese infibulation-practicing populations (chapter 4);

- a determination of the interaction patterns between early Islamic traders and the indigenous population in order to more closely scrutinize the process of cultural and population diffusion (chapter 1);

- a more precise determination both of the de jure and de facto position of women among infibulation practicing populations (chapter 3);

- the relationship between controlling women's sexuality and environment and resource management (chapter 3);

- the question of the universality of the practice of infibulation in those regions where it is known to occur. Specifically, do "client" populations, related to primary infibulating groups, also practice infibulation (e.g., the Somali "sab").? The women of one of these groups (the Midgan) also function as midwives, and are called upon to perform the operation of infibulation (chapter 1);

- the potential relationship between exogamy and infibulation (chapters 3 and 5);

- testing those variables common to infibulation-practicing populations against a wider pastoral population sample; and

- testing the male absenteeism hypothesis (to include a more detailed quali- fication) against a wider pastoral population sample.

The Variables Considered

It is not the intention that the following analysis be interpreted as implying a causal/functional relationship between one or more of the variables considered and the practice of infibulation. It is, however, the intention to explore why these variables compositely occur in infibula- tion-practicing populations, and the extent to which they should be considered as factors complimentary to its practice, and its perpetuation.

The primary variables found to be associated with infibulation in- clude:

- variable XVI:wife retains full membership in her natal group

- variable VIII:male absenteeism

- variable XX:unstable marriages

- variable IX:low position of women

- variable V:sheep and goats herded by (and the responsibility of) the wife.

- variable VII:high brideprice

- variable XII:Islam

- variable XIV:exogamy, which was negatively correlated with infibulation.

Of secondary relevance were variables II (nomadic), XIII (preferred parallel cousin marriage), IV (camel/cattle owners —men), and VI, (bride-price livestock).

Variables XVI and XII

Although the exact reasons for a wife retaining full membership in her natal group are not clear, there is some indication that it is related to Islamic traditions relative to marriage, divorce, inheritance laws, and the general position of women. Mohsen suggests that this practice is related to the "contractual" nature of marriage (in this case related to Islam), which gives the husband exclusive rights to his wife's sexual, labor, and procreational services (but he may have to share this with her natal group), and to her obedience (which he also shares with her father and brother) (1970:224–26). In return, the wife receives (but not exclusive) sexual rights, as well as the rights to maintenance. Similarly, through the woman's retention of membership in her natal group even after marriage, her agnates continue to be largely responsible for her actions. Consequently, they never fully surrender their rights to her services or her fertility ("uxorial and genetricial rights"), which they can transfer (in the event of her divorce) to successive marriages (Lewis, 1961:136; chapter 3, this volume).

Variables XX, XII, and XVI

When a husband cannot provide maintenance, a woman has the right to divorce and to return to her natal home for remarriage. On the other hand, should he not be able to provide maintenance, and the divorce option is not exercised, it is her natal group that will supply her with what she and her children need. Similarly, should a man mistreat his wife, she has the right to return to her natal home. Indeed, since divorce is relatively easy and frequent, and a woman has no independent de jure rights or economic means, the ability to return to her natal home is the only security she has. Of course, she has earned these rights to continued membership in her natal group by forfeiting her rights to inheritance. In this way "a woman secures for herself the continuous security and protection of her kin-family. . . . This security applies to herself and to her children. . . . It . . . is the major guarantee of her marital rights" (Mohsen, 1970:233). Moreover, should a woman be young enough at the death of her spouse, it is her natal family that continues to guarantee her honor and negotiate for her in the event of her remarriage.

Variable VII

Contractual marriage (which may certainly have predecessed the occurrence of Islam in the area) is the case among both Somali and Sudanese populations. The exchange of wealth between the kin group of both bride and groom is prevalent throughout the marriage. (See chapter 3, this volume, and Peters, 1980:144–45.) The bridegroom usually acquires his bridewealth from his father and other members of his lineage. The bridewealth received is distributed accordingly, among the wife's lineage members and is, in part, returned to the husband in the form of the wife's dowry (Lewis, 1962:17). Indeed, a primary function seems to be to provide the couple with a least part of their basic subsistence herds (mainly sheep and goats) (following Goody, 1969: especially 205–08).

Variable V

These herds, which are usually returned to the husband as part of his bride's dowry, remain in his possession. However, they fall under the management and control of his wife, for it is upon these herds that each individual wife and her children depend for subsistence.

Variables IX and XII

The wife retains management rights over these subsistence herds during her husband's lifetime, or the duration of marriage. She has no right to inherit from her husband upon his decease, or to claim restitution or support from him upon divorce. As indicated previously (chapter 3), a wife inherits (or upon divorce is entitled to) less from her husband's estate than from that of her father upon his death.

Variable XVI

It is possibly also for this reason that a woman remains a member of her natal group after marriage, that is, she may at least minimally inherit from her father, whereas she is entitled to nothing upon the death of her husband (except by outright gift prior to his demise, or from his relatives after his death).

Variables IX, XII, and XVI

It must not, however, be thought that women are helpless victims because they have no personal jural identity. As indicated above, even though women are formally the jural responsibility of their patriline (father, brothers, or other male relatives), they are entitled to receive full maintenance, protection, and freedom from responsibility of action. Regardless of the lot of her husband, a woman is "inviolable and . . . entitled, as of right, to a milking camel for sustenance and transport to her relatives" (Lancaster, 1981:59).

On the other hand, since women are jural non-entities, it is their male relatives who have full control over them, to include their future.

> Women are negotiable surrogates for men, for men can never co-operate with others from a different group without justification, friendship is not enough. If a woman is "given" to another group, the giver can then quite legitimately involve himself with them, for co-operation with your sister's husband is permissible because you are simply ensuring her will-being, which is, of course, your jural responsibility. Responsibility for the children is the husband's, but by this time a link has been established that can, in the future, be used to incorporate both groups into one, something that is impossible by any other process. (Lancaster, 1981:59)

Variables XVI, VIII, and V

It is entirely possible that male absenteeism in Islamic northeastern pastoral societies is associated with mixed herding, and women remaining members and the responsibility of their natal household. At least to some extent, it is also associated with the practice of polygamy. Either or both of these (i.e., mixed herding and polygamy) often necessitate the husband's absence for long periods of time (e.g., Young, 1965:118-19). The frequency of polygamy among older, wealthier males may, as Lewis has pointed out, be related to the difficulties of a single woman managing a large herd (unless she has numerous daughters or a widowed mother) (1962a:8; chapter 3, note 8).

Concurrent unions (or younger wives) can certainly help solve the problem of managing large herds. This cohabitation does not, however, alleviate the factor of male absenteeism. On the contrary, since greater wealth, by implication, also involves larger camel herds. Polygamy can also be a factor in lengthy spouse separation where hamlet relocation (due to pasturing requirements) is frequent, and/or a man has two or more wives located in different hamlets. The result of such extended spouse separation is illustrated in Lewis's description of the nomadic hamlet as an unstable unit in which

> a man's several wives may live together in the same hamlet, at other times they move as widely separated units amongst whom the husband shares his time and affection. Again, men attach their families now to one group of close kin, now to another. . . . Each married woman or widow has her own hut . . . and . . . a . . . pen for her flock and the husbandry of sheep and goats is essentially the province of women and unmarried girls. (Lewis, 1962:4ff)

The evidence indicates, however, that the prevalence of mixed herds among pastoral populations in Islamic northeastern Africa is probably the major contributing factor to male absenteeism. Mixed herding involves wealth and subsistence herds having different pasturing requirements. The camel, or wealth herds may *not* be cared for by women. Although their care usually falls to young unmarried males and boys, it is the elder married males who have the final responsibility for these herds, and who are regularly called upon to oversee the moving of them to other pastures, and their sale or acquisition. Similarly, since women have the total responsibility for the household's subsistence herds (sheep and goats), which have different pasturing requirements than camels, a potentially lengthy and/or frequent separation of spouses is often the case.

How these differential herding requirements increase male absenteeism can be gleaned from comparing mixed herd infibulation-practicing pastoral populations with the two noninfibulating pastoral groups (falling within the core of those practicing infibulation the Al Murrah and Rwala of Saudi Arabia (see chapter 4). Among the latter two populations, both subsistence and wealth herds have traditionally been camels. Sheep and goats have only recently been introduced, and then as wealth herds in lieu of camels. These herds are primarily in the care of males. Here, male absenteeism is also related to camel herding (and more recently urban employment), with women restricted to the residence (with the exception of those few unmarried women who help with the herding of camels). This residence is, however, only one unit of a household that retains its unity throughout.

Cole qualifies the difference between these pastoralists and the Kababish of northern Sudan (although the analogy holds for all of the traditional infibulation-practicing populations under consideration).

> Mixed herds require a division of the herding units, at least during certain seasons. The Kababish obtain this at a considerable expense to the individual household, which has to split up during the dry season as some members follow the camels and others stay with the sheep and goats. The Al Murrah achieve this division of labor between households, so that if a sheep and goat herding household owns some camels (as is usual now, for a growing group of the Al Murrah are switching to sheep and goats from camels), they entrust them to the care of a related household that specializes in herding camels. (Cole, 1975:36)

Women are thus usually at home in their tents, within the context of the household regardless of the location of the men who

> are always coming and going, often spending nights away from their households while they are herding, on a hunting trip, or on business in the city. The women almost always remain at home in their tents in the desert, even if their husbands are permanently employed in the city. Indeed, for a wife to reside permanently with her husband in the city signifies their break from tribal society. So long as the wife remains in her tent with the herd, the husband remains a member of the tribe, though he may spend long years away. (Cole, 1975:70)

The Rwala have, traditionally, also been camel herders, but this too is now changing, with increasingly mixed herds of camels and sheep. Although here, as with the Al Murrah, the wife is restricted to the household, in neither case are women "secluded" in their tents (unless males other than kinsmen [agnatic or affinal] are present). Although Cole does not provide information relative to polygamy among the Al Murrah, Lancaster points out that polygamy is currently not the rule among the Rwala, and he is uncertain as to how extensive it was in the past (Lancaster, 1981:132). It may be the case that the degree of male absenteeism relative to polygamous unions, is a further distinguishing factor between the Rwala, the Al Murrah, and the majority of infibulation-practicing populations. But this must remain a question for future study, when more specific information is available to indicate both the precise length and reason for spouse separation (e.g., herding only, or both herding and polygamy) among infibulation-practicing pastoral populations.

It must be stressed that, even though mixed herding proved the primary variable distinguishing infibulating pastoralists from the Al Murrah and Rwala, it cannot be claimed to have that importance in fact. Any potential causal (or functional) relationship between mixed herding and infibulation will require further comparative analysis. Unfortunately, although a comparative analysis might qualify its actual importance, such an analysis can only provide a synchronous evaluation of a variable that may otherwise have historical significance. For example, if we accept that population diffusion resulted in the current distribution of infibulation, then mixed herding among highly mobile populations might have resulted in more extensive spouse separation than is currently the case. If this is viewed in conjunction with raiding and rape, then de Villeneuve may have been right in her assumption that infibulation had a functional purpose: to deter rape (chapter 1, this volume; de Villeneuve, 1937; see also Lewis [1961] on the importance of raiding, feuding, and political alliances among Somali pastoralists, and Harris, 1974:86–87).

Variables XIV, XII, XX, and the Diffusion of the Practice of Infibulation

Although there is no actual basis for assuming a historic association between exogamy and the practice of infibulation, it is the case that, even where preference might have followed the Moslem tradition of patrilateral parallel cousin unions, other forms of cousin, or more distant agnatically related unions regularly occur among pastoralists in Islamic northeastern Africa. This may, of course, simply be a question of availability, or that other extraneous factors necessitate greater flexibility than tradition may allow.

In Middle Eastern societies, for example, the generally expressed preference is for patrilateral parallel cousin unions, but this rule is either not necessarily followed, or is adhered to for other than strictly orthodox reason. Among the Al Murrah, for example, men frequently marry "women who are not their immediate first cousins but who are members of the same lineage. To a much less degree, they also marry women from other lineages and clans" (Cole, 1975:71).

The primary reason the Al Murrah give for preferring parallel cousin unions is that such marriages are more likely to be stable, because the bride does not actually leave to go to another lineage. Although married, she remains within the physical and protected sphere of her own lineage. Similarly, there is less potential for interfamilial conflict; her mother-in-law may likely be her mother's sister. Nevertheless, the frequency of divorce is very high. The Al Murrah attribute this to the daily problems encountered when living together in joint households. Thus, the reasons the Al Murrah give for preferring parallel cousin unions are neutralized by the high frequency, and reasons, for divorce. Cole signals a more important requirement regarding marriage: the Al Murrah insist

on marriage between persons of equal status (which) . . . suggests . . . a caste-like society where integration is achieved more through the economic interdependence of different groups of specialists than through marriage. . . . As long as any marriage is contracted between parties of equal status, even from different tribes, they are considered . . . virtuous, by the Al Murrah. They prefer, nonetheless, that a man marry a woman who is a close relative. (Cole, 1975:72)

Like the Al Murrah, the Rwala will not allow a union of unequal partners. Traditionally, a girl must wed "the nearest young relative whom it is permissible to marry. . . . This is, generally, a son of her father's cousin; should this cousin have no sons or if the grandfather had no brothers, the girl falls to the nearest kinsman descended from the great-grandfather's brother" (Musil, 1928:137). Lancaster indicates that this situation is relevant even today. Marriage preferences are for equal partners, and marriage with the f.f.b.s.s. or d. (father's father's brother's son's son or daughter) is the most popular (Lancaster 1981:43-57 [49-57 addresses the reasons for this preference]).

Peters also notes that, while the literature generally cites the over-whelming prevalence of father's brother's daughter marital unions in the Middle East, plural connections expand and increase the complexity of cousin unions considerably more than is usually assumed (1980:133-34). Moreover, although there may be closeness of kinship in marriage, it

is not consistently with a limited patrilineal range, for many of the more crucial marriages are to women of other corporations. . . . At the heart of the agnatic group . . . there are always women possessing connections with other women and men, some of them the daughters of agnates, others from outside it but linked to women inside it as matrilateral relatives of one sort or another. Apart from this, there is a consistent tendency, once a link with another corporation has been established,to replicate the original marriage with a succession of cross cousin marriages in the same generation or the following ones. . . . Obviously there is no question of this marriage pattern approaching an endogamous condition. (Peters 1980:136-37)

Similarly, there is considerable marital union flexibility among in-fibulation-practicing populations in Islamic northeastern Africa (see chapter 3). In this context, Lewis has proposed interesting additional factors that may have determined marriage unions among the Somali in the past. He conjectures that there is a relationship between marriage unions and the tradition of "marriage by capture" among the Somali: "marriage and fighting are interrelated in as much as those units which exhibit the greatest degree of internal cohesion in fighting also show the greatest degree of exogamy; that as the extent of cohesion decreases in the hierarchy of structural units so intermarriage between collateral segments becomes more and more frequent" Lewis, 1969:112). It would not be unreasonable to also expect marital union flexibility among infibulation-practicing pastoral populations in the Sudan. Indeed, information relative to many pastoral populations in that area seems to indicate that, at least in the past, this was so (see chapter 3 and the appendix). If marital union flexibility and "marriage by capture" was indeed the case, at least historically, among infibulation practicing populations, then we could also anticipate that at least some proportion of brides would, to one extent or other, have been "strangers" to their husbands' lineage.

Under these circumstances, and since infibulation is usually performed prior to puberty and the onset of menarche, it would have (theoretically) guaranteed the virginity and chastity of women. This would have had especial importance where the wife's lack of sequential habitational proximity to her husband's kinsmen, either prior to or after her marriage, precluded their (and her) ability to guarantee her honor (see below). This is, to some extent, substantiated by the fact that in most infibulation-practicing populations, the bridegroom is perfectly within his rights to demand to inspect the infibulation scar of his future wife as a precondition to marriage. He may, on the basis of his inspection, cancel the marriage. Such behavior would seem more at home in cases where the families, although not necessarily strangers, are either unrelated or distantly so, or under conditions of residence mobility. Even a subsequent shift from a flexible marital system to lineage endogamy would not necessarily, initially, obviate the need for infibulation. As has been pointed out elsewhere, infibulation is related both to modesty and the extent to which modesty is enforced, for example, the wearing of the veil and physical seclusion in the residence is related to the degree of sedentarization present (chapter 3).

Pastoral women, of necessity, have generally greater freedom of movement than do sedentary women. Consequently, "the connection of endogamy with modesty and status increases with the growth in the size of the group, its power, and its consciousness of solidarity and vice-versa" (Antoun, 1968:693; see also Lewis, ed. 1980:52).

Antoun makes a relationship between kin group endogamy and the norm of modesty, that endogamy functions not only to "maintain and solidify political power and preserve property within the group," but also guarantees the modesty of women, thus securing the honor and status of her father's group (1968:693). On the other hand, he states that "endogamous kin group marriage usually keeps women within their quarter and away from strangers who might threaten their honor" (Antoun, 1968:693).

If this be the case, then the existence of infibulation in primarily endogamous populations seems rather redundant if it is interpreted as a way of guaranteeing chastity and virginity, which in great part constitutes the indigenous reasons given for its existence (see chapter 1). It would seem more logical to expect its occurrence among populations having more flexible marital unions and where the bride is a "stranger" (stranger here implying that the woman is not agnatically related to her husband, that is, a stranger to her husband's house and lineage group, even though he may be related to her in some other way). Conversely, we might argue that endogamy and infibulation could be paired if extended male absenteeism were also prevalent.

Let us assume, for the moment, that prolonged male absenteeism is requisite to the perpetuation of infibulation, and that, at the very least, marital union flexibility was the norm (historically speaking) among pastoral populations in the geographical region under consideration. If we also assume that Antoun and Lewis are correct in their supposition that increased solidarity and preferred endogamous unions are in some way connected, than the introduction of Islam, combined with an increase in socioeconomic and political stability (in one form or other, e.g., through trading and the development of trading centers), *might* generate a preferential shift to parallel cousin unions (e.g., in the Sudan) (Antoun, 1968:693; Lewis, 1969:112 and 1980:52).

If the practice of infibulation was already a function of prolonged male absenteeism, then infibulation might have been spread in tandem with Islam. Indeed, it might even have been considered a necessary addendum to Islam in association with notions of cleanliness, purity, virginity (chapter 3).

We might also expect to find that the temporal and spatial distribution, as well as the degree of severity of the operation would vary from population to population, depending upon when they were converted to

Islam, the degree to which they were converted to Islam, their indigeneous sociocultural complexion, and their physical distance from the
core area of influence (chapters 1, 2, 3 and the appendix).[1]

Marriage, Status, and the Practice of Infibulation

As indicated in chapter 3, the maintenance of family honor is directly
related to controlling female sexuality. By extension, family honor, like
the nominal identification tag of the family, is publicly borne by the males
of the family, but is primarily earned by the females in their adherence
to lifelong conscription in the private sphere. The spatial mobility of
women will, perforce, be restricted in a cultural milieu where family
honor determines the status and position of its members within society.
Extensive control must be maintained over that element (i.e., women)
that can most deleteriously affect family honor at all levels (e.g., sexual
indiscretion). By extension, active economic participation is out of the
question for women, not only because it invites participation in the public
sphere, but because it initiates loyalties foreign to the private sphere, such
as business interests, interaction with (male) strangers. The latter alone
is sufficient reason to exclude women from all aspects of public sphere
activity.

Consequently, since women can achieve status only within the realm
of marriage, the latter clearly becomes imperative. But the act of marriage
is not enough, for even the minimal status that marriage provides can be
'divorced away' should the woman not be fertile and produce sons. Of
course, a man's status is, to a certain extent, also determined by the size
of his family; especially by the number of sons he sires (chapter 3). "This
is especially true in societies where women reside with their husband's
kin following marriage, separated from their own relatives. . . . In
societies where marriages tend to be unstable, where there is not a great
deal of trust and cooperation between husband and wife . . . women often
give birth in their mother's home" (MacCormack, 1982:9-13). Marriage
instability is an important determinant in the steady production of children, which also acts to keep women in the home. However, even women
who have already borne several children "still feel that their position is
unstable and has to be continuously reinforced by further births, especially of sons. A wife's status increases with the number of children she
produces" (Lewis, 1973:428). It is indeed paradoxical that their children

are all that women have, and yet women have no formal legal rights over their children.

A woman's status is thus twofold. It is determined by her marriageability and by her subsequent fertility, which ideally should provide one or more sons who will care for her in her old age, and provide her with grandchildren, which will increase her status yet further. But marriage is also important for men. Only in this way can a man acquire the necessary home, hearth, labor force, and additional alliances he requires to subsist (Paulitschke, 1880, vol. 1:195; also see chapters 2 and 3). The difference is that for women, marriage is not only a necessity, it is the *only* choice. They are, in the words of El-Saadawi, "reared for the role of marriage which is the supreme function of women in society" (1980:49).

In order to achieve marriage among infibulation-practicing populations (and the right to it must be achieved) a women must first be infibulated. It is this act of infibulation that moves her, literally and figuratively, into the status of an adult, virginal, and marriageable woman (e.g., Lewis 1969a:135; Kennedy, 1978:158). This initial status change also introduces her into the world of women and seclusion, or at least restriction to the private sphere and related activities. It is after infibulation that she takes on the garb and demeanor of an adult woman. The latter explicitly qualifies her sphere of movement as relegated to the private sphere, while the actual operation of infibulation functions to formally seclude her internal space until such time as her husband opens it for conception. Callaway has suggested that men also "own women's internal space," in that the husband "owns the pregnancy . . . of his wife, gaining sole sexual and genetricial rights through marriage and the payment of bridewealth" (Callaway, 1981:182, 185; see also El-Saadawi 1980:205; and Boddy, 1982 and 1989).

This may be related to the fact that women are viewed as minors throughout their lives, in subordination first to the men in their family, then to their husbands, and ultimately to their son(s) (who will theoretically care for them in their old age [Minces, 1980:15–17]). The right of the husband to be the sole guardian (and conqueror) of his wife's internal space is illustrated by an observation made by Godard a century ago. Until marriage, girls were not permitted to mount an animal in order to "prevent the enlargement of their genital organs. Only the husband has the right to dilate his wife" (my translation) (1867:61).

Similarly, the husband's right to this space might also explain why it is so important for the male to open this miniature orifice with his penis, rather than calling for a midwife (for example) to cut the opening to facilitate entry. Potentially more important than the obvious blow to his ego, is the fact that his penis is the conveyor of his sperm or seed, for which his wife acts as the receptacle.

It is also primarily through marriage that a woman can gain the only autonomy and property access she will ever have; she acquires her own household upon marriage, and sometimes even outright ownership of the residence and its contents (e.g., Asad, 1970:43–45; Abdel Ghaffar, 1974:49–52). Moreover, should she be the first wife, her potential for power over other, future wives, and as a future grandmother, is considerable (providing she is fertile). A position as first wife indicates a shared responsibility as head of household. Generally, "the head of the family is territorially associated with the hut of the first wife. . . . Inside, the hut is divided in two by a hide curtain or branch partition meeting the walls near the door. The man sleeps on the side towards the door, leaving the darker more secluded room to this wife" (Lewis, 1969:85).

A married woman also receives full responsibility and usufruct over her flocks, household, and children, in addition to collaborating with her husband on decision making relative to these flocks, the household, and its contents. In this sense, although without rights of formal ownership, she shares with her husband the position of head of household. Her sharing of this responsibility is especially important in pastoral society, where male absenteeism is the rule rather than the exception. As indicated previously, in pastoral society married women and their offspring form an autonomous, basically self-sufficient unit. With her dwelling, the wife and her offspring are capable of splitting and fusing with other similar (lineage-related) units, as the ecological occasion dictates (Lewis, 1973:435). Lewis, citing Colucci, points out that

> the original point of fission is in the family, the death of the father and the marriages of the sons resulting in the rise of new families and the disruption of the parental group. . . . The group of nomadic families which move together splits up by the detachment of families which have become too large to continue as part of the group. It is consistent with the lineage principle that fission should be represented as occurring in the family, since this is the primary source of segmentation in the genealogies. (Lewis, 1969:118)

In this context, the wife's house might be seen to represent the primary, relatively unchanging (although mobile) and most stable unit, only disappearing after the children have moved to other units, or formed their own (e.g., Adan, 1981:137).

It has been posited that the only status position available to women is through marriage, which can only be achieved through infibulation. Infibulation is not, however, a rite of passage in the formal sense, in that there is no corresponding ritual. Unless girls are in the same household or related, each girl is operated on separately. Similarly, in none of the societies practicing infibulation is the operation performed by a male, nor are males present at any point in the procedure. It is a female (usually, though not always, a qualified midwife) who performs the operation. Moreover, it is the women who continue to perpetuate and support this custom, more specifically, it is the older women (especially grandmothers) (Antoun, 1968:683; Godard observed that it was often an old woman who performed the operation, 1867:60-62).

Women carry the primary responsibility for the total socialization, to include infibulation, of female children (until they marry); they are also responsible for male children until they reach the age of seven or eight years (Giorgis, 1981:17; Kennedy, 1978:15; Hayder, 1979:110, Oldfield-Hayes, 1975:631). As such, it is the women who are instrumental in preserving the patriachal unit, which is their primary source of status, identity, and economic security. This is especially the case with respect to grandmothers. Although the position and status of most married women (unless they are the first wife) is relatively low, this is not the case for older women, especially grandmothers, whose status and position should not be underestimated. It is the grandmother who, second only to her husband, is the decision maker relative to the primary household and its wives and children (especially female children) (e.g., Oldfield-Hayes, 1975:624; Hayder, 1979:57). It is also she who usually determines when infibulation will occur, and even that it will occur (e.g., Giorgis, 1981:18; Barclay, 1964:240; Oldfield-Hayes, 1975:620). Also, since the husband, wealth permitting, either has his own section of the house (rural or urban) or, in the case of pastoralists, is usually absent from the tent area, she can often exercise full control over the household and its occupants.

The position of the grandmother (with sons) is the highest status position a woman can achieve. However, all "older" women are usually entitled to more freedom of movement (throughout the private sphere and to some extent into the public sphere) after menopause. At this time, because a woman is no longer fertile, she is also no longer "sexual," and no longer strictly qualifies as a "woman," nor is she a man. In a sense, she reacquires the asexual status she had before infibulation. She becomes socially transparent; because she is no longer a sexual enticement to men, her sexuality (i.e., fertility) can no longer threaten the family honor. Her new status is a reflection of the neutralization of her internal space (the major impurities associated with women are menstruation, afterbirth blood, and childbirth). Hence, after menopause, a woman is no longer formally restricted to a definable social space. She gains the right (at least to some extent) to enter the public sphere of men (and often even the men's house). (Relative to mobility of older women, see Giorgis, 1981:18; Oldfield-Hayes, 1975:624; Hayder, 1979:86.)

We can conclude that a woman's very existence is recognized through the act of being infibulated. Her total social identity can only be achieved by this means. This identity remains fixed until menopause; her only options are to become a wife and mother whose status can be enhanced solely by the production of sons and subsequent grandchildren. After menopause her identity as a (fertile) sexual entity ends, and her freedom of movement increases.

Early Marriage and Infibulation

Although what follows cannot be fully substantiated at the present time, it might provide some useful insights into the possible (historical) purpose of infibulation, and why it occurred primarily among pastoral populations.

Among infibulation-practicing populations, control over the mobility of women (whether physical or spatial) begins at a relatively early age. I suggest that this early control was related to the institution of child brides, with betrothal at, or just prior to, first menarche, and with marriage following some one or two years later, depending upon the solvency of the groom. The potential relationship between infibulation and early marriage would be based upon the following:

- Historically speaking, infibulation was primarily prevalent among pastoral or agro-pastoral populations (chapters 2, 3, and the appendix).

- Infibulation occurs between the ages of four and eleven years (chapters 1-3 and the appendix).

- In the past, most girls were married between twelve and fifteen years (although today females marry between fifteen and twenty years, Magos indicates that child marriages [between eleven and twelve years] are still the norm in the Eritrean lowlands) (Magos, 1981; Lewis, 1969:135; Lewis, 1962a:12; Barclay, 1964:243; Levy, 1931:153; Layish, 1975:14ff.). Since early marriage considerably lengthens the period of fertility, this could have provided an important impetus for early marriages among pastoral populations (see chapter 3:fertility and lactation).

- Orthodox Islamic law offers no prohibition to early marriage. According to Ottoman law (the Mejelle), however, the minimimum age of puberty (nine years for girls and twelve for boys) was also the minimum age for marriage (the maximum age of puberty completed was fifteen years) (Layish, 1975:14).

- The prospective groom is within his rights to inspect the infibulation scar to ensure himself of his future bride's virginity. Should he not be satisfied, he is within his rights to dissolve the engagement (see for example, Lewis, 1962:13; and the appendix, this volume).

- Traditionally, a marriage and bride-price payment is paid in stages, which can last from a number of weeks to one or more years (e.g., Lewis, 1962a:13-15; Lampen, 1933:106; Asad, 1970:57; and chapter 3). In both Somalia and the Sudan, it is usually the woman's family who provides the marriage hut and household goods, and this is often augmented by a dowry gift (including pack camels, sheep, goats, etc.) that is usually extracted from the bridewealth (e.g., Lewis, 1962:16-17). Of course, as indicated in previous sections, the prevalence of a high bride-price and deferred payment is also based on a number of other conditions. Moreover, high bride-price and deferred payment is not restricted only to infibulation-practicing populations.

- There is an extended period of post-marital residence with the wife's natal family for the bride (and sometimes also the groom), lasting at least until the birth of the first (and sometimes subsequent) child(ren). Only thereafter does the new couple formally begin patrilocal married life (chapter 3 and the appendix).

I speculate that, depending upon the time of bethrothal, girls were traditionally infibulated between the ages of four and eleven. When a girl's father was approached for the hand of his daughter, a betrothal fee was paid by the prospective groom, which was either impetus for, or may have even contributed to, the infibulation operation. This initial payment might have taken the form of cash or kind, or may have been symbolic, taking the form of betrothal gifts to the girl, her parents, and perhaps her brother(s). In Somalia, the betrothal fee is usually not more than the equivalent of ten pounds, which is paid to the girl's parents and establishes the engagement (Lewis, 1962:12-13). As noted above, this initial payment might also have covered all or part of the infibulation fee (the formal status and wealth of the girl's family, and that of the prospective bridegroom would no doubt determine whether the operation was performed by a trained midwife, the mother or grandmother of the girl).

This may help to explain why infibulation has traditionally been performed on only individual girls, rather than being a group initiation rite.

After her infibulation, a girl begins her life as an adult woman (see for example Kennedy, 1978:175-76, and 1970:181). Following Cohen, we could interpret the ritual of infibulation as having the additional function of "interfering or weakening a child's identification with its parents" (1964:532-34). This identification is effectively broken at the time of the operation, which transforms the girl into a marriageable (adult) woman (chapter 2). Kennedy points out that among the Nubians, at circumcision, both boys and girls are called bride and groom, and that the ceremony strongly resembles a wedding (1978:157-58). Indeed, among many infibulation-practicing populations throughout the Sudan, the "jirtig" jewelry is worn during circumcision, and otherwise only at weddings (and sometimes by the wife in the seventh month of the first pregnancy) (see the appendix and table 4.1 in chapter 4).

Since infibulation occurred (and still does) prior to puberty, it not only created virginity, but acted as a future guarantee (theoretically at least) of the virginity of the girl in question. This was important given the nature of pastoral life, the prospective bridegroom may not have seen his future bride again until after she had already reached puberty. After his betrothed had reached puberty, the prospective husband, no doubt, wanted to inspect the infibulation scar, not only to assure himself that all was intact, but that infibulation had indeed occurred. Another portion of the bride-price might then be paid, and the marriage would be consummated. The wife continued to reside with her family until (at least) after the birth of the first child. At that time, the final, and perhaps the largest, payment of the bride-price (in livestock) was paid. This not only created the formal blood tie between the two representative kin groups, but was also a good indication of the wife's fertility, which, combined with her services, was that for which he had paid. Only after this final payment had been made would the wife relocate to her husband's home.[2] However, it is not unusual for the husband to pay either or both his mother-in-law/father-in-law an additional fee for permission to depart with his wife (the appendix).

The Composite Variables

Although the variables primarily associated with infibulation are, individually, also present in other social systems, both Islamic and non-Islamic, they are compositely present in infibulation-practicing populations. This is not to imply that they are causal factors leading to infibulation (i.e., that if all these factors are present in a social system females will be infibulated). However, it is the case that they must be present in order to sustain this practice. Consequently, the association of the composite variables with infibulation provides a research embarcation point; this association must be tested against a wider spectrum of pastoral populations.

The way in which these variables are compositely complimentary to this practice can be summarized as follows:

- The preponderance of unstable households is primarily related to the exigencies of differential mixed herd pasturing requirements. The combination of unstable households and the ecological instability of the entire area under consideration results in, often lengthy, periods of spouse separation. Although variable from household to household, this may be exacerbated by polygamy, where the husband must share his time with his other wives, who may or may not reside in the same hamlet. The norm of separate sleeping arrangements for husband and wife also, undoubtedly, succeeds in psychologically distancing the spouses from one another. This is especially so in the case of polygamy, where the husband must share his time equally with all of the households of which he is the sole head.

- Spouse separation, the low position of women, contractual marriage, and the concomitant (usually lifelong) retention of the wife as a member of her natal group combine to undermine marriage stability.

- Although Islam has no relationship to the origin of the practice of infibulation, it has functioned, and continues to function, as a vehicle for its perpetuation. It does this specifically with reference to the overall position of, and attitude toward women (both de jure and de facto). By condoning a low de jure position of women, it effectively alienates them from direct access to economic resources and the public sphere, for example, exclusion from ownership, inheritance, economic wealth, political decision making. Similarly, it is instrumental in perpetuating modesty codes for women, and their direct association with family (and by extension male) honor. In this way Islam gives credence to the necessity to physically restrict women to the private sphere (in sedentary and urban settings this can even involve restricted physical mobility and/or seclusion). It also gives credence to the husband's exclusive rights over his wife's fertility (i.e., her internal space).

Under its auspices, the contractual nature of marriage generally facilitates the ease with which a marriage can be dissolved, as well as charging the husband and his kin group with only minimal jural responsibility for his wife. These same jural rights afford him full ownership of any children she may bear (as part of his patrilineage).

This overall weak social position of women is especially important in any consideration of infibulation: women must "derive their social status and economic security from their roles as wives and mothers" (Gruenbaum, 1982:5). However, they can only achieve this status by being infibulated. Consequently, it is not surprising that it is the women who carry out the practice, and who are its strongest defenders.

Controlled continued restriction to the private sphere (and the exclusion of all males from that sphere) successfully isolates women from the external world, from one another, their husbands and other males, and the potential for education. Even in the pastoral sphere, where women generally have more freedom of movement than in rural or urban areas, the division between camp and tent is very clear: a woman's activities centering primarily around the latter. Indeed, the tent, the subsistence herds for which she is responsible, and her children often comprise the family unit. This is primarily due to the frequent and lengthy male absenteeism associated with varied pasturing requirements (or polygamy).

The economic impotence of women, and their total dependence on their fathers, brothers, husbands, and sons facilitates their being controlled. In short, they are dependent upon and controlled by male relatives throughout their lives. Such social (private sphere) isolation of females also successfully precludes any solidarity of action on their part. This is a major contributing factor in the perpetuation of their ignorance relative not only to health and hygiene, but also to possible alternative life-styles.[3]

The results of this study generally agree with the indigenous interpretation (although not for the same reasons) that infibulation is related to establishing and guaranteeing virginity as well as maintaining chastity. Similarly, it agrees with those academic positions that relate it to:

- the requirement of virginity and chastity in societies where the honor of the family is contingent upon the honor of its women;

- a precaution against rape (either actual or symbolic);

- a necessary preliminary to adult status and marriage.

It can also be concluded that the current distribution of infibulation is the result of a diffusion of populations and social values during the general period of Arab tribal migrations, trading, and indigenous population movements in the geographic area under consideration. Moreover, in the past and currently, the practice of infibulation is perpetuated:

- where absenteeism and household instability constitute the norm, but where the family (both immediate and extended), nevertheless form the basis of the social system;

- where women constitute the mainstay of the family, but are de facto restricted to marriage and the private sphere;

- where women's minimal access to the public sphere, wealth or political or economic decision-making is enhanced and enforced by adherence to the Islamic faith; and

- where a bride retains membership in, and remains the responsibility of, her natal group throughout her life (even after marriage).

Notes

1. Although it is not possible to verify with absolute certainly, it does seem to be the case that the practice of infibulation diffused westward from the Horn region, the operation being more severe in that area, and diminishing in both distribution and severity as one moves westward. Similarly, as one moves westward, the operation, in many cases, represents a later adoption (in some cases occuring during this century) (chapter 1).

2. Lewis informs us that the bulk of the bride price for a first marriage comes from the stock of the young man's family "the allocation being made by his father," and "added to the groom's own navel-knot stock" (1962a:14).
   Such a pattern, although not identical, is by no means alien to the "betrothal marriage" form practiced by the Wodaabe pastoral Fulani (Stenning, 1980:203-05). The procedure for betrothal marriage involves a series of ceremonies, prior to which a boy must be circumcised (carried out on groups of boys between seven and ten years of age without special ritual). After this he is shown those of his father's cattle which will form the nucleus of his own herd.

   The "first betrothal" or preliminary discussions between intending parties to the match is the next stage . . . marked by a homtu ceremony . . . next . . . is the betrothal proper, which occurs when the girl begins to menstruate. This ceremony includes a homtu feast, and also the Islamic wedding ceremony. Then, after an interval, follow the ceremonies of bride removal, at which the couple are first expected to sleep together; this, again, is marked by a homtu feast. The final stage is the home-making, which occurs after the weaning of the couple's first-born. In this, the homestead of the couple is constructed by the co-operative effort of the parties to the marriage, and the herd of the husband is ritually transferred to him. . . . In the course of a betrothal marriage, which sets up a new family unit, all the stages are marked by homtu feasts, but an Islamic ceremony is performed at what may well be regarded as an unimportant stage, the ceremony at which intentions are announced. The other stages all have to do with associating the couple (or in the first instance, the future male herd owner) with the famly herd, or in ritually disassociating them from it in the parts which involve procreation and childbearing. (Stenning, 1980:203–04)

3. In chapter 1 it was pointed out that the Somali client "sab" primarily provide service to the Somali. It is the women of one of these groups (the Midgan) who function as midwives, and who are called upon to perform the operation of infibulation. As was pointed out in that chapter, *if* it could be shown that these women are not themselves infibulated (nor were so in the past), then infibulation might be viewed as a direct status indicator. It would also, simultaneously, devalue the actual and potential status of women engaged in public sphere activities (e.g., working women). This could forestall or discourage women from aspiring to enter the public sphere; working, for women, would have a similar status tag as agricultural work has for pastoral nomads (it is relegated to the domain of slaves).

6

The Future of Infibulation

Social Change and Infibulation

The Islamic background of the populations considered in this study complicates the process of social change relative to women.[1] This has been less so in urban areas, however, (especially of the Sudan) where the combination of (urban and) industrial development, Western profession-alization of governmental and educational agencies, and increased urban migration has had some impact on the cultural environment. But urban development is not rural development. Indeed, it might be more accurate to speak of urban development and rural underdevelopment (primarily due to the extremes of rural poverty) (see especially Chambers, 1983). Consequently, it should come as no surprise that traditional culture traits such as infibulation are more persistently maintained in rural than in urban areas. Similarly, the potential for short-term modification or elim-ination of this trait is also greater in urban than rural areas. *This presumes, of course, that a clear distinction can be made between urban, rural, and pastoral populations.* The extent to which urban and rural/pastoral pop-ulations share a cultural identity, and/or have intense social and economic interaction, will greatly affect the rate at which change can, and will occur. For example, populations occupying the Horn regions (Somalia and the Red Sea coastal area) represent the least sedentary populations under consideration in this study. Similarly, the geographic regions they occupy have the poorest overall potential for viable settlement projects (with the possible exception of the extreme southern regions of Somalia) (see chapters 2, 3 and the appendix). Thus, the rate and potential for settlement of pastoralists is theoretically greater in the Sudan than in Somalia.

Nonetheless, although the pastoral populations in these regions have fewer possibilities for opting for sedentary life, this has not diminished the interaction patterns between towns and pastoralists.

> Towns in northern Somaliland are . . . in no sense independent fastnesses in a nomadic environment. They are indeed, on the contrary, the very nerve centres of pastoral politics and of crucial importance in the nomadic political system. Many feuds have their direct origins in towns, and, even when they have not fighting is frequently directed from villages and settlements where the resident elders control lineage politics. Thus there is in fact no sharp division economic or political, between pastoralists . . . and town-dwellers. . . . Far from lying outside, or on the periphery of pastoral nomadism, towns are the pricipal centres about which the system revolves. . . . Residence in a town does not thus dis-establish the force of clanship and contract, for it does not rupture the economic bonds which link agnates. Permanent townsmen, in most cases still have livestock, particularly camels, in charge of their kinsmen in the interior. Lineage rivalries are as clearly defined and as important in town life as they are outside it. (Lewis, 1961:94)

In the case of Somalia, we would thus expect to find infibulation practiced among both pastoral and town populations, probably with equal intensity. Indeed, although adequate statistics are not available, it does appear that the intensity with which infibulation is practiced, as well as the extent to which the operation varies from simple excision to radical infibulation is different in Somalia and the Sudan. In the former, there seems to be more consistency in both the extent and extreme nature of the operation, all across the pastoral-rural-urban continuum (Dualeh, 1982:2, 12, 17).

Similarly, it is this area which continues to have a generally higher incidence of pastoralism and agro-pastoralism (almost to the complete exclusion of strictly agricultural populations). Consequently, we could expect to find a greater occurrence of infibulation (in intensity and degree) in the urban areas of Somalia. This appears to be the case. (See e.g., Cook, 1979:57; Dualeh, 1982:10; Grassivaro-Gallo, 1986; for Sudan, see e.g., Saadawi, 1980:64; Gruenbaum, 1982; Forni, 1980:22–25; Rushwan, 1983:5,9; Shandall, 1967:184; Cook, 1979:56; Boddy, 1982.)

However, in spite of increasing sedentarization, urbanization, and the (albeit restricted) effects of develop-related programs, change is not occurring rapidly enough for many Western feminists and indigenous activist groups. A number of studies concerned with female circumcision continue to be more involved with its ultimate elimination, than with establishing a clear understanding of its function in the social context. Giorgis, for example, points out that the

> resurgence of campaigns to abolish female circumcision is in part an outgrowth of the general concern about women's health and also of the Western feminists' concern with female sexuality. While the former has generated an objective, analytical contribution to an understanding of the health implications of female circumcision, the latter has in some instances sensationalized the issue by taking it out of the general context of under-development and the oppression of women in underdeveloped societies. (1981:7)

Moreover, "prohibition and legislation have failed to abolish female circumcision partly because they do not offer alternatives for the fundamental transformation of those socio-cultural and economic realities upon which traditional practices such as female circumcision are based" (Giorgis, 1981:7). (The sensationalization of female circumcision, together with legislative action, has more recently also diffused to Europe. In this case, however, it has been applied primarily to circumcision-practicing refugee and immigrant populations [see chapter 7]).

In point of fact, changes in the position of women have been regularly, albeit slowly, occurring throughout the developing world. However, they must occur at the pace set by the indigenous female population, *not* that which western feminists deem necessary. Minces has observed that

> Western feminists have an unfortunate tendency to approach the status of women throughout the world as if it were a single issue. In doing so, they ignore historical factors and other differences in the degree of exploitation . . . and the emancipation of women of various classes and in various countries. . . . Most pre-industrial societies are unfortunately similar in many ways when it comes to the inferior status of women. (Minces, 1982:13-14)

The degree to which social change can occur is also correlated to the feasibility of changing those specific aspects of the sociocultural value structure that most constrain the desired change. Unfortunately, that which forestalls change is also intricately woven into the structural web of the social system. Islam is a case in point, in that "most women in the muslim world continue to be totally subordinated" (Minces, 1982:13-14).

Although it may seem that Islam is the major fiend in this issue, Minces has also pointed out that, while the traditional structure perpetuated by Islam is currently oppressive to both men and women, originally it was the primary source of security (which it continues to be in Islamic

northeastern African societies). In effecting the solidarity and interdependence of family and tribe, no one was theoretically left to fend for
themselves (Minces, 1982:115). Moreover, since women have traditionally been considered minors, and excluded from the public sphere, "it is
hardly surprising that so few of them seek to break out into a world for
which nothing has prepared them" (Minces, 1982:15).

The importance of the family in Islamic society is also true today, for
even the developmental trend has altered neither the tradition of the
family (whether in the nuclear or extended form), nor the lineage as the
most important kinship grouping at all levels of society. And, while this
is also true for urban populations, it is especially in the rural and nomadic
setting that this tradition (and related cultural values) has continued
relatively unimpeded (e.g., Nelson, H., 1973:3; Barclay,1964:68). This
is of particular relevance in the case of northeastern African societies.

The continued importance of family and of women to the maintenance
of the family tradition indicates that any innovative laws (or even
indigenous women's movements) will have little effect on women who
are socially isolated (even the shopping is done by the men), and whose
entire life centers around the (immediate) family (Minces, 1982:42-60).
Mernissi has pointed out that the family was traditionally a self-sufficient
production unit, "whose function it was to mobilize the labour of its
members of both sexes and to place them at the disposal of a patriarch
who was both their employer and their provider" (1982:189-90). But
with increased unemployment, patriarchal authority was seriously weak-
ened, creating "a state of affairs in which women and children are obliged
to work" (Mernissi, 1982:189-90). Apart from the loss of male honor
and status as provider and protector, this has resulted in increased male
emigration to urban areas, and a concomitant increase in the number of
nuclear families. If we can assume that (initial) male emigration ultimately results in the emigration of a man's wife and children, then, given
the exigencies of making a living in an urban area, we might presume
that a man will not be able to afford the upkeep of restricting his wife to
the private sphere. Indeed, she may have to join the labor force herself.

Minces contends that the position of women will ultimately change
(especially in urban and town areas) through a widespread increase in
the number of nuclear families. This will, theoretically, force more
women to enter the labor market to help support the family (1982:108).
Unfortunately, while emigration to urban areas may be increasing, so is

unemployment, which, "aggravated by the high birth rate, is one of the major curses of all predominantly rural and developing countries . . . modernization has simply disrupted the secure traditional family structure without providing any real compensation other than a meagre salary and extra tasks for those who work" (Minces, 1982:108-09). Not only does this help to break down any existing extended family support structure, but it also efficiently blocks the potential for change. This is compounded by the fact that "the husband-wife relationship is probably less equal than in other cultures" (Caldwell, 1981:113). This is further reinforced by the educational system, which is preferential to boys, providing them with a markedly different education than that available to girls (Caldwell, 1981:113). Similarly, because of the different status positions of husband and wife, the Moslem woman will only be allowed to work outside the home as a last, urgent resort.

The relationship between the general position of women and labor has been shown by Sanday to be more than simply a question of "going out to work to supplement the family income." Even where women substantially contribute to subsistence activities, their status is low, and while "contribution to production must be present for female status to develop, other factors must also be present" (Sanday, 1973:1695).

Not surprisingly, when and wherever women are utilized as an unpaid labor force, their status will not, by definition, be high. High status for women lies in their access to the production and control over valued products. This is not the case in Islamic northeastern African societies. For example, Somali women "perform all the menial and heavy work and . . . tend sheep and goats. Somali men considered it beneath their dignity to tend anything but camels, cattle, and ponies—the most valuable economic asset of the Somali" (Sanday, 1973:1696). Unfortunately, "in many societies control is based on a magical or religious title which is in the hands of males. In such societies female status is not likely to develop unless some exogenous influence creates a new demand or results in a re-evaluation of female produce" (Sanday, 1973:1697).

As was pointed out in chapters 3 and 5, the only status arena open to a woman is that of marriage and children, neither of which are available to her unless she has been infibulated. Similarly, her sole economic security comes from her role as wife and mother. The only positions available to her external to this area are that of prostitute (where she risks complete alienation) or midwife. However, it is interesting that perhaps the only socially acceptable independent traditional professional occupation open to women, for the entire area under consideration, is directly associated with procreation: that of midwife. The midwife oversees pregnancy and delivery, and performs the operations of excision and infibulation. It is the latter two upon which her overall income is, in great part, dependent.

Because midwifery is a highly respected profession throughout Africa, the midwife is in a position to exercise considerable influence, especially with the female population, all of whom will (theoretically) be infibulated, and will subsequently strive to become (repeatedly) pregnant. Consequently, any attempt to eradicate this practice must not only contend with the entire female population, but also with the midwives, in whose social and economic interests it is to support the tradition of infibulation and, by extension, the status quo position of women. Similarly, since infibulation is a prerequisite to marriage, which in turn is a moral prerequisite to pregnancy (both of which are imperative for women), the isolation of infibulation as a *social problem to be eradicated* will meet with a similar result as would be obtained should an attempt be made to "eradicate" pregnancy.[2]

Infibulation, Life Expectancy, and General Health Care

Although we do not know the number of deaths that result from the operation of infibulation, there is considerable evidence to indicate that numerous, potentially serious, medical complications are associated with this practice. (For a general overview of both immediate and remote complications see, for example, Verzin, 1975:all; El-Dareer, 1983:132–33; Cook, 1979:58–66.) This is not, however, sufficient reason to presume that infibulation is a major, much less the primary cause of general ill health, sterility, or even death among the majority of women occupying areas where the practice of infibulation is known to be the norm (see chapter 3).

Indeed, throughout the geographic area under consideration, overall knowledge concerning health care and hygiene is minimal, and high mortality rates and short life expectancy (by developed country standards) are the rule. For example, although actual figures for life expectancy vary, those of the UN Economic and Social Council for the Sudan appear to be fairly representative (see table 6.1).

TABLE 6.1: Life Expectancy at Birth (years)

	1950-1955	1975-1980	1980-1985
Male	35.0	45.5	48.0
Female	37.0	47.5	50.0

Source: UN Economic and Social Council Country Programme Profile, 1981 session, p. 3)

In part, this low life expectancy rate is attributable to the inadequate availability of medical facilities, most of which are confined primarily to cities and towns. It is also related to the continued use of traditional methods of diagnosing and treating illness, prevalent at the local level. In addition, although diseases such as typhus, plague, yellow fever, cholera, and smallpox have either been brought under control or eliminated, nutritional deficiency-related diseases, malaria, and general unsanitary conditions continue to be major factors effecting mortality, especially of infants and young children.

Initiating changes at the local level to (a) alleviate the high mortality rate and short life expectancy; (b) increase hygiene; (c) eliminate potential health-detrimental food taboos; and (d) develop general educational programs (attended by both males and females) are aggravated by the lack of facilities, funding, and trained personnel. In the case of Sudan, this is further compounded by the extremely heterogeneous nature of the population, which undermines the development and implementation of programs intended to boost levels of production and raise living standards.

It can only be hoped that general changes in the overall health and hygiene conditions in the area under consideration, combined with educational campaigns will, in the long term, aid in eliminating both the indigenously expressed need and desire for the operation of infibulation. Important in achieving such change is an improvement in the overall medical education required of midwives. It is these midwives who, long before any formal change occurs in the position and status of women, will be able to influence, and to a great extent determine and control, the value placed on female circumcision by both women and men.

The Conditions for Change

The initiation of changes in the position of women will have to take second place to the very basic changes necessary for health and mortality levels. By extension, although a superficial change in the social and economic position of women can occur rapidly and radically, its duration is short-term unless there is a concomitant long-term change in underlying social values (which are neither in the habit of changing overnight, nor with a new government).

Similarly, a move from infibulation to noncircumcision of women represents so radical a change that it is unlikely to be accepted by the majority of women—and men. A far more credible expectation in the context of social change would be a transitional phase involving, for example, the substitution of clitoral excision for infibulation. Once excision becomes viewed as an acceptable substitute, and has been maintained as such over a sufficient period of time (e.g., two generations of women), then a subsequent phase of partial clitoral excision, or even its elimination, could more feasibly be introduced (although this theory could be undermined or prove difficult in light of the growing fundamentalist movement, see chapter 7).

Clearly, what is important here is not that an unsavory practice be eliminated, rather that an attempt be made to understand the nature of culture traits such as infibulation and the degree to which they constitute an integral and even necessary part of the social system. Radically enforcing social change without a concomitant analysis of the functional importance of the culture traits destined for elimination, and without appropriate alternatives, can have serious consequences. For example, we can safely presume that the family constitutes the most primary level of social structure among infibulation-practicing populations. Similarly, because women are generally either restricted to the private sphere, or to activities directly related to it, it is they who form the mainstay of the family. They are responsible for the socialization of children and the management of the residence unit. In short, they populate, represent, and maintain the household. Consequently, their status/rank position is defined and delineated by the private sphere. Any change in this position will, perforce, be related to their access to the public sphere. Infibulation, in this context, is simply one aspect of their identification with the private sphere. Specifically, it is infibulation that provides their access to this sphere. An immediate and radical elimination of infibulation would succeed primarily in confusing women's access even to this sphere.

If the retention of women in the home is deemed necessary for the perpetuation of the family, given that it forms the basis for social welfare, then the elimination of the restraint on women to remain in the home will potentially break down both family solidarity and the social support system.[3] This would ultimately result in the need for the state to take over the welfare of its inhabitants, a situation with which most developing country governments cannot even begin to contend. On the other hand, economic change in developing countries usually affects resource management, requiring increased manpower availability and distribution. This can potentially initiate transformations at the family level. As the cost of living increases, the males of the family are often forced to seek additional employment, either locally or elsewhere. Similarly, the females of the family may be affected. If husbands are no longer in a position to afford a protected environment, women may, in the long term, be forced to engage in, or expand existing cottage industry, or perhaps even to seek employment external to the home (albeit in the form of menial labor). All this would occur in the spirit of supplementing the family income.

Economic growth, which will indirectly initiate changes in the nature and concept of the family, will ultimately also effect the overall position of women; it will increase their access to the public sphere and, of necessity and by association, aid in changing men's attitudes both toward women and themselves.

This is not to imply that changing the status position of women simply involves assigning them menial (albeit paid) labor positions, providing them with a library card, or initiating "self-awareness." Indeed, no change in the position of women can occur in developing Moslem countries unless such change represents an autochthonous development.

Notes

1. Christian colonial rule did not seem to seriously alter this situation. Indeed, it more often had the effect of cementing the Moslem Brotherhood than the converse. This was especially the case when colonial powers established specific administrative regions that were not commensurate with the territorial delineations already in existence (i.e., tribal) (Abdirahman, 1977:244ff).

2. In contrast, Gruenbaum has (correctly) pointed out that, inherent in the attempt to eradicate infibulation, is the perception that it is a *medical problem:* "the view that the practice should or could be 'eradicated,' as if it were a disease, is a particularly medical view. While it is reasonable that arguments against circumcision stress physical risks, the problem nevertheless is one that is not necessarily amenable to medical solutions" (1982:6). It would be interesting to research the evolution of

perceptions about female circumcision, with respect to its treatment as a medical and/or social problem.

3. The presumption here is that in developing countries, national governments do not usually have extensive social welfare programs available to their inhabitants. Thus, the onus of responsibility for the survival of the family falls directly upon the family, more specifically, upon the head of the family. The labor force available to him to maintain this family is, by extension, found within the family, in the form of his wife (wives) and children.

7

The Problem of Altering Cultural Boundaries

It is important to stress that this study began with the question of where, and by whom, infibulation was practiced. Available data indicated that this practice has traditionally been in evidence among pastoral and agro-pastoral populations inhabiting the Horn of Africa and northern Sudan. Moreover, the data reviewed for this study substantiates the findings of Seligman, that infibulation probably originated in, and diffused from, the eastern coastal regions.

However, although I have tacitly assumed that diffusion played a paramount role in the distribution of the practice of infibulation, this does not explain its traditional primary occurrence among pastoral populations. Moreover, the lack of historical and philological data precluded any detailed analysis of population, language, or sociocultural value diffusion. Consequently, this study was (perforce) restricted to exploring why, historically, infibulation primarily occurred among pastoral populations; why it continues to occur among these populations; and why, when these populations are sedentarized, this practice is retained and even diffuses to other sedentary, and urban populations in their proximity.

Infibulation in Context

Viewed from a current perspective, infibulation appears to be an archaic practice that has been (perhaps inadvertently) assimilated and retained by societies currently in the throes of economic development. The societies in which this practice occurs have been here qualified as closed systems, that is, although qualified as economically developing countries, they otherwise function at quite a different level.[1] Moreover, these social systems are fundamentally impervious to the effects of external exposure. In Islamic northeastern Africa, for example, the profane has not only permeated the secular, it has come to be the basis of popular belief. Moreover, the combination of (1) the integration of the written word with oral tradition; (2) the minimal literacy rate; and (3) the access to primarily religious education (and then often only at the oral level) neutralizes the potential effects of external exposure.

The view presented in this volume is that it is the closed nature of Islamic northeast African societies that continues to effect the overall position of women and, by extension, the persistence of the practice of infibulation. In this context, infibulation is perceived as but a symptom of broader developmental problems. Unfortunately, the mutilating characteristics of this practice, and the fact that it is done to young children, has attracted considerable international attention. As such, it has *detracted* from the broader issue of how to generate the overall development that would stimulate social change.

The latter cannot, however, be accomplished without the cooperation of indigenous governments to develop and implement appropriate social policy measures. For example, with respect to developed nations, we could generalize that it is the state which, while self-serving, nevertheless carries the responsibility of the general welfare of its citizens, on whose formal support it depends. In Islamic northeast African societies, it is the immediate family and related community (e.g., lineage, village, tribal confederacy) that does this. In effect, it is the relatively unstable institution of family that forms the basis of this social structure, at the core of which are women. Women thus constitute the reference point of society. The way they conduct themselves determines and reflects the positional hierarchy of the families they represent and, by extension, of themselves.

> The repository of family and lineage honor, the focus of common interest among the men of the family or lineage, is its women. A woman's status defines the status of all the men who are related to her in determinate ways. These men share the consequences of what happens to her, and share therefore the commitment to protect her virtue. She is part of their patrimony. (Schneider, 1970:18)

In short, honor breeds honor, generating the social rules, regulations, and constraints that underpin social solidarity and cohesion.

In this social structural configuration, the amphictyonic principle is Islam. While not the basis for a confederation in the true sense of amphictyony, Islam is the homogenizing principle in the otherwise heterogeneous milieu of the Sudan, and has long been the social and political overlay in tribal Somalia. Aside from historic tradition, the persistence of this role for Islam may be related to its being what

Callaway and Creevey have called an "organic religion": "It does not distinguish between the sacred and the secular, and it does prescribe in detail the rules which should govern family and social life. It was written down by men in pre-industrial society and preserved in this archaic form to the present day. This makes the problem of reform of Islam greater" (1989:111–12).

The combination of Islamic tradition and a social welfare structure dependent upon the institutions of lineage and family acts to strictly delineate the social role of women. Moreover, the central role of women as reproducers in this context means that it is imperative to control their sexuality after marriage, and guarantee their virginity (and thereby their fecundity) well prior to marriage. Where possible, this is accomplished by means of physical seclusion, strict codes of dress and behavior, and, this study contends, being infibulated.[2]

Infibulation: A Social Problem?

In the course of the last decade, many individuals writing about female circumcision have perceived and qualified this practice as a "social problem" requiring political and legal action. They stress the need for the radical and immediate eradication of this practice. Interestingly, this position is usually based upon, and underpinned by, the enumeration of a number of individual cases. These cases usually involve women living in urban communities, with whom contacts have been established through hospitals or clinics, or who are themselves activists in the campaign against female circumcision. In all events, this group comprises a nonrepresentative, indeed, insignificant number of cases.

Consequently, if we qualify a social problem as a "deviation from the norms which are held to be the standards of society" (Horowitz, 1972:531–32), then the practice of infibulation *does not* qualify as such. This is especially so in the context of the social nexus within which it normally occurs: in Islamic northeast African societies, where infibulation *is* a norm falling within the standards of society. It can only be said to be a problem for observers for whom it is in contradistinction to the norms and standards of behavior in their own society. But even here, it is an *individual*, and not a *social* problem; and elevating an anti-infibulation lobby to the level of individual interest groups, indigenous governments, or the international organizational level will not make it so.

In a similar vein, infibulation has recently come to be perceived as a "minority social problem" in those European countries that are housing, usually temporarily, refugees from regions where female circumcision is the norm. That such groups fail to fully comprehend the rights and duties associated with their residence in, for example, the Netherlands, France, or the United Kingdom is compounded by their social isolation, especially in the case of women due to their language limitations and the uncertainty generated by their refugee status. Even when they receive permission (after a period of between two to five years), to remain as immigrants in their country of refuge, they continue to be the victims of conflicting social norms: their own traditions and those of their adopted country. This problem is especially poignant for women coming from societies where female circumcision is the norm, and living in societies where this is viewed as an intolerable and barbaric mutilation, and more importantly, where they can be stripped of their most prized possession— their children. In the United Kingdom and France, female circumcision is prohibited by law, and is formally perceived as mutilation and child abuse. In the Netherlands, there is currently a debate as to the advisability of passing a law prohibiting all forms of female circumcision. In this situation, those female refugees who have already been infibulated, are confronted with a twofold dilemma. Viewed from the western perspective, these women have literally been the "victims" of their own tradition and, it is felt, should logically perceive themselves as such. Consequently (and self-evidently), they should wish to do all in their power to prevent the circumcision (in any form) of their female children.

That this is usually not the case is a source of considerable frustration for (1) feminist activitists; (2) gynecologists confronted with this extreme cultural phenomenon, either in the form of its medical sequelae, or a request to circumcise (in this case infibulate) a (young) female child; (3) voluntary social service agencies mandated to provide assistance and information to refugees; and (4) government, which, when confronted by mass media coverage of female circumcision among refugees and immigrant populations, is pressured to effect a policy decision that will have potentially serious judicial consequences for these (minority) populations. Ironically, in the Netherlands, as in the countries of origin, attention is drawn to the symptoms rather than the problem. In the case of infibulation-practicing Sudan, for example, penal codes were ineffective both in preventing and eliminating this practice. The problem is clearly not to be found in the context of infibulation. In the case of European governments confronted with an incursion of refugees, the problem lies not so much in the confrontation with a singular instance, or even a critical mass of (potential) immigrants. The problem is the inability of these government to formulate policy with respect to the desirability (and capacity) to acculturate and assimilate what appears to be an increasingly regular influx of such populations. Specifically, western governments confronted with this problem have not been able (except by means of penal code) to answer the question of how they plan to deal with a regular influx of populations manifesting a variety of cultural identities, some of which are in direct moral, ethical, and sometimes even legal contradistinction to acceptable practice in the country in which they have sought refuge.

This problem is exacerbated by the generation of advisory reports that do not manifest an adequate qualification and structuring of the problem (let alone its analysis and solution). A recent example is the Bartels and Haaijer report on Somali (female) refugees in the Netherlands (commissioned by the Center for Health Care of Refugees in conjunction with the Ministry for Welfare, Public Health and Culture). This report was generated *not* because of the overwhelming cases of requests for circumcision or emergency medical consequences resulting from operations performed in the home, *nor* because of the critical masses of female Somali immigrants/refugees in the Netherlands (ca. 1869 women and female children (all ages) as of 20 February 1992). Moreover, it does not comprise a representative sample, neither of the refugee women currently residing in the Netherlands, nor of the majority of women residing in Somalia, for whom this practice is the norm. What then, we may ask, *was* the basis for generating this report? According to Bartels and Haaijer, it was "practical and medical-ethical" (1992:5). It would appear, then, that it is based on a *perceived potential social (minority) problem*, not of the Somali refugees as such, but of host nation activist feminist groups concerned with human (female) rights issues, and a handful of medical or ethical/morally concerned gynecologists. Needless to say, this does not simplify the task of voluntary social service organizations who have to deal with refugees on one to one, and small group levels. The refugee response to such media and other concerned coverage can, ironically, generally be described as confused, fearful, and oppressive.

Islam: The Problem of Change

In Islam, the Koran, which identifies that which consitutes normative behavior, has traditionally had absolute authority. The main problem has been one of interpretation. Norm-giving sources of interpretation today include traditionalism, modernism, secularism, and fundamentalism. Consequently, there still does not exist a clear distinction between the sacred and the secular, and there has been no real fundamental change in the immutability of traditional Islamic law (Callaway and Creevey, 1989:88-90). This has become exacerbated, in recent years, by the fact that this law has "increasingly become a fundamental symbol of Muslim identity," a concept that has gained wide social and geographical relevance (Callaway and Creevey, 1989:109). This is especially apparent in the fundamentalist movement, which understands Islam to be a "social order." Thus, for example, the position of women is sanctioned by the religion if it is deemed to be part of God's social order. Moreover, "if the laws of Islam distinguish between men and women, they are an expression of a natural, innate difference between the sexes" (Hjärpe, 1983:12-14). Accordingly, while both men and women may be entitled to certain rights and privileges, for example, access to education, this should occur at separate institutions.

Fundamentalism is especially important in the context of this study because it is gaining strength in much of the area where infibulation is practiced. In the Sudan, for example, there is an attempt to Islamicize the state and society, the goal being to substantively develop an Islamic national identity. This is manifest, in the case of the Sudan, by the formation of a "legal commission to revise existing laws to bring them into closer conformity with the Shari'a" (Lapidus, 1988:859). Of course, the problem of fundamentalism is less due to its nature, than to the fact that it predominates in areas where Islam constitutes a popular religion and the majority of the population are illiterate.

As could be expected under these conditions, the push for social change inconsistent with the Koran and the Sunna (traditions) inevitably generates conflict, especially when it concerns matters of family, honor, marriage, and women (Hjärpe, 1983:21). In addition, Lapidus has pointed out that the traditional status position of women also works against change and, in the context of growing fundamentalism, can even countermand the attempt.

Limited education, illiteracy, economic dependency, lack of employment opportunities, social segregation and male hostility to the social or political involvement of
women inhibit contemporary trends. Some of the deepest barriers to change are the
cultural values with which both men and women are imbued from childhood . . .
concepts of male superiority and family honor remain potent . . . the highest values
in regard to women stress . . . fertility and motherhood, and imbue women with the
expectation of security, protection, and esteem in the family context. (Lapidus,
1988:897)

The Future of Infibulation in a Closed Cultural System

If we accept, in the context of the foregoing, that Islamic northeast
African societies constitute closed cultural systems, then we must return
to the question posed in chapter 3: what effect has this had, and does this
continue to have, on the position of women in these societies, especially
with respect to the practice of infibulation?

Infibulation has been shown to be part and parcel of the reproductive
process, a process which is of paramount importance in these societies.
The subordination of (or rigid social control over) women has its basis
in the central position they hold in this process. However, the concept
"subordination" is relative and, as such, must be perceived in context.
Thus, because their primary concern is with reproduction, women "at
least as much as men, have always been instrumental in the construction
and transformation of social institutions. They may have lacked a strategy
to put this power to work in their own interests, but as social scientists
we too have lacked the means of understanding their potentialities"
(Robertson, 1991:105). Consequently, a direct attack at a singular practice that is symptomatic of a broad and intricate structural web is not only
futile, but can even be counterproductive. This is especially the case in
closed societies, where tradition is sanctioned by religious authority, and
where a barely secularized, self-servicing state system manifests little or
no policy development designed to improve the overall welfare and
quality of life of its citizens. In this context, the best we may hope for
with respect to the practice of infibulation has been aptly pointed out by
Gruenbaum.

It may yet be that Sunna circumcision becomes more common and more closely
associated with Islam. It is ironic that this should occur as the result of a fundamentalist
movement which has at the same time worked against the position of women. . . . In
this situation, the gradual abandonment of pharonic circumcision for Sunna, although
it may be an improvement in terms of health effects, may actually add to the long-term
tenacity of some form of the practice by more firmly associating it with religion and

by further increasing women's economic dependency on men. (Gruenbaum, 1988:313-14)

Equally significant, both in the indigenous context, and in the case of refugee/immigrant populations in Europe is the

> ideological use of female circumcision in the maintenance of ethnic identity. . . . This is significant not only because this might serve to preserve the practice to bolster ethnic identity in a multicultural society, but also because in a class-stratified society where ethnicity confers privilege, the boundaries of that ethnicity may be guarded and individuals defined by their adherence to identifying customary practices, motivating insiders to preserve and assimilators to adopt them. I believe that circumcision currently serves as such a marker of ethnic identity, associated with class privilege; if I am correct, this can be expected to constitute another obstacle to change or even a motivation for further spread of the practice. (Gruenbaum, 1988:314)

The situation has been further exacerbated in both the national and international contexts by the all too often radical feminist coverage this practice has received. In the words of Buckley and Gottlieb, it seems more likely that the attitudes reflected in such considerations of female circumcision "tell us more about the ways in which our own culture symbolizes perceived threat than about any cross-cultural actuality" (1988:21).

It has been the thesis of this study that any analysis of infibulation must find its basis in an historical consideration of the contextual environment of the populations concerned (i.e., their sociocultural, political, and economic complexion). Available data indicates that the vast majority of those populations practicing infibulation, although currently distributed all along the pastoral-rural-urban continuum, have had (or continue to have) a recent pastoral, or agro-pastoral tradition. Although many of these populations are now sedentary, as either rural or urban inhabitants, the practice of infibulation continues to be retained. Perhaps the single most influencing factor in the retention of this practice has been Islam. Not only has it greatly influenced the social, political, and legal systems, but it has also incorporated, as an albeit unofficially sanctioned norm, the (archaic) indigenous practice of infibulation.

In conclusion, I would contend that infibulation can only occur and persist in closed social systems where paramount importance is attached

• to family;

• to the maintenance of family honor;

• to the perpetuation (and honor) of its patrimony;

and where women play a central role in the maintenance and propagation of this system. Moreover, where the protection of women falls to those males related to them by blood or marriage, because they are viewed (by men and themselves) as having neither the means nor the right to protect themselves.

In Islamic northeastern Africa, these factors, combined with the exigencies of mixed herd pasturing, results in women who are unprotected, both as children and as married adults. Consequently, not only their initial virginity and their subsequent chastity, but also the paternity of their children is potentially open to question. Infibulation, if not actually, then at least symbolically implies (1) initial virginity (virgins are made, not born); (2) perpetual chastity (it is difficult to easily rape an infibulated woman); and (3) a relatively successful seal over that area of a woman in which a man and his lineage have invested—her womb.

In the course of history, infibulation-practicing pastoral populations became sedentarized, and/or developed and maintained close network interactions with sedentarized populations (in some cases even exercising political control over them, e.g., the Ruf'a (see chapter 3). Because they concurrently retained their primary social values, especially with respect to family, marriage, and women, not only did they perpetuate the practice of infibulation, but they were also instrumental in its wider dissemination.[3]

While we could logically expect that increased environmental, economic, and political stability will influence, if not generate, a decrease in the prevalence and intensity of this practice, the question arises as to the extent to which such changes are feasible in the foreseeable future.

Notes

1. In this context, for example, the physical control over women (together with the development of codes of honor and shame) has been associated with the continued use of outdated and primitive technology at all levels of subsistence, and with ecologically related community organizational problems (e.g., regulating access to natural resources for both human and animal populations) (respectively, Mernissi, 1982:183–184, and Schneider, 1970:4–5). Resource access organizational problems are, in turn, related to social organizational flexibility (e.g., group segmentation, contractual relationships, ritual kinship, etc.). Interestingly, infibulation has traditionally been prevalent primarily among populations inhabiting environments that are both unpredictable and harsh to the extreme. While this is not to imply that such a relationship is causal, it is certainly the case that environment is an important variable in the long-term perpetuation of infibulation. Moreover, both the environ-

ment and the degree to which technological development (and its broad utilization) can be marshaled to mitigate the effects of the harsh environment in northeastern Africa will greatly determine the potential for economic development in this region.

2. Of course, infibulation, while considered to both create and guarantee virginity, will not necessarily stop a female from having pre- or extramarital coitus. However, its combination with seclusion (where possible) and a strict modesty code for females after the age of seven certainly represents a powerful physical and psychological deterrent to illicit sexual activities.

3. The prevalence of (1) the Islamic faith among sedentary populations; (2) the associated general view of family, marriage, and women; (3) environmental instability, requiring even these populations to be more agro-pastoral than agricultural when sedentarized, may even have encouraged the adoption of the practice of infibulation.

Appendix

Physical Geography

Sudan

The greater part of modern Sudan consists of a large plain, which is usually divided into three zones. The first of these is the rocky and semidesert area to the north of Atbara (excluding the Red Sea Hills area), which receives an annual rainfall of less than one inch and supports only minimal vegetation. South of this region the rainfall increases (progressively as one moves further south) and the topography changes from semidesert to savanna. The area between the Red Sea, the Nile, and the Atbara river is Beja country, which stretches southward to the Abyssinian highlands and to the desert of Aswan in the north. The northern and Red Sea Hills portion of Beja country is arid and largely uninhabitable, while the southern regions evidence richer vegetation. Rain cultivation is possible in the penninsula (Gezira) area between the Blue and White Niles. This region of low-rainfall woodland savannah is now the principal cotton growing area of the Sudan, and is consequently of great importance to the Sudanese economy. To the south of this area is a clay belt, stretching eastward from southern Darfur to the rain-lands and semidesert region just east of the Blue and main Niles (the Red Sea Hills separate this plain from the narrow coastal strip). Dry season ranges from twelve months in the north to less than three months along the southern border.

Ethiopia

Trimingham (1952:1-5) distinguishes the following five principle regions in Ethiopia:

1. Ethiopian-Kaffa plateau, which includes Tigrai, Amhara, Gojam, Shoa, and Jimma-Kaffa (the historical region of Abyssinia and the Sidama Kingdoms);

2. to the west, the Ethiopian highlands descend to the plains of the Nilotic Sudan, and consist of open plateaus and valleys (this area traditionally housed the original Hamitic population);

3. the Eastern Rift valley, which runs from the Danakin depression in the north (through Lakes Stephaia and Rudolfs) and on into the great equatorial lakes in the south;

4. to the north of the Rift valley is the third region, the Dankali depression itself, which includes Eritrean Dankalia, Ethiopian Dankali ('Afar), and Aussa; (this is an arid, sandy, rocky wasteland in which even nomadic tribes have trouble existing); and

5. the central massif between the Rift valley depression and the Galla-Somali plateau.

He comments that the

> physical structure and relief of northeast Africa explain the directions of the migratory movements of its peoples. It was easy to move about the Galla-Somali plateau or the 'Afar plain, it was possible to reach the heights of the central massif, but it was a very different matter if migrants wished to attain the Ethiopian massif against the wishes of its inhabitants, for the walls of the Tigrai, Shoa, Gurage, Gamo, and Barodda offer almost impenetrable obstacles to migratory movements. (Trimingham, 1952:3)

In addition, the latter also offered impenetrable obstacles to the general spread of Islam and infibulation, neither of which are overwhelmingly prevalent among these populations (and although there are numerous Moslem villages in the highland area, they by no means constitute a majority).

Many of the populations of the highland interior of Ethiopia have their origins in the immigrations of the Gallas (then nomads) beginning in the sixteenth century. These Galla in turn originated from what is now the Somali Republic (Lipsky, 1962:6) (see below—Somalia).

Eritrea

Eritrea is an area that is land-joined to the Sudan by a broad open border of steppe and hill tract. The Ethiopian land frontier is established by river beds (which are usually dry), with the southern part of Eritrea being a portion of the Ethiopian massif. The countryside, like the inhabitants, are partly Ethiopian and partly Sudanese. Longrigg says of Eritrea: "Had Italians never landed at Massawa, Eritrea would today be partly, as always before, the ill-governed, or non-governed northernmost province of Ethiopia" (Longrigg, 1945:3). He divides the country's land surface into four primary types: (1) south central core of the plateau highland; (2) Red Sea Coastal plain; (3) broken hill country forming the north and midwest of the main triangle; (4) broad plains of western face.

Djibouti

Its surroundings at one time comprised the area of French Somaliland. On one side it faces the Red Sea, while inland it has frontiers with Eritrea to the north, Somalia to the south, and Ethiopia to the west and south. Generally speaking, it exhibits a coastal desert region landscape similar to other such areas on the Horn of Africa. Rainfall is scarce and irregular, and varies with altitude.

Somalia

Lewis (1969:56) divides the northern regions of Somalia into three main zones: (1) the arid maritime plains (between the mountains and the sea), which afford pasture for only a few months per year; (2) the maritime range (parallel to the northern coast and intersected by inland plains); and (3) the raised southern plateaus, with extensive pastures leading into the richer pastures of the central plains of the "Haud and Sawl Haud," the main grazing areas of northern Somalia.

The less arid southern regions he divides into five zones:

* the shore area, with shifting sand-banks;
* the hills and short plains of consolidated sand (the first inland zone);
* the sand steppe;
* the black alluvial soil along the rivers;
* the area between the Jubal and lower bend of the Shebelle, constituting the richest pastures of Somalia. Northeast and farther inland are the fertile areas of Bur Hakaba and the Baidoa plateau. These latter are the main centers of cultivation and sedentary and semisedentary cultivating tribes, as well as residual Negroid populations.

Islam

Sudan

Moslem Arabs have, for centuries, entered the area of Sudan in small numbers from upper Egypt. By 643 A.D. the armies of Islam had invaded and penetrated the area of Nubia.[1] When the Mamelukes seized power in the mid-ninth century, many of these Arab populations moved south into the hinterlands. "On the northernmost reaches of the river they gained a moral and cultural ascendency, intermarried with the local population, acquired lands, and in general prepared the way for their own eventual control" (MacMichael 1954:24). Although their initial primary influence appears restricted to the northern regions, by the fifteenth and sixteenth centuries Arabic had become the lingua franca in the northern and central zones. This migration of Arab populations into the area continued through the fifteenth century, effectively adding not only to the numerical Moslem Arab population, but also to the dispersion and (gaining) influence of the Islamic faith. Generally, those that settled in this region intermarried with the indigenous population (in addition to often taking slaves as concubines). The sources regarding the number and nature of Arab immigrants arriving in the area, or to what extent their arrival constituted peaceful infiltration or invasion are, however, extremely limited in quantity, and delimiting in terms of providing sufficient data to establish relevant conclusions. That the sources are silent regarding actual invasions may be indicative of long-term peaceful infiltration and assimilation.

The Arab representatives in the Sudan were not only tribal, however, for Arab merchants had been engaged in commercial enterprises there since the early centuries of Islam. Indeed, it is highly possible that their primary interest in the area was to acquire slaves, for the Sudan blacks or al-Nuba, as they were known, were in considerable demand as laborers, domestic servants, and troops (Hasan, 1967:42; Ashtor, 1976:24). The booming slave trade in the area evolved such that deep penetration into the interior of the region became necessary (in addition to effecting agreements with tribal heads to supply slaves). Although many of these slaves no doubt originated in regions other than the Sudan (even though the general name given them was "Nubians"), the effects of the slave trade on the population level in the Sudan must nevertheless have been quite staggering. Mrs. Petherick, while traveling through the Sudan and Central Africa in 1869 recalls sighting a boatload of slaves taken from the south, and Baggara tribesmen, who were carrying off no less than five hundred captives, twelve thousand head of cattle, grain supplies, and so forth. In the same context, she remarks passing numerous deserted villages in the southern Sudan, where the entire population had been taken off into slavery. She qualified these populations as Dinkas (Petherick, 1869, vol. 2:13, 95–97). Similarly, McLoughlin states that slaves came primarily from southern (negroid) populations. On the receiving end were "1. Nomads: (a) central and western Sudan cattle (and some camel) Arab nomads; (b) Hadendowa peoples in the eastern Sudan. 2. Moslem agriculturalists along the Nile north of Khartoum . . . along the White and Blue Niles south of Khartoum . . . urban Khartoum and Omdurman" (McLoughlin, 1962:360).

Hasan is of the opinon that the slave trade deprived the general region of its younger population, such that when Arab tribes began to penetrate the area in large numbers, active resistence to them was minimal. Similarly, that this Arab tribal penetration was possible, and due primarily to the extensive knowledge acquired by Arab traders of the region's geography (pasture areas, access routes, etc.) (1967:49–50). Moreover, if the Arab penetration was concomitant with a depopulation of the area as a result of the increasing slave trade, it seems highly likely that these immigrants either infiltrated basically uninhabited areas, or rapidly began to constitute the majority of the population in the Sudan, especially in the north. One thing would appear to be certain, however: until the end of the fifteenth century the general process of Islamization in the area was primarily accomplished by tribal migration and traders. Unfortunately, we have no information about the degree to which even these populations were "Islamized," with respect to their level of literacy, and/or their knowledge of Islamic dogma. We do, however, have some comparative possibilities relative to culture traits that have been perpetuated in this area, and that were neither peculiar to the original Arab population, nor to their regions of origin (Seligman, 1913). Of course, it remains difficult to determine the precise nature of, and degree to which, indigenous traditions were modified by the adoption of Islam.

Table A.1 represents an overview of the proportions of adherents to various religions (reproduced from Allgemeine Statistik Des Auslandes, Laenderberichte, Sudan, 1966:57).

TABLE A.1: Population According to Religious Affiliation[*]

Affiliation	1955	Representation between . . . and . . .	
	(1000)	(1000)	(1000)
Moslem (1)	7,296	9,300	9,600
Nature-religious	2,740	3,300	3,700
Catholic	184	100	260
Protestant	30	30	60
Orthodox	10	15	10
Jewish	3	5	10

* Approximations following Sudanese census information
(1) Sunni, Mahdist, and other sects.

Generally speaking, two-thirds of the population are Sunni Moslems, living in the Arab north. Approximately 25 percent (southern population) is pagan, with another 5 percent (approximately) encompassing minority groups that are Christian, Jewish, etc.

Ethiopia, Eritrea, Djibouti

Table A.2 contains a distribution of religions in Eritrea and Ethiopia (albeit from 1952).

TABLE A.2: Distribution of Religions in Eritrea and Ethopia (1952)

	Christian	Muslim	Jews	Pagans	Total
Eritrea[2]	390,000	359,000	-	16,500	765,500
Ethiopia: Abyssinia	2,900,000	300,000	60,000	-	3,260,000
Galla-Sidama	200,000	500,000	-	800,000	1,500,000
Harar Prov.	306,170	780,000	-	431,663	1,517,833
Danakalia	-	50,000	-	-	50,000
NW. Margin	-	75,000	-	80,0	
SW. Margin	50,000	40,000		400,000	490,000

Source: J. Trimingham, 1952:15

It is important to remember that the form of Islam (or any of the other higher religions) practiced in the areas considered by this study is not necessarily the orthodox form, neither in practice nor doctrine. We are, in all of these instances, dealing with "African" Moslems who profess a religion that they received secondhand. Although most of the population of Ethiopia (including Eritrea and Djibouti and excluding Somalia) is non-Moslem, the region is almost entirely surrounded by Moslems. Islam is the primary religion in the northern Sudan, Egypt, Arabia, and Kenya coastal areas, with the southern Sudan and northwestern Kenya being pagan (Trimingham, 1952:30).

The populations practicing Islam in this area include all the indigenous tribes of the lower-lying districts of Eritrea and the Red Sea coast. These include the Barja, Beja tribes such as the Beni 'Amir and Bait Asgede (Habab, Ad Takles, Ad of), Tamaryamwo, two-thirds of the Bilen, the Mansa, Bait Juk, Marya, and Saho. In the Abyssinian highlands (most of which is Christian), there do exist a number of Moslem villages, and communities of Moslems can be found in all larger towns and cities. It is also the case that populations on the Sudanese border have, to one degree or other, been influenced by Islam (e.g., Beni Shangul country wherein the Berta and some western Galla are now Moslems). In the eastern steppe and desert area, all of the nomadic 'Afar (Danakil) and Somali are Moslems. The southern region, only, has remained primarily pagan.

> Along the line passing from Harar first up the Hawash, and then south of Addis Ababa through the Gurage country to Gore Harar in the south-east is a strong Muslim centre which has influenced all the surrounding galla tribes (Ala, Nolle, Jaso, Itu, and Enia). Half of the Galla of the provinces of Arusi and Bali are at least nominally Muslim. Another strong Islamic centre is found in the region of the River Gibe . . . whilst in the surrounding areas of Bunno, Nonno, Waliso, Botor, and Gurage are Muslim minorities. Amongst the Sidama tribes only the Haiya of Qabena, the Alaba, Garo, and Tambaro are Muslim, and they in little more than name. (Trimingham, 1952:31)

The slave trade and the development of Moslem coastal trading areas by Arab traders and artisans strongly influenced the spread of Islam in this area, especially along the coast. In addition, the early conversion (fourteenth century) of portions of the Saho, 'Afar, and Somali tribes aided in spreading Islam among the tribal populations of the area. Not to be forgotten is the overall effect of the extensive Arab nomadic migrations of the sixteenth century. During this same period the Galla tribes, although not yet Moslem, also begin to migrate into this area in large numbers. By the nineteenth century the Galla in the eastern highlands (Wallo, Yajju, Raya) and in southwestern Ethiopia, as well as the nomadic 'Afar and Somali tribes had all converted to Islam. The Somali had been an important factor in the spread of Islam in southern Ethiopia. The Galla in the Harar region were nominally Islamic but the vast numbers of nomadic Galla of the south and west remained pagan, (Trimingham notes that the Arusi did not become Moslems until the second half of the nineteenth century)[3] (Trimingham, 1952:110).

Generally speaking, the overall weakness of the Islamic development in Ethiopia was ultimately due to the strong cultural cohesion of the later Christian state. Initially, however, the lowland area was not particularly appealing for migrant populations due to the "unattractiveness of the Dankali plains, for, compared to the Sudan, very little of the Ethiopian plains is of a type to attract even nomadic Arab tribes. Also their natural migrational trends took them northwards and so eventually, like the Bani Hilal, through Egypt to North Africa and the Sudan" (Trimingham, 1952:139).

Somalia

Islamic influence in the northern portion of Somalia was in evidence by the ninth century. Here again, many centuries of trading relations with Arabia established commercial colonies along the coast. By the tenth century, in addition to a Moslem state in the northern regions, there was another in the south, centered around the town of Mogadishu. Thus, the expansion and conversion to Islam reached early completion in this area, with the result that the majority of the population is Moslem (table A.3).

TABLE A.3: Distribution of Religions in Somalia (1952)

	Christian	Muslim	Jews	Pagans	Total
Somalia:					
Italian	200	750,000	-	10,000	760,200
British	-	345,000	-	-	345,00
French	-	46,391	-	-	46,391

(The figures for pagans primarily relates to the negroid agricultural populations in the south)
Source: J. Trimingham, 1952:15

Demographic Data: Sudan

The Northern Populations

The six northern provinces (approximately 12 million people) traditionally included the Northern, the Blue Nile, Kassala, Khartoum (province), Darfur, and Kordofan. The populations in these provinces include
the Arab tribes (the Ja'aliyyin and Juhayna groups, with the latter being
primarily nomadic or seminomadic), the (Arabized) Nubians, the Beja,
and various non-Arab tribal groups.

The Nubian populations. The inhabitants of "Nubia" (the area along
the Nile Banks from Aswan to Debba and Korti) comprise the "Berberines" (or Barabra) in the north (the Kenuzi, Sukkot, and Mahas), and the
Danaqla (inhabitants of Dongola) in the south (the latter distinguish
themselves from the Barabra).[4] These populations, although primarily
sedentary agriculturalists, also often maintain herds of varying size and
composition. Murdock informs us that while only men work in the fields
among the Barabra, women participate in the herding and milking of
livestock (1959:162). As with many of the following populations, the
Nubians appear to have originally been matrilineal. Trimingham outlines
the various attributes usually associated with matrilineality (e.g., marriage ceremonies at the home of the bride, extended matrilocal residence,
birth of the first child at the home of the mother, the authority of the uncle,
return to the uncle's house at divorce, etc.) (1949:179).

Among the Barabra marriage also involves a bride-price (usually paid
in livestock), in addition to a period of matrilocal residence (with
bride-service) prior to patrilocal residence. Similarly, Reid noted that
among the camel breeding arab populations generally "it is customary to
leave the daughter with her parents until she has borne two or three
children. . . . Finally, after the birth of two or three children, the wife is
moved to her husband's house, leaving one or more of her children with
her mother" (1935:122). There is also a general preference for local
endogamy, and parallel (or cross) cousin marriage (Reid:1935:120). The
preference for parallel cousin marriage appears primarily related to the
general conversion to Islam. Delmet suggests that cross-cousin marriages were probably the preference prior to the spread of Islam (1979:34;
see also Tubiana, 1968:12). "The Kabbabish only abandoned exogamy
after they adopted Islam. . . . In Guli, as in Dar Fung, it was no longer

possible to practice exogamy after the demographic disaster at the close of the 19th century, which favoured the adoption of the Islamic model" (my translation) (Delmet, 1979:47). Murdock (1959:163) notes that the Barabra "subject girls to clitoridectomy, excision of the labia minora, and infibulation"; and Seligman (1913:639) tells us that the "Barabra, the Beja, the Arab and even the darker so-called 'Arab' tribes of the Sudan" all practice infibulation. (See also Rueppell, 1829:42–43.) *The Danagla* are inhabitants of Dongola (Northern Province). Crowfoot indicates that females are circumcised in Dongola district, but the severity varies.

> The consummation of the marriage depends largely on the severity with which she has been circumcised. If this operation has been very severe, consummation may not take place at all during the 40 days of the marriage ceremony. . . . In villages, the tas-him, which may be delayed for a year to two after the wedding used, I am told, to be itself an occasion for domestic feasting and rejoicing, but public opinion has changed not altogether for the better. Many prefer being brutal to incurring the risk of ridicule (1922:8–9). (Tas-him refers to the aid of a midwife being sought when the infibulation has been so severe that normal consummation of the marriage is not possible. The tas-him is often delayed for up to one year.)

Similarly Pallme (1844:60,61,81), when describing the "jirtig" marriage ceremony among the Danagla, informs us that if "the bride belongs to one of the tribes who practice circumcision, she is certainly forced to subject herself to a fresh operation twenty days before her marriage" (1844:81).[5]

But then, a few pages later (1844:84), he recounts that circumcision of females occurs when the girls are between five and seven, and is "attended with festivities, for which no expense is shunned." In a footnote he mentions that the girls are "excised," although his discription of the operation is more in conjunction with what we know about infibulation than simple clitoral excision. It is possible that Pallme is either referring to two (or more) different populations here (for on pp. 60 and 81 [1844] he mentions that the women of the "Dongolavi" are treated badly, especially if they do not produce offspring), or that that which he calls "excision" is, in fact, infibulation. Similarly, as there are very few references to festivities in conjunction with infibulation of females, it may very well be that Pallme is referring to subpopulations of the Dangala, some of which infibulate, while others "excise" their females. Rüssegger also describes festivities associated with infibulation among the Dangala (1843:495).

Trimingham (1949:4) informs us that all females are infibulated among the Berberines (e.g., the Sukkot and Mahas, who inhabit the north), and the Danagla (which MacMichael suggests are related to the Danakil of the northern Somali coast [MacMichael, 1967:13n]). Cadalvene and de Breuvery also report infibulation being praticed in "Dongola" (1844:227–28), as does Godard (1867:60). None of these references mentions the existence of related festivities, however.

The Majasare are found in Lower Nubia (Northern Province), and in large numbers around Khartoum. They are divided into two groups, the northern and southern Mahas (the former still spoke Nubian in 1922, while the southern branch spoke Arabic) (Crowfoot, 1922:13). The northern group are often employed as servants in Egypt, while the southern branch are primarily cultivators. Since in both cases the "tas-him" may be invoked, we can presume that both the southern and northern populations infibulate their females (Crowfoot, 1922: 13). Wedding custom in both groups also dictates that the female reside with her parents for at least one year after the marriage.

The Beja. East of the Nubian groups lies Beja country, the population of which represents the first group of Arab tribes to occupy the north (Trimingham, 1949:4). Although some sections of the Beja have adopted sedentary or seminomadic cultivating life-styles (primarily in Eritrea), the majority remain nomadic. The Beja, like many other populations of northern Sudan are thought to have had a matrilinear system prior to their conversion to Islam, the process of patrilinearity beginning and developing through intermarriage with incoming Arabs (Hasan: 1980:118). Generally speaking, all Beja groups are nominal Moslems, polygynous, follow the Moslem practice of preferred parallel cousin marriage, and are known to pay substantial bridewealth, in the form of livestock. Both the levirate and the sororate are customary. They are patrilineal and residence is patrilocal after from one to three years of matrilocal residence, which usually includes bride-service, although this varies from group to group. The four major tribes are, respectively, the Bisharin, the Ammar'ar, the Hadendoa, and the Beni Amer. Gamst informs us that, socioeconomically speaking, there are four types of Beja (1984:132). These are the camel and sheep herders of the north (practicing minimal cultivation), the cattle, sheep, and camel herders of the south (who are either rain horticulturalists or riverine cultivators [agro-pastoralists]), the permanent or semipermanently settled group (also with flocks), and those who, in recent years, have begun to occupy town and urban centers. Although insufficient information is available concerning the circumcision practices of each of these individual groups and their subgroups, Gamst indicates that infibulation is widely practiced among the Beja (1984:134).

The Ababda, although not actually Beja, are very closely related to them. They primarily inhabit Upper Egypt, but have several branches in the Sudan. The majority are camel nomads. Here also, the "jirtig" marriage ceremony is prevalent, and consummation of the marriage may take up to one year.[6]

Browne noted that the nomadic "Bega" practiced female "excision" (1799:172), whereas Cloudsley states that all Beja practice "infibulation" on girls at age two (1981:84). W.T. Clark, in his 1938 study of the Beja notes that the Amarar and Bisharin circumcise both boys and girls as babies (although he does not qualify what type of operation the girls undergo).[7] On the other hand, Murray, in 1935, observed that "until recently . . . ten or twelve boys, of seven or eight years of age, were circumcised together" (1935:176-79).

It may be that the confusion surrounding circumcision practices among the Beja is a result of treating the Beja as one homogeneous population. It is also possible that, under the influence of Islam, the practice of circumcising boys, and excising girls shortly after birth was adopted. In the case of girls, a second, more radical, operation would follow when an acceptable age was reached, between four and eleven (e.g., Pallme, 1844:86; Lewis, 1962a:13fn). Gamst (1984:134) noted that clitoridectomies, involving "a minor or major removal of tissue and infibulation are practiced upon females, the former operation taking place in infancy. Males may be circumcised just after birth or later in boyhood, when they are segregated in a special house with the performer of the operation." Of course it is not unlikely that in Browne's time females were only excised (MacMichael also refers to Bega females being "excised"), with males being circumcised just prior to puberty (MacMichael, 1967:172). Subsequently, in conjunction with conversion to Islam, infant circumcision of both males and excision of females may have become prevalent. It should be noted, however, that there was no "general" conversion to Islam, and the various Beja populations converted at different times.

Adawi tells us that the Beja were matrilineal, removed the right testicle of the male, and circumcised their females, but that it seems that these "customs ended when the Arabs began to settle among the Beja and intermarried with them" (1954:9).

In sum, available data does not indicate specifically which Beja populations infibulate, and which excise, their females. There does, however, seem to be a correlation between the "jirtig" ceremony tradition and the infibulation of females; and we do know that the Ababda, Bisharin, and the Hadendoa have the 'jirtig' ceremony and practice infibulation (Murray, 1927:44-45; see also Nalder, 1935:240-41 for a discussion of the jirtig).[8]

The Beni Amer are primarily camel and cattle nomadic. Those who are cultivators inhabit the territory that extends south of Tokar and Khor Baraka into Eritrea, where they are one of the more important elements in the population. In the border area of Sudan/Eritrea, their territory is desert and semidesert, the Beni Amer in this area being nomadic. Because the Beni Amer are a loosely tied confederation of tribes, having varying origins, it is not possible to give a general account of their tribal life and customs (Paul, 1950:234). Milk is the staple diet of all hill Beni Amer (their cattle, although not prolific, produce very rich milk), with the cattle herded and milked by men only. Marriage preference among the Beni Amer is with a paternal cousin. After the marriage, the bride and bridegroom spend seven nights and days in their own house, but the marriage may not actually be consummated until up to one year later (Paul, 1950:234). This is a common factor of all "jirtig" marriage ceremonies. Goldsmith also mentions the "jirtig" ceremony in conjunction with marriage among the Beni Amer (see note 5.; and Goldsmith, 1920:294). After the marriage, the bride continues living in her father's house for at least one year, or until the remainder of the bride-price has been paid. Infibulation is practiced by this group (e.g., Münzinger, 1864:323-24).

The Bisharin are camel nomadic, to varying degrees, with some groups being seminomadic minimal cultivators. The two primary divisions are the Um Ali and the Um Nagi (four clans of which are camel herders, with the rest being agro-pastoral). Minimal cultivation, when practiced, is done by women. Only men may engage in herding and milking. Sandars informs us that in his time the Hannar section owned and cultivated a number of wadis (east of the Abu Hamad and between

W. Amur and Obak), even though the primary wealth source was in the
form of camels and sheep (1933:146). The Rubatab, with whom they
were on good terms, were generally found cultivating with them (such
contact might explain the existence of infibulation among the Rubatab).
Murray states that the Bisharin also have a "jirtig" marriage ceremony,
and that girls are infibulated (without ceremony) (Murray, 1935:177). He
noted that married women among the Bisharin have considerable freedom of movement, which they do not have among all other branches of
the Beja (Murray, 1927:39-45).

The Hadendoa are camel nomads, who also practice minimal cultivation. They are located primarily in Kassala province, in the wide area of
the Red Sea Hills, extending from Aswan to the borders of Eritrea and
Kassala. This group is more closely related to the Bisharin than they are
to the Beni 'Amir. They practice infibulation (e.g., Seligman,
1913:640n).

The other major grouping of Arab tribes of the northern Sudan has
been divided by H.A. MacMichael into two main categories: Ja'aliyyin
and Juhayna. (The population categories outlined below were extracted
from MacMichael, 1967:197-47; and MacMichael, 1967a:51-214.)[9]

Ja'aliyyin Group. This group represents the largest and most widely
distributed, and includes most of the northern riverine and Kordofan
sedentary populations. MacMichael tells us that this group absorbed an
older, more sedentary, heterogeneous population (1967:237).
Trimingham qualifies this group as not practicing infibulation (1949:4).
As will be seen below, however, available information, although not
always specific as to type, does indicate female circumcision being
practiced among many of the tribes in this group. Unfortunately, the
extent to which this practice is a result of Islamic/Juhayna group influence cannot, at present, be determined. Some of the major tribes included
in this category follow.

The Batahin is a seminomadic tribe between Khartoum and Atbara.
They cultivate and own large herds of camels, cattle, sheep and goats.

The Gawama'a, Gima'a, and Gamu'ia occupy the west bank of the
Nile south of Omdurman, and are sedentary (prior to the Mahdia they
were cultivators and cattleherders). MacMichael mentions, however, that
there are still some branches of these tribes who are camel and cattle
breeders. The Gima'a are semisedentary, and appear to have adopted

many customs from the Baggara. There is some evidence that a portion of the Gawama'a moved into the area of Bornu and Wadai, in Chad, and DarFur, in Sudan in the early part of the seventeenth century (MacMichael 1923:22).

The Ja'aliyyin "tribe" are riverine, located between the mouth of the Atbara and the Shabluka cataract. They currently engage in variable economic activities, but the nucleus of the tribe remain cultivators and cattle herdsmen. Burkhardt described them as primarily nomadic, however (1831:279). Generally, they have a similar tribal organization as their neighbors, the Batahin, the Shukria, etc. Here again, although some agro-pastoral sections of this group maintain mutual independence, others evidence sedentary/pastoral interaction. MacMichael noted that the Ja'aliyyin families "who cultivate the Nile banks live the ordinary life of the sedentary villager and send such flocks as they possess eastward in charge of their semi-nomadic kinsfolk" (1967:235). Among the Ja'aliyyin, patrilocal residence after an initial period of matrilocal residence is the rule.

The Rubatab and Manasir are riverine tribes (between the fourth cataract and the Atbara/Nile junction: Northern Province).

The Rubatab are agriculturalists. Parallel cousin marriage is generally prescribed (regardless of age disparity). As with most other tribal groups in the Sudan, the newly married couple (or at least the bride) live with her parents for at least one year. Circumcision for males occurs usually between the ages of fourteen and sixteen, while for females it is earlier. Ceremonial feasting is associated only with male circumcision. Females are infibulated without any related festivities (Crowfoot, 1918:133). MacMichael mentions that the 'Awadia section of the Rubatab is camel nomadic (1967:210). In a footnote he indicates that in the middle of the last century they were far more numerous than even the Ababda (1967:210n6). Because of the genealogical proximity of the 'Awadia to the Rubatab, and their large numbers (at least during the last century), it may be relatively safe to assume that the majority of the Rubatab were, at one time, camel nomads.

The Manasir are also agriculturalists, and have been considered a subtribe of the Shaiqiyya, although they are not actually related to them. In 1887, C. Wilson reported that the Manasir claimed kinship with the 'Ababda (MacMichael, 1967:209n)

The Shaiquiyya are, controversially, considered originally a nomadic tribe of Beja origin (Ibrahim, 1979:112-15). Today, they represent a diverse population engaged in a variety of economic activities. Many are cultivators and cattle herders, but traditionally they seem to have been camel nomads (Murdock, 1959:411). The Shaiquiyya infibulate their females (Crowfoot, 1922:17; Ibrahim, 1979:57). Generally, they are patrilineal with preferred parallel cousin marriage (or other close relation). Patrilocal residence is the rule, after an initial period of matrilocal residence, and during the last months of pregnancy, when the wife returns to her father's cluster. They have the jirtig ceremony in conjunction with marriage, circumcision, and birth.

Juhayna Group. This group includes most of the camel-owning/herding nomads of Kordofan as well as certain nomads inhabiting Sennar Province in the southern Gezira. The Juhaina generally represent nomadic Arab immigrants, who retained and preserved their tribal system from generation to generation (MacMichael, 1967:237).

Trimingham states that infibulation occurs among these populations, although, as in the previous population divisions, he is not specific as to which populations do or do not infibulate. (1949:4) (See also Thurnwald, 1940:260, who mentions that all "Abbala" [camel herders] and "Baggara" [cattle herders] infibulate except the Tungur.

The Awamra, Khawalda, 'Amarna, and the Fadnia are included here as an indication of the subsistence patterns in the Gezira area prior to its development, although I could find no indication of the current existence of these tribes (the first three were relatively insignificant in number, even in MacMichaels time). The first three are agro-pastoral, and the latter had a sedentary and a nomadic branch.

The Baggara (the word itself means "cattlemen") is used to denote a large group of closely related nomadic and seminomadic cattle herding tribes inhabiting a large area that stretches from the White Nile to Lake Chad (south of the thirteenth parallel of latitude). In the following discussion, I have followed MacMichael's designation and distribution of the Baggara (1967:273-300). As there is insufficient information available about these populations individually, they will be treated as a group below (although where possible, specific information about a specific subgroup is included).

The Baggara, never ardent cultivators, are dependent (as are many primarily nomadic populations) on the markets of the settled population for grains, cloth, tools, and so forth. Nevertheless, their basic subsistence comes from their animals (cattle, sheep, and goats). Here again, the society is patrilineal, patriarchal, and residence is patrilocal (although prior matrilocal residence for the bride is not unusual). Parallel cousin marriage is preferred (but this preference can only be confirmed for those Baggara inhabiting the Sudan). The jirtig (marriage) ceremony does not seem to occur among the Baggara groups. The branches of Baggara in Chad are located in the regions of Wadai, Bornu, and Baguirmi (the Beni Helba, Beni Khuzam, Nawaiba, Beni Rashid and Ziud, the Salamat, etc.). MacMichael points out that historically there has been considerable confusion as to who the Baggara actually were, and he suggests, as one possibility, that

> when the Arabs entered the central states they came no doubt with their camels and sheep: cattle they presumably had none, or but few. As they would have been a nuisance to the sedentary population cultivating the central belt and would have had themselves no security for their herds, they naturally gravitated, some to the more barren spaces of the north, and some to the forests and bogs of the south. The camel of course cannot exist in the south because of the tsetse fly . . . and such Arabs as went there imitated the indigenous population and took to cattle-rearing. . . . Thus it arises that, for instance, the Mahamid and the Mahria are independent nomad tribes of camel-owners in northern Darfur and Wadai, while other Mahamid and Mahria compose two-thirds of the Rizaykat in southern Darfur. (1967:273–74)

The Mahamid and Mahria (Rizaykat) population in southern Darfur are agro-pastoral. In addition to the Mahamid and Mahria in northern Darfur and Wadai, three other camel nomadic tribes (in the same geographic area) are related to the Baggara. These are the Nawaiba, the 'Eraykat, and the 'Atayfat.

The Mahamid are located in Wadai and northwestern Darfur. they are camel nomads who also have herds of cattle and horses. They are Moslems. Infant mortality among this group is extremely high, as is the incidence of rape. Girls are married at approximately twelve years of age, and Courtecuisse describes the lot of these young women, who "suffer a veritable legal violation, inflicted upon them by their husbands, during the consummation of their marriage" (Courtecuisse, 1971:105). The status of women generally is extremely low. They are relegated to the camp, as only men are permitted to tend and pasture the animals. Courtecuisse informs us that bride-price is payable in animals, that children are suckled as long as possible, and that young girls are infibulated between the ages of eight and ten years (Courtecuisse, 1971:99–

109). I could find no information, however, concerning marriage preference (e.g., parallel/cross cousin, etc.), or residence patterns.

The Salamat now inhabit Bornu, Chad district, Bakirmi, and southern
Wadai, having migrated to these areas from Darfur. Although the major-
ity of the Salamat branches are baggara (with sheep), some branches are
camel-owning nomads (e.g., sections of the Beni Rashid and Ziud)
(MacMichael, 1967:296). Barth noted that the Salamat-Shoa infibulate
(Shoa is the local name for all semisedentary Baggara Arabs of Bornu,
Baguirmi, Chad district, and southern Wadai) (1857, vol. 2:570). A.
LeBeuf (1959:88) and Nachtigal (1971, vol. 4:74) inform us that in Wadai
province (Chad), young girls undergo clitoral excision, but not infibulation, and that circumcision of females is not practiced at all in Bornu
(Chad). In her demographic delineation of Wadai, LeBeuf includes the
"Ouadaiens, Mimi, Tama, Massalit, Mararit, Soungor, Marfa, Zaghawa,
Daza, Dadjo, Arabes" (LeBeuf, 1959:76-78). Livestock, the principle
wealth in the Wadai area is in the hands of the Arab population. The
remaining population is essentially agricultural (LeBeuf, 1959:81). All
of the population of Wadai are at least nominal Moslems. In her delineation of the Arab population (in southeastern, and south central Chad),
LeBeuf includes the "Hassauna, Djoheina, Beni Hemat, Beni Khozam,
Salamat, Ouled Rachid, Misirie, Mahamid, Mawaibe, Mahariye, and the
Eregat." These groups she generally qualifies as seminomadic pastoralists, with agriculture occurring primarily in the south, but remaining a
secondary activity (LeBeuf, 1959:90-95). The descent system is patrilineal, and residence is patrilocal, but consummation of the marriage is
delayed, indicating prolonged matrilocal residence after marriage for the
bride. Although she is not specific about the length of the delay, it no
doubt is related to the age of the bride. LeBeuf qualifies these tribes as
being exogamous (that is, the "kasim bet" is exogamous: "the kasim bet
or kasim nar are general terms signifying 'members of the same house'
[bet], or 'those who share the same hearth' [nar]") (LeBeuf, 1959:96)
(my translation). LeBeuf further informs us that all of these tribes excise
their females between the ages of six and eight years.

As to the practice of circumcision among the Baggara generally,
Yuzbashi informs us that the Baggara did not always infibulate their
females.

The Baggara, whose original home is in the west formerly practiced the "sunna" form
of circumcision, but the "pharonic" method gradually came into use through the

influence of traders and other inhabitants of northern Sudan with whom they came into contact. The Messeria, being the most easterly of the tribes in question, were the first to adopt this practice, and after it had become universal among them, they passed it on to their neighbours, the Fellaita section of the Homr, whence it made its way to the Agaira section of the same tribe. At the time of my first visit to Muglad, in 1917, I found that the Agaira were still practicing the "sunna" method, and made every effort to convince the Nzir Nimr Ali Gulla of the atrociousness of the pharonic custom and the damage and suffering which it inflicts on the women. I earnestly advised him to use all his influence to prevent it from spreading amongst his section. He appeared to be convinced by my arguments and promised to do his best; I regret to say however, that during my next visit in 1918, I found that the "pharonic" custom had made its appearance there and was given a hearty welcome. The reasons given for the adoption of this form of circumcision are (1) that it is supposed to be a protection against untimely pregnancy, and (2) that it is regarded as rendering the victim more attractive to men. (1922:203–04)

The Dar-Hamid were entirely nomadic until the early part of the ninteenth century (and many still are). Those that are still camel nomads also practice minimal cultivation. They are found primarily in central Kordofan. MacMichael points out that in the recent past a portion of this group was with the Kababish in Dongola, while larger sections were attached to the western Kawahla, and incorporated as a subtribe of the Kababish in Kordofan (1967:256). These sections were still nomadic in the early part of this century (see also LeBeuf, 1947:430–39).

The Dubasiin are found in the northern Gezira and are related to the Shukriyya (although the nature of the relationship is unclear). They were generally nomadic until this century (their grazing area lying south of Khartoum), when they became agro-pastoral. This group has also been included because of their location in the Gezira area.

The Hawazma spend the greater part of the year living in the area of Bedayria villages to the north of the Nuba Hills. They appear to be seminomadic cattle herders (I have no information as to the amount [if any] of camels they may have). Nadel informs us that the Hawazma branch of the Baggara practice infibulation, and that they passed this practice on to the Tira-Mande (Nuba) (1947:486–87).

The Kababish are camel owning nomads, and are widely distributed in Kordofan and Darfur. In addition, some groups are found in Dongola Province, where a certain number are sedentary, but the majority are camel nomads. This population is representative of the regularized interaction between town and nomadic populations, and Holt notes that "their wide range, across the north-western trade-routes, made the tribe a factor of some importance in the commercial and political history of the Sudan, especially in the nineteenth century" (Holt, 1961:10). The Kababish are thought to have been matrilineal prior to adopting Islam. Asad informs us that parallel cousin marriage is the preferred form (1970:59), and Parkyns intimates it (1851:272–73), although this may not have been strictly enforced in the past. Parkyns noted that a young man, ready for marriage,

> starts off, and passes in review all the pretty girls of the tribe, until he finds one unequalled in qualities and accomplishments, both personal and mental. The personal qualities she should have are, thick legs, a broad and heavy stern like a dutch boat, eyes . . . like an ox's, and her copper coloured skin shining from the dilka, which blackens her clothes and leaves an odour a mile off, and an enormous quantity of wool in a bush on her head well plastered with suet, and well scented with some spice or essential oil to prevent its stinking. (1851:266–67)

Asad found that after the first stage of the wedding, the bride continues to live with her parents for up to several years (during which time she is maintained by her father). The length of her residence in her father's house "depends in part on the age of the groom, and on his capacity to establish his own household, and in part on the mother's readiness to part with her daughter" (Asad, 1970:59–60). The Kababish practice infibulation, without festivity, and circumcise their males, with festivity (e.g., Parkyns, 1851:266).

The Lahawiin are related to the Rufa'a and are primarily camel nomadic. They are located near el Fasher on the Atbara (although one portion of them appear to be more sedentary, living on the east bank of the White Nile). The nomadic section was attached to the Kababish for several generations, living in northern Kordofan, but in 1910 they moved eastwards over the Nile. They now fall under Shukriyya control.

The Messallamia are also distantly related to the Dar-Hamid. They live in the Gezira, on the White Nile, and on the eastern side of the lower reaches of the Blue Nile. Those in Gezira and the White Nile are sedentary, the rest being agro-pastoral. Hasan includes this group, along with the Dughaym (cousins of the Kenana), the Kenana, and the Kawahla as among the first Arab populations to penetrate the Gezira region. Although it is not known exactly when they arrived, the Kenana appear in Upper Egypt by the mid-thirteenth century. MacMichael states that the Mesallamia, east of the Blue Nile, are "chiefly nomadic in their habits, and until about the middle of the nineteenth century were entirely so" (1967:270). Their main wealth is in the form of sheep and goats, but they also have numbers of camels and cattle. They are noted to infibulate (Widstrand, 1964:106).

The Rufa'a, although historically almost entirely nomadic, are now settled to a considerable extent. Holt mentions that some of them became sedentary in the fifteenth century, but that until the ninteenth century the bulk of the Rufa'a remained entirely nomadic. Similarly, the town of Rufa'a was originally a tribal settlement, of which the southern section remains largely nomadic (Holt, 1961:9). The Rufa'a fall into two general groups, the northern and the southern. The former is settled in villages in the Blue Nile province, with the latter being more nomadic than sedentary. MacMichael points out that among the sedentary Rufa'a, although some villages are made up of only Rufa'a, other villages comprise a combination of Rufa'a, Mahas, Ja'alyyin, Danagla, and others (1967:240). The nomadic Rufa'a are camel, cattle, sheep and goat herders. These groups, as with most herding populations (especially those with camels), send their young men out with the herds, usually far from where the tents are pitched. They may spend two or more months with the grazing herds, while only a few will remain behind in the settlement to look after the women, children, aged, and weaker animals. The women here, as among most camel herding populations, always remain in the settlement area. The Rufa'a generally are patrilineal, with parallel cousin preferred marriage (or someone in the same close rela-tion). The rule is patrilocal residence, but only after the birth of the first child. Until then the wife remains in residence in her father's cluster. The Rufa'a also have the jirtig ceremony at marriage (personal communica-tion from Abdel Ghaffar). Circumcision of girls is practiced (Abdel Ghaffar, 1974:42), and Widstrand (1964:106 [referencing Hassan, 1893]) informs us that the Rufa'a infibulate their females.

The Shenabla are located in the northeastern part of the Blue Nile province, near the White Nile. The majority are camel nomads and are related to the Dar-Hamid. MacMichael points out that in the eighteenth century

> when all the Northern Kordofan tribes were nomad camel-owners the Shenabla severed their connection with Dar Hamid: part migrated to the east banks of the White Nile and and settled near Shatt and Zerayka: others joined the Kababish in the north. Of the former colony again some afterwards joined the Mesallamia, and some, namely the Gihaysat, attached themselves to the Hamar 'Asakir in the west . . . The party who joined the Kababish remained nomads with that tribe until the "Mahdia." They then

... threw in their lot with their kinsfold on the river. .... The bulk of the tribe are still
nomad camel-owners, but they also own land near the White Nile. (1967a:206)

The situation described above was not uncommon, and is indicative not
only of the fairly recent settlement of entire groups or sections thereof,
but also of their fluid interactions with neighboring or related groups.

The Shukriyya are found in Kassala province, although the majority
inhabit the area between the Blue Nile and the Atbara. They are primarily
nomadic camel and cattle herders, although sections of them have been
sedentarized. This group, as most other Arab groups, is polygynous and
patrilocal (with an initial period of matrilocal residence). Very little
information is available concerning the social structure and traditions of
this group, and even the 1983 study of female circumcision in the Sudan
has a very small sample for Shukriyyan women (although of the sample,
the majority have been, and continue to infibulate their daughters)
(Rushwan, 1983:191–97). Crowfoot (and later, Trimingham) briefly
mentions them in his discussion of the jirtig ceremony, which he says the
Shukriyya do not have (1922:22; see also note 8 [although Trimingham
may have taken his information directly from Crowfoot]).

Other Arab Groups. The Ababda inhabit Upper Egypt, with several
branches in the Sudan. They are primarily camel nomads. Because of
their close relationship to the Beja, they have been included with them.

The Hasania groups (with the exception of those on the west bank of
the White Nile Province, who are cattle herders) are primarily camel
nomads with sheep and some cattle. In 1878, Marno noted that the
"Hassanie" (the Hasania division of the Kawahla group) infibulate
(referenced in MacMichael, 1967:328). Widstrand (referencing
Hartmann), also mentions infibulation among the Bayuda Desert
Hasania Arabs, and among one settled Hasania tribe (the Awlad Kahil)
in the White Nile Province (1964:107).

The Hawawira are camel nomads living in Dogola. They move with
the Kababish in the rainy season.

The Kawahla are widely distributed in northern Sudan, and fall into
two primary groups. The most important of these are the nomadic
camel-herders of Kordofan. Of the other group, those south of Sennar
and on the banks of the Atbara are nomadic, while others have become
sedentary, occupying areas along the White Nile and in the Gezira. The
Ababda and Bisharin of the east also appear to be related to this group.

The Kenana are divided into two groups, both of which are primarily cattle herders. The larger division owns cattle, camels and sheep, and lives to the south of Sennar. The other group lives in Kordofan, and grazes with the Hawazma (Baggara). Crowfoot (1925:125) indicates that the Kenana infibulate (see also Trimingham 1964:83).

The Kerrarish are related to the Ababda. Although originally in Upper Egypt, they now graze their camels and flocks in the area west of Dongola. Others have settled on the Nile, to the south of the Mahas.

The Kerriat appear to be a heterogeneous camel nomadic group, whose grazing grounds are the area west and north of Omdurman, east of the Wadi el Mukaddam.

The Rashaida are relatively recent Arabian immigrants to the Sudan (having arrived in 1846). They are camel nomads living between Tokar and the Eritrean border; as well as on the Atbara and the Kash.

Non-Arab Populations. Of the non-Arab populations MacMichael includes many of those tribes inhabiting Darfur and the eastern Chad borderland (e.g., the Bedayat [in the northern portion of Darfur and the Chad border area], the Zaghawa [in northern Darfur], the Midob [northeastern corner of Darfur], the Berti [eastern Darfur], the Tungur [central Darfur], the Dagu [central Darfur], the Birked [central Darfur], the Beyko [southern Darfur]). In addition to these tribes are the Fellata (largely represented in Darfur), of whom the majority (as in West Africa), are cattle-owning nomads although some are sedentary. Additionally, he includes the western frontier tribes (e.g., the Kimr [western Darfur], the Tama [eastern Chad border area], the Masalit [western Darfur and Chad border area], and the Fur themselves (MacMichael, 1967:52–115).

The Bedayat can be found in the northern portion of Darfur and the Chad border. They are primarily nomadic camel breeders, and appear to be related to the Zaghawa. They adopted Islam in the course of this century but are not completely Islamized, and sections of them remain pagan. They only circumcise (i.e., excise) their females if they have been promised in marriage to a Zaghawa (Fuchs, 1961:76). They are patrilineal, and basically patrilocal, although a lengthy (or sometimes permanent) initial period of matrilocal residence is usual.

The Berti are located in Northern Darfur, are Moslems, and are fully sedentary agriculturalists. The Berti marriage and residence pattern described below is, to a considerable extent, representative of that which occurs throughout the Sudan (although there are, no doubt, exceptions to this pattern). They are polygynous, and parallel cousin (cross-cousin, or other close relation) marriage is preferred (although this may be more directly related to the adoption of Islam than to an indigenous development). Marriage for boys occurs between the ages of twenty and twenty-four, and for girls between eighteen and twenty-two (Holy, 1984:159). Weddings occur in three stages. The first stage is the payment of the first part of the bridewealth, which occurs on the occasion of the wedding ceremony. The spouses subsequently continue living with their respective families, and do not consummate their marriage until approximatley six months later, in a hut built for them in the household of the bride's parents.

This second stage of the wedding usually occurs after the harvest. After the marriage is consummated the husband returns to his own homestead, visiting the wife regularly (the frequency of these visits depend on the distance of his family homestead from that of his wife's). During this period the husband will also perform "bride-service." Usually, one or more offspring are born to the couple during this second phase of the wedding, with the average time between the first and final wedding stages being up to four years. Before the final phase occurs, the wife continues to be a member of her natal home, and only becomes associated with her husbands group after the final stage of the wedding. Similarly, the husband remains in his natal home. The final stage of the wedding occurs only after the final payment of the bridewealth (Holy, 1974:2–4, 71–73, 112, and 1984:159).[10] In the case of polygynous families, they are "never in the same village if the husband is still sexually active. . . . The homesteads of subsequent wives remain in the village of the wives' parents; all secondary homesteads of polygynists are uxorilocal" (Holy 1974:111). The Berti have not been included as infibulation-practicing in this study for two reasons: (1) I was only able to find a single source for this population (Holy); (2) Holy makes no mention of this practice among the Berti in earlier publications (see Holy, 1991:164ff. for a description of infibulation among the Berti). Thus, it is unclear whether infibulation constitutes a very recent adoption among the Berti (also see Holy, 1988 for a detailed consideration of gender and ritual, characteristic for most of the populations under consideration in this study).

The Dagu can primarily be found in central Darfur and eastern Chad, where they represent one of the oldest communities (Berre, 1984:219). Approximately 90 percent of them are sedentary, with those owning considerable stock entrusting these to Arabs (in exchange for grazing rights in their fields) (Berre, 1984:220).

The Dagu are Moslems. They practice male circumcision and clitoral excision on females. The position of women is generally low, although they do not wear veils. Should a husband take more than one wife, each occupies a separate residence (often in a different village).

The Fur, from whom Darfur takes its name, comprise the most numerous sedentary population in its western region. They are nominal Moslems. In the territory of DarFur "the circumcision of females, either partial or entire, was not uncommon, but the Fur proper did not practice it" (El Tunisi, referenced in MacMichael, 1967:107). Also found among the Fur, as among the Arab nomads and the sedentary populations throughout the northern Sudan, is the mother/father-in-law avoidance by a man/ woman respectively. MacMichael points out that it is "particularly taboo for a man to eat with his mother-in-law, or a woman with her father-in-law" (1967:106).

Although avoidance of in-laws of the same sex is less extreme, some distance is maintained. Murdock informs us that the Fur are organized in matrilocal extended families (1959:143). Haaland, however, states that although the groom moves to his wife's village in bride-service to her family (for approximately one year), the preferred residence is virilocal (1984:267). The bride-service may, however, and often does, lead to permanent settlement with the wife's family. The children (girls indefinitely, and boys until between eight and ten) are the responsibility of the mother, as was the case in all of the above populations. It is she who must provide for their subsistence from the produce of the fields worked by her. Similarly, there is a tendency for daughters to succeed to their mother's fields, upon the death of the latter (Barth, 1967:151–53). Marriage is not prescribed according to exogamous or endogamous clans or lineages (Haaland, 1984:267).

The Masalit of western Darfur and Chad. The Masalit are Moslems and, like the Fur, are sedentary agriculturalists, with both men and women cultivating, owning lands and animals, and making consumption decisions (Tully, 1984:501; Haaland, 1984:266). In neither case is the family "united in joint estate under one person's control, but rather a system of rights and duties between husband and wife, parent and child. Men must provide housing and most cash goods for their wives and children, while women are primarily responsible for the domestic needs and food for the family" (Tully, 1984:501; and for the "Fur" see Haaland, 1984:266).

Marriage usually occurs for both men and women in their early twenties, with the bridewealth distributed to the bride, her mother, and other relatives. Here again, bride-service (matrilocal residence) lasts for at least one year (or until after the birth of the first child). After the bride service period, matrilocal residence may become permanent, or the couple may settle near the husband's family. The residence will usually be determined by the position and availability of fields (Tully, 1984:501). I can find no evidence for circumcision among the Masalit.

The Meidob inhabit the north eastern corner of Darfur. They appear to be related to the Nubians, in that most of their sections claim Mahas origin (from Dongola). There are both agro-pastoral and seminomadic Midob. The latter maintain regular connections with the Berti, from whom they purchase most of their corn. Women participate in the herding and milking of livestock.

Although they are Moslems, Thelwall informs us that the Meidob were not effectively Islamized until well into the last century, which probably explains the continued existence of a matrilinear system of inheritance (1984:505). Parallel cousin marriage (father's brother's daughter/son) seems to be preferred, with residence determined by the "physical settlement pattern and the marital/kin status" (Thelwall, 1984:506). Both sexes are circumcised, with girls being excised (MacMichael, 1967:60; Murdock, 1959:163).

The Nuba are located in the hills of northern Kordofan, and are pagan (although recent conversions to Islam have occurred among many sections). They are primarily agricultural, with supplementary animal husbandry. Polygyny, and both patrilineal and matrilineal descent patterns, can be found among these populations. No form of cousin marriage is permitted, and residence, as in most of the Sudan, is patrilocal after the birth of the first child. Marriage involves a bride-price paid in livestock, in addition to a minimal bride-service. The Nuba may well represent an autochthonous "Sudanese" population (Nadel, 1947:3–6). Murdock hypothesizes that

> the inhabitants of the Nuba Hills have no archaeological record and only a very brief history. Protected by their mountainment, they have remained relatively untouched by the movements of peoples and cultures in the Nile Valley and between the latter and the central Sudan. They thus constitute a sort of cultural eddy or backwash and

probably retain many cultural characteristics of the Nile Negroes before the latter felt
the impact of Pharaonic civilization. (1959:164)

Given the above, and if Murdock's reconstruction of the social structural
development of the Nuba (summarized below) is accepted as indicative
of the general autochthonous structure, then infibulation can only with
difficulty be seen as an originally indigenous trait (1959:168-69).

The Mesakin tribe of the Talodi group (one of the most southern and
least disturbed Nuba tribes) is used by Murdock to illustrate the original
Nuba social structure. Its most characteristic features would have been
"matrilineal descent, initially matrilocal but permanently avunculocal
residence, bride-service rather than bride-price, monogamy, and Iroquois
cousin terminology" (1959:168).

For the next developmental phase, he cites the Talodi proper, and the
Korongo tribe of the tuntum group (both neighbors of the Mesakin). In
this phase, cattle have been introduced into the area, and are presumed
to have been owned and tended by men (considerably strengthening their
economic and social position).

This factor of cattle ownership initiated patrilineal inheritance and
patrilocal residence, as well as creating the possibility for polygyny.
Characteristics here include

> modest bride-price, limited polygyny, mixed rules of inheritance, and a moderate
> incidence of patrilocal residence, although they still adhere strictly to matrilineal
> descent. The Iroquois pattern of designating cousins, losing its original support in
> kin-group localization, yielded to the practice, either of extending sibling terms to
> cousins, as among the Lofofa, or of applying descriptive terminology (Murdock,
> 1959:168).

The Tullishi tribe of the Tumtum group represent the next phase.
Bridewealth has become substantial, and patrilocal residence has become
the norm. The final phase of this process is represented by the Koalib
group (Heiban, Koalib, Moro, Otoro, and Tira). Here polygyny is general
(with more than 50 percent of all men possessing plural wives), and
patrilineal descent is prevalent.

In none of these phases does circumcision occur. Nuba children, in
general, are still not circumcised today (except among those sections
directly influenced by Arab populations) (Sagar, 1922:148; see also
Cailliaud, 1826:22-23). Nadel mentions that clitoridectomy "is . . .
practised by the Arab tribes in the west and south-west of Kordofan

(Messirya and Humr), and has spread to their Nuba neighbours, the peoples of Kamdang, the Miri, and the Daju" (1947:486).[11]

The Tungur are an agro-pastoral, Moslem group living in central Darfur, Bornu and Wadai. They are thought to have originated in Dongola (MacMichael, 1967:66). After their arrival in Darfur they apparently intermarried with the Fur to a considerable extent. They circumcise males between the ages of eight and sixteen years, but do not circumcise their females (LeBeuf, 1959:98; J. Tubiana, 1984:799).[12]

The Zaghawa are found to the south of the Bedayat, but are mixed with them. They are primarily located in Chad and Darfur. Those in Darfur are agro-pastoral, having both camels and cattle (as well as sheep and goats). The Zaghawa of Chad are primarily seminomadic cattle herdsmen, cultivating when climatic conditions permit, but who also hunt and gather. The gathering is done primarily by the women, who often set off in small groups (or alone) to gather wild plants, a task which may last a month or more.

The status of women among this group is especially low (they are regarded as a necessary evil) (MacMichael, 1967a:114).

Milking of the cows, goats, and ewes in the villages is done by the women only and, although both men and women may milk the camels, this task is usually done by the men (Tubiana, 1977).

Both the Zaghawa and the Bedayat (they refer to themselves collectively as "Beri") have (had) slaves, and endogamous castes of smiths. They practice polygyny when they can afford it, and still retain the custom of levirate. Marriage generally involves a high bride-price (especially among the Zaghawa), and both parallel and cross-cousin marriage was taboo until fairly recently (M-J. Tubiana, 1984:156). Generally speaking, patrilocal residence is the rule (preceded by a period of matrilocal residence). Although Fuchs (1961:76 referenced above) indicates female circumcision, Tubiana informs us that although male circumcision is practiced, "female circumcision is practiced only among the daughters of royal clans" (1984:157). Chapelle reports that the Zaghawa do infibulate their females, and although he uses the term *excise*, his description is closer to infibulation, "the ablation of the clitoris and the labia minora" (Chapelle, 1980:142). He associates its occurrence in Chad primarily (though not entirely) with the introduction of Islam (1980:142). Tubiana (personal communication, 1985) informed me that circumcision was not, to her knowledge, generally practiced among the

Zaghawa. As a consequence, I have not included the Zaghawa in the listing of infibulation-practicing populations.

The Southern Populations

The three southern provinces (comprising approximately 4 million people) have traditionally included the Bahr el Ghazal, Equatoria, and the Upper Nile. The tribal groups inhabiting these southern provinces are either agriculturalists, or agro-pastoral.

The population, although very diverse, is genetically and culturally related to black Africa. Barbour points out that much of the population diversity can, in part, be explained by the tse-tse fly of the Ironstone Plateau, and the swamps of the southern clay plains, both of which have inhibited communication and discouraged the creation or maintenance of large political units (1964:209). In addition, much of the communication inhibition between the south and the north of the Sudan finds its origin in the slave trade. During this period the southern populations found themselves regularly hunted by their northern compatriots.

Generally speaking, infibulation (unless very recently adopted) is not practiced by the tribes of the southern provinces (nor could I find any reference to its practice there in the available literature—either recent or historical). However, among some groups clitoral excision is now practiced, as well as male circumcision (Seligman, 1932; El-Dareer, 1983).

A short discussion of some of the primary southern groups follows, together with a brief overview of their marriage, residence, and subsistence patterns. Seligman has delineated four groups of primarily pagan populations (although there has been some degree of Islamization and Arabization) (1932). These are:

The Nilotes. These groups are all cattle-herding/cultivating, semisedentary pastoralists.

The Shilluk, the Nuer, and the Dinka are all agro-pastoral. None of these circumcise their females, and only the Dinka circumcise their males.

The Nilo-Hamites are primarily cattle herdsmen, but they also practice agriculture.

The Bari, Kuku, Nyupo, Kakwa all live in the southern Bahr el Jebel (Equatoria province). All are agro-pastoral, pagan, polygamous (number of wives is unlimited, but two or three is common), and patrilineal. Child betrothal is common, with partial payment of bride-price commencing when the girl is eight to ten years of age (final payment is usually made some four to eight years later, when the girl has reached puberty).

The Turkana live in the southeastern corner of the Sudan, (Equatoria Province). They are a pagan, seminomadic, primarily cattle-herding people (who also have camels, donkeys, sheep, and goats). They also practice some minimal cultivation. Nevertheless, their principle diet is composed of milk and meat. They are polygamous, and generally live in small groups of from three to ten family units. They are not known to have practiced circumcision (White, 1920:219).

The Negroid Tribes of the Blue and Upper Nile Provinces. The Berta are agro-pastoral. Some sections of this group now practice circumcision and clitoridectomy (Murdock, 1959:173; Bender, 1975:14)

The Fung, although there is some confusion as to who is included in this group, are qualified by MacMichael as a mixed negroid race, who are primarily agro-pastoral, and located primarily in the Sennar mountains (1967a:230). They circumcise their females, but it appears restricted to excision of part of the clitoris (Seligman, 1932:388–89).

The Ingassana are agro-pastoralists living in the Tabi Hills in the Dar Fung area (Blue Nile Province). According to Bender, they were, until recently, "basically sedentary agriculturalists" (1975:11). Pre-pubescent betrothal is not unusual. Both sexes are circumcised between eleven and thirteen years of age. Females undergo clitoral excision (Seligman, 1932:430; Murdock, 1959:173; Bender, 1975:14).

The amount of bride-price and the duration of bride-service varies from section to section in this general population. Marriage to all cousins is forbidden. Polygyny is acceptable and practiced among some groups, while monogamy predominates in others (there is no general rule of thumb). Patrilocal residence, in addition to approximately one year of initial matrilocal residence, appears to be the norm.

The Southwestern Group. The Azande are agricultural and practice husbandry. Females are not circumcised. Males are circumcised from twelve years of age (Seligman, 1932:518; Bower, 1923:250; Brock, 1918:250).

The Bongo-Mittu are agricultural, with husbandry. Males are circumcised, but Seligman states that it is not an indigenous trait, having been adopted from the Azande (1932:465). Females are not circumcised. Evans-Pritchard said that although circumcision (of males) was unknown "throughout the entire river district . . . today it is coming in from the Azande to the south, who in their turn borrowed the custom from the Amdi in the Congo" (1929:8).

The Kreich Nakka, Banda, Binga, Kara, Ferogi, Kreich Jebel, Kreich Hofrat, and the Bornu are inhabitants of the western Bahr el Gazal (and are actually north of the "south-western" populations). Of these groups, all practice clitoral excision of girls except the Binga and the Kara (who were acquiring the custom at the time of Bower's report) (Bower, 1923:249–50).

Demographic Data: Northeast Africa and the Horn

Ethiopia

The majority of the population in Ethiopia does not practice infibulation. Those that do, often occupy other (neighboring) territories as well. Where the majority of a given population occupies another territory, e.g., Saho and 'Afar, they have been included thereunder. Consequently, only those populations, the majority of which occupy Ethiopian territory, have been included below.

MAP 10: Estimated Distribution of Listed Populations Sudan/Eastern Chad

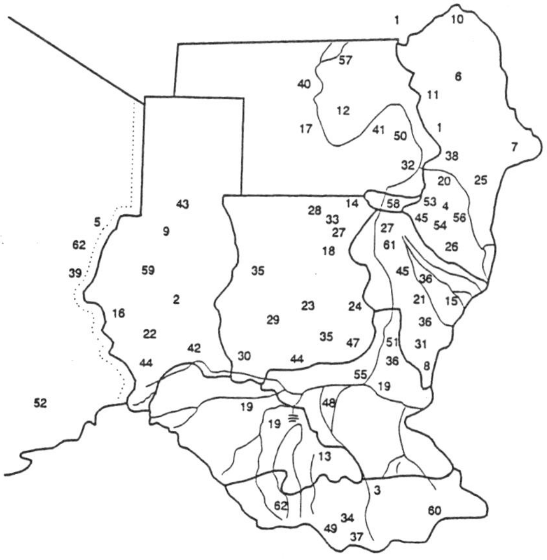

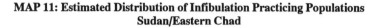

**MAP 11: Estimated Distribution of Infibulation Practicing Populations
Sudan/Eastern Chad**

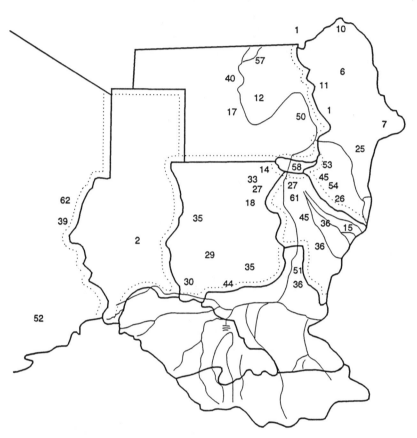

The Amhara and the Tigrai are related populations inhabiting the highland provinces (the latter also inhabits northern Eritrea). Of the two, the Amhara are the dominant group in modern Ethiopia. Both are agriculturalists and primarily Christians, although the Tigrai include some Moslems. Animal husbandry, although practiced, plays a secondary role in groups (even Moslem Tigrai) forbid first cousin marriage, and although Moslem groups practice polygyny, the Christian population is (at least theoretically) monogamous. Both groups circumcise males, and many practice clitoral excision.

TABLE A.4 - Labels Used in Maps 10 and 11

1	Ababda	32	Ja'aliyyin
2	BAGGARA	33	Kababish
3	Bari	34	Kakwa
4	Batahin	35	Kawahla
5	Bedayat	36	Kenana
6	BEJA	37	Kuku
7	Beni Amer	38	Lahawiin
8	Berta	39	Mahamid
9	Berti	40	Mahas
10	Bisharin (Umm Ali)	41	Manasir
11	Bisharin (Umm Nagi)	42	Masalit
12	Bisharin	43	Meidob
13	Bongo	44	Mesiriya
14	Burri Al Lamaab	45	Messalamia
15	Burun	46	NUBIANS
16	Dagu	47	NUBA
17	Danagla	48	Nuer
18	Dar Hamid	49	Nyupo
19	Dinka	50	Rubatab
20	Dubasiin	51	Rufa'a
21	FUNG	52	Salamat
22	FUR	53	Shaquiya
23	Gawama'a	54	Shenabla
24	Gima'a	55	Shilluk
25	Hadendoa	56	Shukriya
26	Hallali	57	Sukkot
27	Hasania	58	Three Towns
28	Hawawir	59	Tungur
29	Hawazma	60	Turkana
30	Humr	61	Umm Fila
31	Ingassana	62	Zaghawa
		63	Zande

The Dasenetsch (also called Dasanik, Geleba, Reschiat, Marille) inhabit the lower Omo Basin of southwestern Ethiopia. They are semi-nomadic cattle herders, although some groups are agro-pastoral (Jensen, 1947:79; Carr, 1977:9). They are exogamous and polygynous (the number of wives ranging from one to five, although Carr reports that the majority of men interviewed had from one to three wives) (1977:120). Carr indicates that females are circumcised although she does not indicate which type of circumcision is performed (1977:146).

The Falasha represent a negroid Jewish population located in north-central Ethiopia (Tigrai and Begemder Provinces). They are agriculturalists and craftsmen. Simoons states that girls are excised (clitoris), and are marriageable at nine years of age (boys being eligible at seventeen) (1960:23,38). Apart from the Ke'mant (a pagan Jewish population in Begemder Province who practice clitoral excision), there was no other mention of female circumcision in these regions.

The Galla (also called Oromo) are the largest ethnic group in Ethiopia. They currently occupy the southwest and south central regions. Although the majority are now agriculturalists, they are thought to have originally been pastoral. Those who have remained pastoral are primarily pagan, while those settled in highland Ethiopia have become either Moslems or Christians (Murdock, 1959:325).

The pastoral groups are either seminomadic or completely nomadic cattle herders (although the Arusi, Borana, and that group which Murdock terms the "Bararetta," also have camels and horses)[13] (Murdock, 1959:325). These groups are generally polygynous, with each wife occupying a separate dwelling. They are exogamous.

Although the evidence relative to the practice of infibulation among Galla populations is conflicting, there are some generalizations that can be made. Most Galla populations cicumcise males and perform clitoral excision on females (although Murdock says they also sometimes infibulate) (Murdock, 1959:326). It seems that those Galla living closest to the Somali (Islamized Galla) perform this most extreme form of circumcision on their females (e.g., the Galla of Harrar and of Shoa), whereas the pagan Galla do not infibulate their females (Jensen, 1947:80; Widstrand, 1964:100).

The Sidamo peoples inhabit the southwest region of the Ethiopian plateau, and, although a heterogeneous population, they are collectively known as Sidamo. They all practice intensive agricultural (many of them with terraced irrigated fields), and husbandry (although this is of secondary subsistence importance). Here again, exogamy is the rule. Generally, polygyny is practiced, with each wife having her own house. The Sidamo, like the Galla and Somali, traditionally had hereditary slaves. With the exception of the Gibe and Kafa (who practice clitoral excision), female circumcision does not appear to occur.[14]

The Somali represent a small part of the population (+/-6 percent), and are included in the discussion under Somalia. Those in Ethiopia, like their counterparts in Somalia, practice infibulation.

Eritrea

The 'Afar (Danakil) are distributed along the coastal area of the Red Sea in Eritrea, and the Ethiopian border region. Specifically, they "occupy the eastern lowland desert parts of the Ethiopian provinces of Shoa, Wollo and Tigre, as well as northern Harar Province, southern Eritrea, and Djibouti" (Pastner, 1984:10-14).

They represent a Moslem, camel nomadic population (although there are a few cattle herders and agro-pastoralists among them) (Chedeville, 1966:173). The primary areas they inhabit have been described by Lewis as "unfertile desert traversed by lava streams and interspersed with volcanoes, hot springs, salt lakes and depressions. The only region in which cultivation can be practised is in the south along the Awash river" (1969:160). Their diet reflects this environment. "In the interior the nomad lives exlcusively on milk and meat; a handful of durra obtained by barter is a luxury. A favourite delicacy is a concoction of ghee and red pepper mixed in curdled milk; bush fruits are also eaten. On the coast and in Aussa dates and tobacco are available, and coffee seems fairly common" (Lewis, 1969:162).

The 'Afar represent a population that has been only minimally studied, and the information available to us is thus fragmentary and often inconsistent (Lewis, 1969:165; Trimingham, 1952:173; Pastner, 1984:10). The information we have indicates that, although they do not form an ethnic unit, they are loosely grouped into tribes (for alliance/defense purposes). They are polygynous, and follow the Islamic tradition of a maximum of four wives, however, as is true for the entire area under consideration, each wife has her own hut. Residence (as with the other populations) is patrilocal with an initial period of matrilocal residence, usually until after the birth of the first child (although sometimes longer) (Chedeville, 1966:188; Lewis, 1969:165).

Although the 'Afar appear to be primarily patrilineal, bilateral reckoning is important (Chedeville, 1966:189). Lewis (1969:163) states that the tendency is toward tribal endogamy, whereas Chedeville (1966:191) indicates a preference for tribal exogamy. Both agree, however, that cross-cousin (patrilateral cross cousins) marriages are preferred (Lewis, 1969:163; Chedeville, 1966:191).[15] Chedeville adds that although parallel patrilateral and matrilateral cross-cousin marriages are not considered incestuous, the southern 'Afar strongly disapprove of both.

Generally, the position of women resembles that of the Somali. They have virtually no legal rights, neither in terms of marriage, divorce, or inheritance, nor can they own any means of production. Lewis states that all girls undergo infibulation, generally in their eighth year, but in some tribes just after birth, and are eligible for marriage in their tenth year (1969:167–69; also see Kesby, 1977:66; and Magos, 1981:33).[16]

In Paulitschke's time, however, girls were apparently infibulated at around the age of three, and were "defibulated" just prior to marriage at the age of fifteen or sixteen (Paulitschke, 1893, vol. 1:175). He informs us that defibulation along the coastal areas was accomplished by a Midgan woman with a sharp knife just prior to consummation, but that in the interior, "the bridegroom de-infibulates the bride, who is held by two of his friends" (my translation) (1893, vol. 1:175). Curiously enough, around the city of Harar, "widows are re-infibulated in the same manner as the original operation. Nowhere else is this practice in evidence, not even among the Somali and the 'Afar" (my translation) (Paulitschke, 1893, vol. 1:175). The infibulation of widows in an "urban" area could be indicative either of their youth (reinfibulation facilitating remarriage), or their entry into the world of prostitution (out of economic necessity).

The Beni 'Amer are described above, in the section on Sudan.

The Bilen (Bogos) are located in north central Eritrea, in the Keren area. Trimingham informs us that they (were) agricultural (1952:164). He refers to them as nomadic herdsmen, included in the tribal federations of "Bilen, Marya, Mansa, Bait Asgade, and Bani 'Amir." He also mentions that they were Christians until the middle of the last century, when, under political duress, they began to convert to Islam (1952:165).

Infibulation has been noted among this group by Jensen (1947: 809), and Münzinger (1864:144). Given the above, it is impossible to determine whether or not infibulation was introduced after the Bilen entered the tribal federations (and were converted to Islam). Muenzinger's observations do not enlighten us, as they were made after conversion had taken place. The Beni 'Amer may have considerably influenced the Bilen and other tribes in the area of northern Eritrea, for Crowfoot found that the "Eritrean tribes, whose wedding rites present striking resemblances to the Sudanese rites . . . are the Mensa with sub-tribes Bet Ebrahe and the Bet Shakan, the Red and Black Marea, the Bet Guk, and the Bilan or Bogos" (1922:17). He qualifies all of these populations as being primarily pastoral, practicing some cultivation. They all circumcise their women in the same way "as the Arabs of the Sudan" (1922:17). However, there is a major difference between the wedding customs. Specifically, in the Eritrean custom the bride is removed by the bridegroom early in the wedding procedure, which is not the case in the Sudan (1922:21). Crowfoot was of the opinion, however, that this early departure of the bride was "a new element in these customs and that the Sudan group represents the older patterns" (1922:22).

The Kunama inhabit northwestern Eritrea, along the northern Ethiopian and eastern Sudan border. They are pagan and agro-pastoralists. Their importance lies in the fact that they are an example of a more "primitive negroid people which has remained uninfluenced by the highly developed peoples who have exploited them" (Trimingham, 1952:14).

They are exogamous and matrilineal. Although Jensen (1947:794) (nonspecifically) includes them in the groups that infibulate, Widstrand (1964:105), in conjunction with Münzinger (1864:387), specifically states that they do not infibulate.

The Saho primarily inhabit the northeastern Eritrea coastland, and in the summer months they migrate considerably inland. They are seminomadic pastoralists who are becoming sedentary (Lewis, 1969:174; Trimingham, 1952:178). Virtually nothing is known about them. Trimingham indicates that the women are veiled and secluded in their huts (1952:179). Kesby (1977:66) and Jensen (1947:809) inform us that the Saho practice infibulation.

Somali

The Northern Somali. There are six important clan families in Somalia, four of which, the Darod, Ishaak, Dir, and Hawiya, together constitute an estimated 75 percent of the total population of Somalia (Nelson, 1982:76). The majority of these are widely distributed pastoralists (with an increasing minority being settled cultivators). The more southern relatives of this group are the Hawiya and the trans-Juba Darod (see map

12).[17] These Somali are located primarily in northern Somalia, and are predominantly pastoral nomadic camel breeders.

> Camel breeding predominates in the dry plains of northern and central Somalia and is supplemented in the rugged mountains and coastal zones of the extreme north by sheep and goat herding Cattle breeding predominates where water is more abundant (and rainfall generally more reliable), specifically in most of the southern region between the Jubba and Shabeelle Rivers and in a small section of the north-west around Borama. (Cassanelli, 1982:14)

Animal husbandry has historically been the basis of the Somali economy (whether pastoralist or cultivator), with wealth and status reckoned in terms of stock. Camels and cattle are generally tended only by men (but cattle are sometimes also milked by young girls), and sheep and goats are usually tended exclusively by women and young girls. Where cultivation exists it is done by clients (in the past by slaves), but never by the "noble Somali" (Lewis, 1969:67, 76).

The Darod are found primarily in the trans-Juba region. They are nomadic pastoralists (and cattle breeders when located in the central and southern regions). Some of the trans-Juba Darod tribes are interdependent with Negroid and Hawiya agriculturalists in the area (Lewis, 1969:20).

The Geri consist of two groups, one is nomadic, and the other is agricultural. There is very little information available regarding this population. Murdock includes them among the "infibulating" Somali (1959:320–21).

The Kablalla comprise the Kombe-Harti and Kumade confederacies. The origins of the former are in the northern regions of Somalia where only minimal cultivation is possible, and the majority of the population is pastoral nomadic. The Kumade group includes both nomadic pastoral and "cultivator" subsections. Lewis notes that there is very little ethnographic information available on the Kumade (1969:23).

The Marehan has one group north of the Shebelle, and the other south of the Juba. They are nomads with camels, sheep, goats, and some cattle (especially in the south where they are in regular contact with riverine cultivators).

The Mijertein are a subconfederacy of the Kombe-Harti. They are nomadic pastoralists dependent upon camels, sheep, goats, and some cattle. The Mijertein circumcise both males and females.

**MAP 12 - Estimated Distribution of Populations
Practicing Infibulation in the Horn**

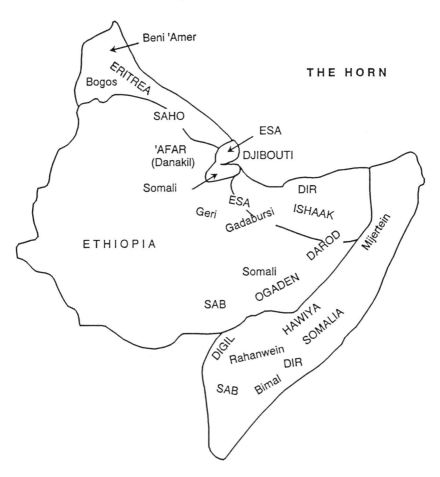

Mijertein boys are circumcised in their seventh year; the ceremony is not a collective rite and appears to have no connection with age-sets. In the north, however, and in trans-Juba, circumcision seems to be associated with initiation into an age-grade organization. . . . In the case of the Mijertein, the chief significance of circumcision seems to be to Tumal (blacksmiths), Yibir (hunters and leather-workers), and to set a limit on marriage, since the uncircumcised boy, being haram (ritually impure) cannot contract marriage. (Lewis 1969:105, 134)

The infibulation of girls takes place between the ages of six and eight, without ceremony or festivities, and with only women present.

The Ishaak, located in northwest central Somalia, are almost entirely nomadic pastoralists.

The Dir, the oldest of the Somali stock, are represented by three surviving tribes: the Esa, the Gadabursi, and the Bimal.

The Esa ('Iise) (Dir) are located in northwest Somalia, Djibouti, and in the Harar Province of Ethiopia. They are divided into two geographical groups, the Black Esa, living in the west toward the 'Afar and Ethiopia, and the White Esa, located along the coastal Guban plains. Although this population has generally been qualified as wealthy camel-owning pastoral nomads (Lewis, 1969:25; 1962:46). Lewis, in his study of the social organization of the Esa, mentions that the Black Esa possess more camels and cattle than the White, who have large flocks of sheep and goats (Lewis, 1961a:75). Nevertheless, the Esa, as a whole, are socioculturally similar to all other northern Somali; they are exogamous, divorce is common, and the levirate (and sororate) is practiced. Patrilocal residence after a period of matrilocal residence is usual (Burton, 1894:70-89).

The Gadabursi (Dir) are also located in northwestern Somali. They are primarily pastoral, but do seem to cultivate to some extent.

The Bimal are the southern representatives of the Dir, and are located on the Shebelle (around Merca), and between Juba River and the Tunni of Brava. Although the former group cultivates, the Bimal as a whole are camel nomads. Hess points out that the Bimal could retain their pastoralist life-style only because Bantu slaves cultivated their fields. Similarly, the Somali as a whole have a traditional disdain for agiculture, and a concomitant tradition of slaves to cultivate available fields, without which they would have been at bare subsistence level (Hess, 1966:87).

The Hawiya can also be found in the south, and are centered around and along the Shebelle (the Hawiya, under government influence, are becoming increasingly agricultural). Although some Hawiya tribes are nomadic, the majority might properly be termed agro-pastoral (Lewis qualified their economy as intermediate between nomadic pastoralism [dominant among the northern Darod], and the agricultural [southern] Rahanwein [1969:28]).

Agriculture in Somalia. Although pastoralism has historically been the most common (and most esteemed) life-style, cultivation has also regularly been practiced (although relegated primarily to the southern regions along the Juba and Shabelle rivers). Even though a considerable amount of the population in this area originates outside Somalia (they have been linguistically assimilated, and consider themselves Moslems), to a very considerable extent it derives "from immigrant waves of northern nomadic pastoral Somali who have settled on the land and adopted cultivation in the most fertile region of southern Somalia." And, concomitant with this immigration, they also adopted the social structure of the indigenous population, forming "large, stable politico-legal groups . . . a hierarchical . . . authority system . . . and the . . . adoption of foreign clients in group formation" (Lewis, 1969:59ff.). Lewis informs us that these characteristics are either rare or absent in northern pastoral Somali social structure. The southern populations are heterogeneous in agnatic composition, and form territorially based political units (confederations of lineages), which are loosely linked and noncorporate. Thus, the

> southern equivalent to the northern Somali clan is essentially a land-based unit, and frequently the names in its shallow quasi-genealogical framework refer directly to territorial sections rather than to genealogical segments in a true sense. . . . Acquisition of rights to arable land in the south requires, if a person is not already a member of a land-holding group, that he should seek admission as an adopted client in the clan of his choice. In return for receiving a grant of land for cultivation, the client has formally to undertake to accept joint responsibility with other members in the payment and receipt of all damages involving his clan of adoption. (Lewis, 1980:246)

Although within each land-based unit there is a population representative of the "founder population," these united "clans" are essentially formed from "layer upon layer of adopted clients" (Lewis, 1980:247). Additionally, this loose form of agnatic kinship results in a high degree of clan endogamy (parallel and cross-cousin marriage), which is in direct contrast to the northern Somali practices (Lewis, 1969a:60–71).

> Since marriage is here regarded as a means of strengthening weak existing ties, rather than as in the north of supplementing strong agnation, there is no objection to the characteristic pattern of Muslim patrilateral parallel-cousin marriage which, with matrilateral cross-cousin marriage, is practised preferentially . . . however . . . there seems to be little difference in the high degree of marriage instability. (Lewis, 1980:247)

Agriculture is the primary activity of the southern Sab (Rahanwein and Digil), while the Hawiya (Somali) are agro-pastoral. The propensity of agriculture in the south relates primarily to regional suitability for agrarian exploitation:

In the north . . . the total area cultivated is 800 sq. miles, a negligible figure within a total environment of 68,000 sq. miles. . . . In the south it is reckoned that 7,500,000 hectares (about 30,000 sq. miles), that is, 15% of the total area of Somalia, is suitable for cultivation, and of this only about 400,000 hectares are at present devoted to agriculture. (Lewis, 1969:71)

The Sab. The Sab represent a heterogeneous population inhabiting the southernmost regions of Somalia, along the Juba and Shabelle Rivers. The Digil (parent family of the Sab) is comprised of various populations, with the Rahanwein representing the most numerous tribal cluster (Lewis, 1969:32, and 1980:241–42).[18]

The range of herding movements among the agro-pastoral Sab is considerably more circumscribed than in the north. In the southern river area pastoral life revolves around small villages, where the attachment to the land is generally stronger (Lewis, 1969:32; Cassanelli, 1982:21). According to Cassanelli, it is the occupation and right to land that identifies a group and underlies its solidarity.

Indeed, it appears that many southern "clans" were formed by the coming together of nomadic groups of disparate genealogical origins over a considerable period of time. The immigrants occupied adjacent tracts of grazing and farm land and made alliances with neighbors who were not necessarily agnatic kinsmen. The result was a series of confederated communities whose cohesiveness rested as much on territorial proximity as on genealogical affiliation. In contrast to the strictly pastoral regions of the north where clans could best be defined as kinship groups which might be need not be territorial units, the typical clan in the south was a territorial unit which might but need not be an actual kinship group. (Cassanelli, 1982:22)

This is also reflected in the manner in which agricultural work is organized among most (though not all) of the Sab tribes. Here, in contrast to what occurs in the north, and among the southern Hawiye, cooperative work-parties comprise tribesmen and attached clients.

The Digil group comprises the Dabarre, Dubdere, Irole, Dagine, Osman, Jiddu, Dube, and Tunne. The first three are primarily cattle, sheep, goat, and some camel pastoralists (some of whom also practice minimal cultivation). The others, with the exception of the Tunni, also appear to be primarily pastoral and small in number. The Tunni are agro-pastoral.

The Rahanwein generally qualify as agro-pastoralists, with one group, the Helai (largest and most important of the Rahanwein tribes), being agriculturalists (with stock).

Other Populations in Somalia.[19] *Negroid peoples* primarily "inhabit the hinterland between the rivers. . . . They cultivate during the rains and hunt in the dry season. Both the Hawiya and Digil despise them, and there seems good reason to regard them as a pre-Cushite aboriginal population" (Lewis, 1969:42). These populations represent a combination of pre-Cushitic negroid inhabitants and freed slaves. Although they have (to a certain extent) been assimilated as clients of the Somali population, they have apparently retained a number of indigenous customs and ritual practices. Cerulli noted that many of these populations had been completely assimilated (1934:183). Unfortunately, information concerning the social organization and customs of these populations is minimal (Lewis, 1965:30–31; Lewis, 1969:41; Cassannelli, 1982:14, 164–66; Jensen, 1947:796).

The Somali have designated the principal groups on the Shebelle as the Shidle, Kabole (Kavole), Rer Issa, Makanne, and Shebelle, and those on the Juba, as the WaGosha, Boni (WaBoni), and Gobawein (Lewis, 1969:32). All of these populations are primary cultivators, although the WaBoni engage mostly in hunting and fishing, as does the WaRibi, a similar negroid population dispersed throughout Jubaland.

According to Grottanelli, although circumcision of both males and females (clitoridectomy) does occur among the negroid populations of "Abyssinia, Eritrea, and Somaliland," "infibulation, prevalent among the Somali, is only practiced by those Bantu in clientship to the Somali" (my translation) (1947:846).

Outcast Groups include, for example, the Midgan (representing the most numerous group, and who are occupied as hunters and leather-workers). The outcast groups are usually attached to nobel tribes through patron/client relations. They perform specific duties, in return for payment and permission to remain in the tribally controlled territory. It is a Midgan woman who infibulates, and performs subsequent defibulation and any requested reinfibulation operations (Lewis, 1969:53; Deschamps, 1948:30; Kirk, 1904:97).

Comparative Data

The Borana are a Galla tribe, located in Ethiopian highlands, in the Wallo region. They are primarily pastoral (although Kesby [1977:61] notes that at one time they were "only" pastoral). A high bride-price in livestock is required for marriage. They are exogamous, practice the levirate, and are polygamous, although like other Galla, the general rule is one wife. Divorce is unusual. Huntingford informs us that (according to his sources) clitoridectomy only is performed on Galla girls, with the exception of the Galla of Harar and of Shoa, who practice infibulation (and who are in close contact and interaction with the Somali and Danakil) (1955:41).

The Rendille are mixed-herd pastoralists located in northern Kenya. Camel are the most important animal they keep. Their diet consists primarily of milk, blood, and meat, mostly from the camel. Camels are cared for by young men, and goats and sheep are collectively care for by unmarried women (Tanaka, 1982:4–5). They are patrilineal and patrilocal. Inheritance is limited to the eldest son. Migration results in regular fission and fusion of camp membership. Marriage occurs at a late age, which Tanaka attributes to the low reproduction rate of the animals (1982:6).

The Gabra are pastoral nomads on the Kenya-Ethiopian border. They keep camels, goats and sheep, and do not cultivate. Exogamy is practiced, and all cousin marriage is prohibited, although Harako points out that after marriage, there is no sexual taboo between cousins. Indeed, there is generally a limited sex taboo on women after marriage (1982:65). The age of first marriage is approximately thirty for males and fifteen for females. Both girls and boys are circumcised, boys between fifteen and eighteen years, and girls between twelve and fifteen years. Betrothal of girls occurs very early, ofttimes while they are still in infancy, or before circumcision. Polygyny is practiced, and matrilocal residence is the rule for at least one year (Harako, 1982:67). There is a postpartum taboo of two to three years after the birth of each child, during which time the husband sleeps outside, or immigrates for a time. Divorce is rare. Harako points out that this rare occurrence of divorce is also prevalent among the Borano and Rendill, and may be general among Galla-speaking peoples (1982:68).

The Turkana are located in northwestern Kenya, and are mixed-herd nomadic pastoralists, keeping camel, cattle, goats, and sheep. Here again, there is regular fusion and fission of residence groups, with families typically divided into two parts, one with cattle and the other with browsing stock (Gulliver, 1974a:352). "At least one wife (of the family head, a son or a dependent) should live at each homestead, and at least one adult male; these two supervise the domestic and watering, and the pastoral and herding sides of life respectively" (Gulliver, 1974a:352). The Turkana are polygynous and virilocal, the wife becoming part of the husband's family. Men marry fairly late. Although the Turkana and the neighboring populations (Gabra, Samburu, Dassanetch, Rendille, Borana, and Somali) are all pure pastoralists, only the Rendille, Gabra, and Somali rely primarily on camel products for subsistence (Torry, 1973:31–32).

The Kaffa represent an ancient kingdom in southwest Ethiopia, whose inhabitants are also often referred to as Kaffa (they are in fact divided into four subtribes). They are agro-pastoral. The pagan Kaffa may practice either polygamy or monogamy. Bride-price is usually in the form of livestock. The Moslem Kaffa practice the levirate, and among the pagan Kaffa, the wife (wives) of the deceased are inherited by his eldest son. Huntingford informs us that they do not practice infibulation, but girls are excised (1955:115).

The Barabaig are located in Tanzania and are basically agriculturalists. Although they have not been included in the tables, I have included them here for general information, since their circumcision and weaning patterns are indicative of Bantu tribes in general. Among the Barabaig, weaning takes place at about two years of age, and girls are already domestically productive by the age of four or five. Girls undergo clitoral excision between two and six years of age, with no related ceremony or ritual. The circumcision of boys, however, involves an elaborate ceremony (Klima, 1970:51–63). Girls are married by thirteen or fourteen years of age, while boys marry much later, at around twenty-four years of age.

The Tuareg are mostly nomadic pastoralists with camels, sheep and goats, and where possible, cattle. They are segmentary, and loosely Moslem. They are endogamous, preferring cousin marriage of all forms. Women hold a high position, are not secluded, and have no qualms about premarital sex (thus, there is no high status accorded virginity). Murphy relates the generally high status accorded women to the traditional matrilineality of the Tuareg (1968:357). After marriage, the couple may periodically reside with the families of either bride or groom, although most Tuareg profess patrilocality. A period of matrilocal residence in the initial phase of a marriage is common. (Nicolaisen, 1963:142; Murphy, 1968:365; Slavin, 1973:29).

The Al Murrah are bedouin located in the Empty Quarter of the Arabian Penninsula. Their importance to this study lies in the harshness of their environment, comparable to that of the Horn region. They are camel nomads, and their diet is primarily made up of milk, dates, and rice or bread with animal fat poured over it (Cole, 1975:27). The Al Murrah differ from the northeast African herders in that they keep only camels. This is an important point, as it is only with mixed herds that a division of the herding unit is necessary, and a concomitant division of the household. Here again, no adult females work with the camels, as that is the province of men. Marriage is usually within the lineage, but not always (Cole, 1975:71). Marriage usually takes place between the ages of eighteen and thirty for men, and at age eighteen for women. After marriage the bride moves to her husband's household until she is due to give birth to her first child, which she does in her parents' household. Divorce is frequent. Generally, the position of women is higher than among village or urban Moslem groups, and women are not secluded. The tent belongs to the senior women, and no man resides in a tent without a woman (single men reside in someone else's tent). The tent is subdivided into sections, with each married woman having her own, where she, her husband and their young children sleep. Male guests and postpubescent males sleep in the men's section. Except for sleeping, men and women spend very little time together. Residence is virilocal.

The Rwala are camel nomads located on the Arabian Penninsula. Here again, the tent is the responsiblity, and under control of the wife. Milk is their main nourishment. They are polygynous. Children remain with their mother until their seventh year, after which the boys are separated from the women (Musil, 1928:255). Marriage among the Rwala, as with the other populations included in this study, is an important element in the social identity of both men and women. "Neither sex, unless the circum- stances are exceptional, can live an independent life unless married. Women have no jural identity and therefore only exist in their father's or brother's shadow. Men cannot lead independent lives until they have a tent of their own and they cannot run a tent unless they have a wife" (Lancaster, 1981:48). Marriage for men usually occurs between twenty and twenty-five years of age, while girls are considered marriageable from fifteen or sixteen years (Lancaster, 1981:48).

The Fulani are west African cattle nomads. They are polygamous, Moslem, and patrilineal. Women are often betrothed and married in childhood (often prior to menstruation), but the wife returns to her father's homestead for the birth of her first child. She remains there for 2 to 2 1/2 years, during which time she has no contact with her husband. After this period she returns to his homestead to formally take up her position as his wife. Women generally seem to have a high status, and divorce may be initiated by both sexes (although it is easier for the male) (Stenning, 1959: 4, 112, 114, 116-20, 148).

Notes

1. Historically, a distinction is made between Lower and Upper Nubia. These areas had separate histories up to the early ninteenth century. Lower Nubia included territory to the north and south of the current Egyptian-Sudanese frontier, while Upper Nubia (above the third Cataract) fell under the control of the Funj rulers of Sennar (Holt, 1961:3).
2. These figures generally coincide with those given by Longrigg (1945:appendix C).
3. Harar was annexed by the Egyptians in 1875 and, although their occupation of the region was transitory, they apparently had a considerable effect on the diffusion of Islam in that area.

    The Galla of the region had tried to resist the invaders, but after various fights . . . they had to submit. The Egyptians managed to decoy their chiefs into Harar and threw them into prison, then forced them to dissolve their parliament . . . cut off their . . . long hair, and submit to circumcision. A great number perferred to be killed rather than be thus humiliated, but after three or four years they were reduced to such misery that the majority submitted. (Trimingham 1952:121)

4. The Nubians, along with the Nobatae (Nuba), are mentioned by Budge to have lived in the deserts on the west of the Nile. The Nobatae were a nomadic tribe living in the western desert (by the third century A.D.), and apparently came from Dar Fur and Kordofan (Budge, 1907, vol. 2:176). MacMichael informs us that there is "a quite definite probability that the Libya races, the ancient Temehu, and Nobatae . . . had comingled. Throughout history the nomads of the west, Libyans or Berbers have maintained an intimate connection with the dwellers of the Nile valley" (1967:25).
5. Briefly, in the ceremony of the "jirtig" the bride and bridegroom are dressed in the clothes and ornaments appropriate for the marriage state. On the right wrist a silver bracelet with a blue-green stone is worn. This is called a jirtig, and it (as well as the other ornaments) are removed at the end of the wedding (usually on the fortieth day after the initial wedding ceremony). The jirtig ornaments are only worn for the first marriage. The jirtig (and the marriage apparel) is also usually worn at circumcision by both males and females. Additionally, a similar jirtig ceremony is performed during the seventh month of pregnancy (Crowfoot [1922:1–28] and Trimingham [1949:182–83 provide more detailed information concerning the jirtig ceremony).
6. The marriage ceremony among the Ababda is sometimes combined with circumcision ceremonies for boys. Both festivities have the same name—'irs (the ordinary

arabic name for combined ceremony may occur because of the great poverty of the Ababda [Murray, 1927:54]).

7. Clark also mentions that the women of the Beja "retain little of the respect and importance they had in early Began culture" (1938:8).

8. Murray notes that the "jirtig" ceremony is prevalent throughout the northern Sudan (1927:45), and Trimingham (1949:182) informs us that the jirtig wedding is common in most of the northern Sudan "amongst the riverain tribes (Mahas, Danaqla, Ja'aliyyin, and Sha'iqiyya), in Northern and Central Kordofan, the Blue and White Niles, and the Beni 'Amir. It has been adopted by most of the camel-nomads, but not the Shukriyya, the Baqqara, the Bedawie speaking Beja, nor the Nubian kenuz and Sukkot in Egyptian Nubia".

9. The tribal listing provided here is partial. See MacMichael (1967:200–347, and 1967a:51–214) for a complete listing and description of the (historical) interrelations between the various tribal units comprising this group. It is highly likely that much of the tribal information presented here is now outdated, some of it perhaps no longer even valid. However, to my knowledge, no contemporary publication(s) (relative to the tribal populations of the northern Sudan) exist that can either supplement, replace, or compete with the MacMichael texts cited above. Moreover, the tribal listing has been culled to include only those tribes for which there is information relative to "female circumcision," or those which are of comparative value or historically related relevance.

10. The average time between the second and final stage is four years, depending upon how long the mother of the bride can prevent the third phase from occuring. Holy relates this latter point to preferred virilocal residence: "it is the wife's parents' domestic group which is mostly likely to lose" (1974:113).

11. The Messiriya and Humr are Baggara, and only one section of the Daju appear to practice it.

12. Carbou (1912, vol. 2:17, 22) states that "excision of girls is not universally practiced by the Arabs and 'Ouadaiens'; the 'Toundjour', also of Arab origin, do not conform to this practice" (my translation).

13. Jensen (1947:791) notes that the Borana (the southernmost Galla) live in an area which, for the last few centuries, might be designated as "the core area" of the original Galla nomads.

14. Although Murdock (1959:189) states that the Kafa perform clitoral excision, Widstrand (1964:101) cites two references to Huntingford, the first of which states that the Kafa infibulate, whereas the second states that they do not. Because of this discrepancy they have not here been included as practicing infibulation.

15. Matrilateral parallel cousins (the children of all the mother's sisters). Patrilateral parallel cousins (the children of all the father's brothers). Patrilateral cross cousins (the children of the father's sister).

16. Paulitschke noted (at the end of the last century) that the "northern 'Danakil' on the 'Zula and Hamfili-Fai' borders, like the 'Afar of the interior, do not infibulate" (my translation) (1893, vol. 1:272, footnote 245). His sources would appear to be questionable, however, since he informs us of the manner in which "defibulation" occurs in the "binnenlande" (see quoted text).

17. The Hawiya are colaterally descended, with the Dir, from a common ancestor. The largest group, representative of the Dir family is the Esa (northern Somalia). The Dir are important for having given rise to the Ishaak and Darod tribal families.

18. Although the Rahanwein are a subgroup of the Digil, they have grown to be considerably more numerous and important than their parent group, the Digil (Lewis, 1969:32).
19. Although the Afar and Saho are related to the Somali, they primarily inhabit Ethiopia and Eritrea, and hence are treated thereunder.

Bibliography

Abbas Ahmed, M.

1980   *White Nile Arabs: Political Leadership and Economic Change.* London:Athlone Press and New Jersey Humanities Press.

Abdel Ghaffar, M.

1973   Tribal and Sedentary Elites: A Bridge between Two Communities. In *The Desert and the Sown*, edited by C. Nelson. UC Berkeley:Research Series No. l, Institute of International Studies, Berkeley.

1974   *Shaykhs and Followers: Political Struggle in the Rufa'a al-Hoi Nazirate in the Sudan.* Khartoum:Khartoum University Press.

1976   The Question of Pastoral Nomadism in the Sudan. In *Some Aspects of Pastoral Nomadism in the Sudan*, edited by A. Ghaffar and M. Ahmed, 75-96. The Sudan National Population Committee and The Economic and Social Research Council, Khartoum, Sudan.

Abdi A., Sheik-Abdi.

1984   The Somalis. In *Muslim Peoples*, edited by R. Weekes, 699-705. Connecticut:Greenwood Press.

Abdirahman, H.A.

1977   The Arab Factor in Somali History: The Origins and the Development of Arab Enterprise and Cultural Influences in the Somali Peninsula. Ph.D, diss., UCLA. Ann Arbor, MI:University Microfilms.

Abernethy, V.

1979   *Population Pressure and Cultural Adjustment.* New York:Human Sciences Press.

Abou-Zeid, A.

1959   The Sedentarization of Nomads in the Western Desert of Egypt. *UNESCO International Social Science Journal* 11, no. 4:550-58.

Abramzon, S.

1978   Family Group, Family, and Individual Property Categories among Nomads. In *The Nomadic Alternative*, edited by W. Weissleder, 179-88. Paris:Mouton.

Abu-Lughod, L.

1986   *Veiled Sentiments.* London:University of California Press Adams, W. Y.

1977   *Nubia, Corridor to Africa.* Princeton, NJ:Princeton University Press.

Adan, A.

1981   Women and Words. *UFAHAMU, Journal of African Activist Association* 10, no. 3, Spring:115-41.

Adawi, al, I. A.

1954   Description of the Sudan by Muslim Geographers and Travellers. *Sudan Notes and Records* 35, pt. II, Dec.

Ahmed, A., and D. Hart.

1984   *Islam in Tribal Societies.* London:Routledge and Kegan Paul.

AIDOS/SWDO.

1989   Female Circumcision. Strategies to Bring about Change. Proceedings of the International Seminar on Female Circumcision. Mogadishu, Somalia.

Allaix, H.

1935   Les mutilations sexuelle: Subincision, circoncision, hyménotomie, clitoridectomie. Paris:Edit. du Lien médical.

Allgemeine Statistik Des Auslandes.

1966   Länderberrichte Sudan. Statistisches Budesamt Wiesbaden. Stuttgart, Germany:W. Kohlhammer.

Allman, J.

1987   *Women's Status and Fertility in the Muslim World.* New York:Praeger.

Almagor, U.

1978   *Pastoral Partners: Affinity and Bond Partnership among the Dassanetch of South-west Ethiopia.* UK:Manchester University Press.

Ammar, Hammed.

1954   *Growing Up in an Egyptian Village.* London:Routledge and Kegan Paul.

AMRFI.

1974   African Medical and Research Foundation, International Medical Development. Mali.

Ander, R., M. Buvinic and N. Youssef, N., eds.

1972   *Women's Roles and Population Trends in the Third World.* London:Croom Helm.

Anker, R.

1982   Demographic Change and the Role of Women: A Research Programme in Developing Countries. In, *Women's Roles and Population Trends in the Third World*, edited by R. Anker, M. Buvinic, and N. Youssef, 29–54. London:Croom Helm.

Antoun, R. T.

1965   Conservatism and Change in the Village Community: A Jordanian Case Study. *Human Organisation* 24:4–10.

1967   Social Organization and the Life Cycle in an Arab Village. *Ethnology* 6:294–308.

1968   On the Modesty of Women in Arab Muslim Villages: A Study in the Accommodation of Tradition. *American Anthropologist* 70:671–97.

Arberry, A. J.
1955   *The Koran Interpreted.* 2 vols. New York:Macmillan Co.

Ardener, S., ed.
1981   *Women and Space: Ground Rules and Social Maps.* London:Croom Helm.

Arens, W.
1975   The Waswahili: The Social History of an Ethnic Group. *Africa* 45:426-37.

Asad, T.
1966   A Note on the History of the Kababish Arabs. *Sudan Notes and Records* 47:79-88.

1970   *The Kababish Arabs.* London:C. Hurst and Co.

1972   *Anthropology and the Colonial Encounter.* London:D. Wolton.

1979   Equality in Nomadic Social Systems: Notes. In *Pastoral Production and Society, Equip Ecologie et Anthropologie des Societes Pastorales.* Proceedings of the international meeting on nomadic pastoralism, Paris, 419-28. London:Cambridge University Press.

Ashtor, E.
1976   *A Social and Economic History of the Near East in the Middle Ages.* London:Collins.

Assaad, F.
1982   The Sexual Mutilation of Women. *World Health Forum* 3, no. 4:391-94, Geneva:W.H.O.

Assaad, M. B.
1980   Female Circumcision in Egypt: Social Implications, Current Research, and Prospects for Change. *Studies in Family Planning* II (1), 3-16.

Asuen, M.
1977   Maternal Septicaemia and Death After Circumcision. *Tropical Doctor*, 7, no. 4:177-78.

Aswad, B.
1970   Social and Ecological Aspects in the Formation of Islam. In *Peoples and Cultures of the Middle East*, Vol. 1, edited by L. Sweet, 53-74. New York:The Natural History Press.

Aziz, F.A.
1980   Gynecologic and Obstetric Complications of Female Circumcision. *International Journal of Gynaecology and Obstetrics.* 17:560-63.

Azizah al-Hibri, ed.
1982   *Women and Islam.* Oxford:Pergamon Press.

Badan-Unat, N. A., ed.
1981   *Women in Turkish Society.* Leiden, Netherlands:Brill.

Baffoun, A.

1982   Women and Social Change in the Muslim Arab World. In *Women and Islam*, edited by A. al-Hibri, 227–42. Oxford:Pergamon Press.

Bagge, S.

1904   The Circumcision Ceremony among the Naivasha Masai. *Journal of Royal Anthropological Institute* 34:167–69.

Barbour, K.

1964   North and South in Sudan: A Study in Human Contrasts. *Annals of the Association of American Geographers* 54, no. 2, June:209–26.

1980   The Sudan since Independence. *Journal of Modern African Studies* 18, no. 1:73–97.

Barclay, H.

1964   *Buurri al Lamaab*. Ithaca, NY:Cornell Univiversity Press.

Barrett, R.

1974   *Benabarre: The Modernization of a Spanish Village. Case Studies in Anthropology.* Chicago:Holt, Rinehart and Winston.

Bartels, K., and I Haaijer, I.

1992   *'S Lands wijs 's lands eer? Vrouwenbesnijdenis en Somalische vrouwen in Nederland.* Rijswijk:Report by the Centrum Gezondheidszorg Vluchtelingen.

Barth, F.

1961   *Nomads of South Persia: The Basseri Tribe of the Khamseh Confederacy.* Boston:The Little Brown Series in Anthropology.

1961a   Fathers Brothers Daughters Marriage in Kurdistan. In *Peoples and Cultures of the Middle East.* Vol. 1, edited by L. Sweet, 127–36, New York:The Natural History Press.

1967   Economic Spheres in Darfur. In *ASA Monographs* 6, Themes in Economic Anthropology, edited by R. Firth, 149–74. London:Tavistock publications.

Barth, H.

1857   *Travels and Discoveries in North and Central Africa, 1849–55.* 3 vols. Gotha, Germany:Justus Perthes.

Bascom, W.

1969   *The Yoruba of Southwestern Nigeria.* Chicago:Holt, Rinehart and Winston.

Bascom, W., and M. Herskovitz, eds.

1958   *Continuity and Change in African Cultures.* Chicago:University of Chicago Press.

Bates, D.

1968   The Role of the State in Peasant-Nomad Mutualism. In *Man in Adaptation: The Cultural Present.* 2nd ed., edited by Y. Cohen, 285–96. Chicago,:Aldine.

Baumann, H., and R. Thurnwald.

1940   *Völkerkunde von Afrika.* Essen, Germany:Essener Verlagsanstalt.

Baxter, P., and U. Almagor, eds.

1978   *Age, Generation and Time: Some Features of East African Age Organisations.* London:C. Hurst & Co. Ltd.

Bayoumi, A.

1979   *The History of Sudan Health Services.* Nairobi:Kenya Literature Bureau.

1981   Female Circumcision: Ways of Giving Up the Practice. *Women Speaking* 5:4-6.

Bazin-Tardieu, D.

1975   *Femmes Du Mali.* Ottowa, Canada:Lemeac Inc.

Beachey, R.

1976   *A Collection of Documents on the Slave Trade of Eastern Africa.* London:Rex Collings.

1976a   *The Slave Trade of Eastern Africa.* London:Rex Collings.

Beasley, I.

1976   Female Circumcision. *Women Speaking* 4:21-2.

Beattie, J.

1956   Ethnographic and Sociological Research in East Africa: A Review. *Africa* 26, 3:265-76.

Beke, C. T.

1843   On the Countries South of Abbyssinia. *Journal of the Royal Geographic Society,* 13:254-69.

Bender, M.

1975   *The Ethiopian Nilo-Saharans.* Addis Ababa, Ethiopia:np.

Bentwich, N.

1945   *Ethiopia, Eritrea, and Somaliland.* London:Gollanz.

Bernatzik, H.

1947   *Afrika, Handbuch der Angewandten Völkerkunde.* 2 vols. Innsbruck, Austria:Schlüsselverlag Ges. M.B.H. (See especially vol. 2:779-887, *Ostafrika,* by A. Jensen, C. Rossini, V. Grottanelli, and E. Pauli.)

Berre, H.

1984   The Daju. In *Muslim Peoples,* edited by R. Weekes, 219-22. Westport, CT:Greenwood Press.

Beshah, T., and H. Harbeson.

1978   Afar Pastoralists in Transition and the Ethiopian Revolution. *Journal of African Studies,* no. 5, 3:249-67.

Bettelheim, B.

1954   *Symbolic Wounds.* Chicago:The Free Press.

Bidney, D.

1953   *Theoretical Anthropology.* Chicago:Schocken Books.

Bieber, F.

1920   *Kaffa.* Muenster, Germany:Aschendorffschen Verlagsbuchhandlung.

Boddy, J.

1982   Women as Oasis: The Symbolic Context of Pharaonic Circumcision in Rural
        Northern Sudan. *American Ethnologist* 9:683–98.

1989   *Wombs and Alien Spirits: Women, Men, and the Zar Cult in Northern Sudan.*
        Madison:The University of Wisconsin Press.

Bossen, L.

1979   Women in Modernizing Societies. In *Women & Society, An Anthropological
        Reader*, edited by S. Tiffany. Montreala:Eden Press.

Bosworth, C.E., E. van Dozel, B. Lewis, and Ch. Pellat, eds.

1979   *The Encyclopedia of Islam.* New Edition. Leiden, Netherlands:Brill.

Bouhdiba, Abdel Wahab.

1985   *Sexuality in Islam.* London:Routledge and Kegan Paul.

Bower, J.

1923   Circumcision Schools in the West Bahr el Gazal. *Sudan Notes and Records*
        6:249–50.

Brain, J.L.

1977   Sex, Incest, and Death: Initiation Rites Reconsidered. *Current Anthropology*
        18 (2), june:191–208.

Brandstroem, P., J. Hultin, and J. Lindstroem.

1979   *Aspects of Agro-Pastoralism in East Africa.* Research Report no. 5, Nordiska
        Afrika Institutet, Uppsala Offset Center AB, Uppsala.

Brehm, A.

1975   *Reisen im Sudan, 1847 bis 1852.* Tübingen/Basel:Horst Erdmann verlag,
        reissue.

Brock, R.

1918   Some Notes on the Zande Tribes as Found in the Meridi District (Bahr el
        Ghazal province). *Sudan Notes and Records* 1, no. 4:249–62.

Brotmacher, L.

1955   Medical Practice among the Somalis. *Bulletin of the History of Medicine* 29
        (3), May-June:197–229.

Brown, J. K.

1963   A Cross-cultural Study of Female Initiation Rites. *American Anthropologist*
        65:837–53.

Browne, W.

1799   *Travels in Africa, Egypt, and Syria from 1792 to 1798.* London:np.

1814   Journey to Dar-Fur: A Kingdom in the Interior of Africa. In *J. Pinkerton, Voyages* 15:108–62 and 827–38.

Bruce, J.

1790   *Travels to Discover the Source of the Nile 1768–1773.* In 5 vols, Edinburgh:J. Ruthnen, printers.

Bruce, J. W.

1979   *A Bibliographical Guide to the Customary Law of the Sudan.* Customary Law Project, University of Khartoum, Faculty of Law.

Brumpt, E.

1904   Mission du Bourg de Bozas de la Mer Route a l'Atlantique a travers l'Afrique tropicale. *Bulletin Sociologique Normande Geographie* 26:153–79.

Bryk, F.

1931   *Die Beschneidung bei Mann und Weib.* Neubrandenburg, Germany:Verlag Gustav Feller.

Buckley, T., and A. Gottlieb.

1988   A Critical Appraisal of Theories of Menstrual Symbolism. In *Blood Magic: The Anthropology of Menstruation,* edited by T. Buckley and A. Gottlieb, 1–50, Los Angeles:University of California Press.

Budge, E.

1907   *The Egyptian Sudan.* 2 vols., London:Kegan, Paul, Trench, Truebner & Co. Ltd.

Bullough, V., ed.

1976   *Sexual Variance in Society and History.* New York:J. Wiley & Sons (especially pp. 205–44).

Burkhardt, J.

1831   *Travels in Nubia.* London:John Murray.

Burns, T.R., T. Baumgartner, and P. Deville.

1985   *Man, Decisions, Society: The Theory of Actor-System Dynamics for Social Scientists.* New York: Gordon and Breach Science Publishers.

Burton, R.

1894   *First Footsteps in East Africa.* 2 vols., London:Tylston & Edwards (1966 edition published by Routledge & Kegan Paul, London).

1964   *Personal Narrative of a Pilgrimage to al-Madinah and Mecca.* 2 vols. New York:Dover (reissue of 1893 publication).

1982   *The Perfumed Garden (of the Shaykh Nefzawi).* London:Book Club Associates. (reissue of 1886 publication).

Burton, R. W., and J.W. Whiting.

1961   The Absent Father and Cross-sex Identity. *Merill-Palmer Quarterly of Behavior and Development* 7 (2):85–95.

Cadalvene, E., and J. de Breuvery.

    1844   Nubie, une noce a Dongolah. *Revue de l'Orient* III:224–33.

Cailliaud, M.

    1826   *Voyage a Meroe, au Fleuve Blanc.* 4 vols. Paris:par autorisation du roi, a l'Imprimarie royal.

Caldwell, J.

    1981   Fertility in Africa. In *Fertility Decline in the Less Developed Countries*, edited by N. Eberstadt. New York:Praeger.

Callaway, H.

    1981   Spatial Domains and Women's Mobility in Yorubaland, Nigeria. In *Women and Space, Ground Rules and Social Maps*, edited by S. Ardener, 168–86. London:Croom Helm.

Callaway, B., and L. Creevey.

    1989   Women and the State in Islamic West Africa. In *Women, the State and Development*, edited by S.E.M. Charlton, J. Everett, and K. Staudt, 86–113. New York:State University of New York Press.

Canaan, T.

    1931   Unwritten Laws Affecting the Arab Woman of Palestine. *Journal of the Palestine Oriental Society* 11:172–203.

Caplan, A.

    1976   Boys' Circumcision and Girls' Puberty Rites among the Swahili of Mafia Island, Tanzania. *Africa* 46:21–33.

Carbou, H.

    1912   *La Region du Tchad et du Oudai.* 2 vols. Paris:E. Levoux.

Carlstein, T.

    1982   *Time Resources, Society and Ecology. Preindustrial Societies*, vol. 1. London:George Allen & Unwin.

Carr, C. J.

    1977   *Pastoralism in Crisis: The Dasanetch and Their Ethiopian Lands.* Chicago:University of Chicago, Department of Geography.

Cassanelli, L.

    1980   Towns and Trading Centers in Somalia: A Nomadic Perspective. Paper for 23d. Annual Meeting of the African Studies Association, Philadelphia, PA, 15–18 Oct.

    1982   *The Shaping of Somali Society: Reconstructing the History of a Pastoral People, 1600–1900.* Philadelphia:University of Pennsylvania Press.

Cerulli, E.

    1934   Gruppi etnici negri nella Somalia. *Archivio per l'Antropologia e la Etnologia* 64, no. 1–4:177–84.

    1957   *Somalia.* 2 vols. Roma:Instituto Poligrafico dello Stato P.V.

Cerulli, Ernesta.

1956   *Peoples of South-west Ethiopia and its Borderland. North-eastern Africa, Part III.* London:International African Institute.

Chambers, R.

1983   *Rural Development: Putting the Last First.* London:Longman.

Chapelle, J.

1980   *Le Peuple Tchadien.* Paris:Editions L'Harmattan.

Chedeville, E.

1966   Quelques faits de l'organisation social des 'Afar. *Africa* 36:173–95.

Chorley, R., and P. Haggett, eds.

1967   *Socio-Economic Models in Geography.* London:Methuen & Co. Ltd.

Clark, W.T.

1938   Manners, Customs and Beliefs of the Northern Bega. *Sudan Notes and Records* 21, pt. I:1–31.

Cloudsley, A.

1981   *Woman of Omdurman: Victims of Circumcision.* London:Published by author.

Cohen, Y.

1964   The Establishment of Identity in a Social Nexus. The Special Case of Initiation Ceremonies and Their Relation to Value and Legal Systems. *American Anthropologist* 66:529–52.

1964a   *The Transition from Childhood to Adolescence: A Cross-cultural Study of Initiation Ceremonies, Legal Systems, and Incest Taboos.* Chicago:Aldine.

Cole, D.

1975   *Nomads of the Nomads.* Illinois:AHM Publ. Corp.

1984   Alliance and Descent in the Middle East and the 'Problem' of Patrilateral Parallel Cousin Marriage. In *Islam in Tribal Societies, From the Atlas to the Indus,* edited by A. Ahmed and D. Hart, 169–86. London:Routledge and Kegan Paul.

Coleman, J.S.

1990   *Foundations of Social Theory.* Cambridge, MA:Belknap press of Harvard University Press.

Comaroff, J.

1980   *The Meaning of Marriage Payments.* London:Academic Press.

Constantinides, P.

1980   Zaar and the Adaptation of Women to Urban Life in Northern Sudan. In *Urbanization and Urban Life in the Sudan,* edited by V. Pons, 647–71. Development Studies and Research Centre, University of Khartoum, and Department of Sociology and Social Anthropology, University of Hull.

Cook, R.

1979   Damage to Physical Health from Pharaonic Circumcision (infibulation) of Females. A Review of the Medical Literature. In *WHO/EMRO Technical Publication*, no. 2, (ref. as such below):53-105.

Coulson, N.

1964   *A History of Islamic Law.* Edinburgh:Edinburgh University Press.

Courtecuisse, L.

1971   *Quelques Populations de la Republique Du Tchad.* Paris:C.H.E.A.M. III.

Crawford, O.G.

1951   *The Fung Kingdom of Senna.* Gloucester, UK:John Bellows.

Crawley, A.

1895   Sexual Taboo: A Study in the Relations of the Sexes. *Journal of the Royal Anthropological Institute*, vol. 24:430-45.

Crow, B., and M. Thorpe, eds.

1988   *Survival and Change in the Third World.* New York:Oxford University Press.

Crowfoot, J.

1918   Customs of the Rubatab. *Sudan Notes and Records*, 1:119-34.

1920   Angels of the Nile. *Sudan Notes and Records* 2, no. 3:183-92, 1919. Beliefs about the Mansions of the Moon. *Sudan Notes and Records*, 3:271-79.

1922   Wedding Customs in the Northern Sudan. *Sudan Notes and Records* 5: 1-28.

1925   Further Notes on Pottery. *Sudan Notes and Records* 3:125-36.

Culwick, G.

1939   New Ways for Old in the Treatment of Adolescent African Girls. *Africa* 12, October, 4:425-32.

Cunnison, I.

1966   *Baggara Arabs: Power and the Lineage in a Sudanese Nomad Tribe.* Oxford:Clarendon Press.

1972   Some social aspects of nomadism in a Baggara tribe. In *Some Aspects of Pastoral Nomadism in the Sudan*, edited by A. Ghaffar. Khartoum, Sudan:Khartoum University Press.

Cunnison, I., and W. James, eds.

1972   *Essays in Sudanese Ethnography.* London:Hurst.

Cutner, L.P.

1985   Female Genital Mutilation. *Obstetrical and Gynaecologic. Survey* 40 (7):437-43.

Dahl, G.

1979   Ecology and Equality: The Boran Case. In *Pastoral Production and Society, Equipe Ecologie et Anthropologie des Societes Pastorales.* Proceedings of the international meeting on nomadic pastoralism, Paris, 261-82. London:Cambridge University Press.

Dahl, G., and A. Hjort.

1976   *Having Herds: Pastoral Herd Growth and Household Economy.* University of Stockholm:Stockholm Studies in Social Anthropology.

D'Ashur, S.

1989   *Silent Tears.* London:Black Women's Health Action Project.

David, A.

1978   *L'infibulation en République de Djibouti.* Medical thesis no. 131, University of Bordeaux II.

Davis, K.

1937   The Sociology of Prostitution. *American Sociological Review* 2, October:744–55.

Dawood, N.

1974   The Koran. Penguin Classics. Harmondsworth:Penguin Books Ltd.

De Villeneuve, A.

1937   Etude sur une coutume Somalie: Les femmes cousues. *Journal de la Societe des Africanistes* 6:15–32.

Delaney, C.

1988   Mortal Flow: Menstruation in Turkish Village Society. In *Blood Magic: The Anthropology of Menstruation,* edited by T. Buckley and A. Gottlieb, 75–93. Los Angeles:University of California Press.

Delemarre-v.d. Waal, H.

1984   *Central Regulation of Human Puberty.* Nieuwkoop:De Boer.

Delmet, C.

1979   Islamisation et matrilinearite au Dar Fung (Soudan). *L'Homme* 19, no. 2:33–51.

Deng, F.

1971   *Tradition and Modernization.* New Haven:Yale University Press.

1978   Africans of Two-worlds: The Dinka in Afro-Arab Sudan. New Haven, CT:Yale University Press.

Deschamps, H.

1948   *Cote des Somalis.* Paris:Editions Berger-Levrault.

Dieck, A.

1981   Beschneidung van Frauen und Männer in vor-und frühgeschichtlicher Zeit. *Curare* 4:77–84.

Djibouti Post Report.

1981   January. Washington, DC:U.S. Dept. of State publication.

Dorjahn, V.

1958   Fertility, Polygyny and Their Interrelations in Temne Society. *American Anthropologist* 60:838–60.

Douglas, M.

1966   *Purity and Danger: An Analysis of Concepts of Pollution and Taboo.* London:Routledge and Kegan Paul.

1982   *In the Active Voice.* London:Routledge and Kegan Paul.

1982a   *Essays in the Sociology of Perception.* London:Routledge and Kegan Paul.

Douglas, M., and P. Kaberry, eds.

1969   *Man In Africa.* London:Tavistock Publications.

Drake-Brockman, R.

1912   *British Somaliland.* London:Hurst & Blackett.

Driver, H.E.

1969   Girls Puberty Rites and Matrilocal Residence. *American Anthropologist* 71, no. 6:905–07.

Dualeh, A.

1982   *Sisters in Affliction: Circumcision and Infibulation of Women in Africa.* London:Zed Press.

Duisburg, A. V.

1947   Mittel Sudan und Zentral sahara. In *Afrika.* Vol. I, edited by H. Bernatzik, 471–99. Innsbrück, Austria:Schluesselverlag, Ges. M.B.H.

Eberstadt, N., ed.

1981   *Fertility Decline in the Less Developed Countries.* New York:Praeger.

Ed-Din, Nazirah Zein.

1982   Removing the Veil and Veiling. In *Women and Islam,* edited by A. al-Hibri, 221–26. Oxford:Pergamon Press.

Edel, M.

1968   African tribalism. In *Readings in Anthropology. Cultural Anthropology.* 2d ed. Vol. 2, edited by M. Fried, 518–31. New York:Thomas Y. Crowell Co.

Edgerton, R.

1965   Cultural vs. Ecological Factors in the Expression of Values, Attitudes, and Personality Characteristics. *American Anthropologist* 67:442–47.

Edney, J. J., and M.A. Buda.

1976   Distinguising Territoriality and Privacy: Two Studies. *Human Ecology* 4, no. 4:283–96.

Edwards, F.

1922   The Foundation of Khartoum. *Sudan Notes and Records* 5, no. 1:157–62.

El-Awad Galal-al-Din, M.

1970   Living Conditions of Nomadic, Semi-nomadic and Settled Tribal Groups. In *Readings in Arab M.E. Societies and Cultures,* edited by A.M. Lutfiyya and C. Churchill. Paris:Mouton.

1980   A Socio-economic Explanation of High Fertility Rates in Greater Khartoum. In *Urbanization and Urban Life in the Sudan*, edited by V. Pons. UK:University of Hull Department of Sociology and Social Anthropology.

El-Dareer, A.

1978   Female Circumcision and Current Preventive Efforts in the Sudan. Paper for 21st Annual Meeting of African Studies Assoc., Baltimore, MD., 1-4 November.

1979   Preliminary Report on a Study on Prevalence and Epidemiology of Female Circumcision in Sudan Today. Paper presented at the W.H.O. Seminar on Traditional Practices Affecting the Health of Women and Children, Khartoum, Sudan, 10-15 December.

1982   *Woman, Why do You Weep?* Circumcision and its Consequences. London:Zed Press.

1983   Attitudes of Sudanese People to the Practice of Female Circumcision. *International Journal of Epidemiology* 12 (2), June:138-44.

1983a   Complications of Female Circumcision in the Sudan. *Tropical Doctor*, July, 13:131-33.

El-Tayib, D.G.

1987   Women's Dress in the Northern Sudan. In *The Sudanese Woman*, edited by S. Kenyon, 40-66. Khartoum, Sudan:Graduate College Publications no. 19, University of Khartoum.

Ellen, R.

1982   *Environment, Subsistence and System: The Ecology of Small-Scale Social Formations.* Cambridge,UK:Cambridge University Press.

Elliott, F.

1913   Jubaland and its Inhabitants. *The Geographical Journal*, January, no. 41:554-61.

Ember, C., and M. Ember.

1983   *Marriage, Family, and Kinship: Comparative Studies of Social Organization.* New Haven:HRAF Press.

Ember, M., and C. Ember.

1971   The Conditions Favoring Matrilocal Versus Partilocal Residence. *American Anthropologist*, 73:571-94.

Epstein, T.

1982   A Social Anthropological Approach to Women's Roles and Status in Developing Countries: The Domestic Cycle. In *Women's Roles and Population Trends in the Third World*, edited by R. Anker, M. Buvinic, and N. Youssef. 151-72. London:Croom Helm.

Erlich, M.

1986   *La Femme Blessée: Essai sur les mutilations sexuelle féminines.* Paris: Editions L'Harmattan.

Evans-Pritchard, E.

1927   Preliminary Account of the Ingassana. *Sudan Notes and Records* 10:69–85.

1929   The Bongo. *Sudan Notes and Records* 12, pt. 1:1–62.

1935   An Ethnological Survey of the Sudan. In *The Anglo-Egyptian Sudan From Within*, edited by J. Hamilton, 79–93. London:Faber and Faber.

1948   A Note on Ingassana Marriage Customs. (Recorded in 1926). *Sudan Notes and Records* 21, pt. 2:307–14.

1965   *The Position of Women in Primitive Societies and Other Essays in Social Anthropology.* London:Faber & Faber Ltd.

Farran, C.

1963   *Matrimonial Laws of the Sudan.* London:Butterworths.

Ferrandi, U.

1903   *Study of the Gassar Gudde.* Rome:Lughi Emporio Commerciale sul Guida.

Filer, L.

1977   Relationship of Nutrition to Lactation and Newborn Development. In *Nutritional Impacts on Women: Throughout life with Emphasis on Reproduction*, edited by Moghissi and Evans, 151–59. Bethesda, MD:Medical Dept., Harper and Row.

Firth, R.

1959   *We the Tikopia.* London:Allen & Unwin.

Fleming, G. J.

1919   Beni Amer Marriage Custom. *Sudan Notes and Records* 2, 1 (Notes):74–76.

Forni, E.

1980   Women's Role in the Economic, Social, and Political Development of Somalia. *Afrika Spectrum* 15, 1:19–28.

Fortes, M., and E. Evans-Pritchard, eds.

1955   *African Political Systems.* 5th ed. London:Oxford University Press.

Fox, G.

1977   Nice Girl: Social Control of Women through a Value Construct. *Signs* 2, no. 2, Summer:805–17.

Frisch, R.

1974   The Critical Weight at Menarch and the Initiation of the Adolescent Growth Spurt, and the Control of Puberty. In *The Control of the Onset of Puberty*, edited by M. Grumbach, G. Frave, and F. Mayer. New York:Wiley Interstate.

1981   Population, Nutrition and Fecundity: Significance for Interpretation of Changes in Fertility. In *Fertility Decline in the Less Developed Countries*, edited by N. Eberstad. New York:Praeger.

Frisch, R., and G. Wyshah.

1980   Delayed Menarch and Amenorrhea in Ballet Dancers. *New England Journal of Medicine*, 303:17–19.

Fuchs, P.

1961   *Die Völker Der Südost-Sahara.* Wien, Austria:Wilhelm Braumueller.

Fuller, A.

1961   *Buarij, Portrait of a Lebanese Village.* Cambridge, MA:Harvard University Press.

Fyzee, A.

1960   *Outlines of Muhammadan Law.* London:Oxford University Press.

Galaty, J., D. Aronson, P. Salzman, and A. Chouinard, eds.

1981   The Future of Pastoral Peoples. Proceedings of a Conference Held in Nairobi, Kenya, 4-8 August 1980. International Research Centre, Ottowa, Canada.

Gamst, F.

1969   *The Qemant: A Pagan-Hebraic Peasantry of Ethiopia.* Chicago:Holt, Rinehart and Winston.

1984   The Beja. In *Muslim People, A World Ethnographic Survey.* 2d ed., edited by R. Weekes, 130-37. Westport, CT:Greenwood Press.

Garfinkel, H.

1967   *Studies in Ethnomethodology.* Englewood Cliffs, NJ:Prentice Hall, Inc.

Geiser, P.

1967   Some Impressions Concerning the Nature and Extent of Urbanisation and Stabilisation in Nubian Society. In *Contemporary Egyptian Nubia,* edited by R. Fernea, 143-69. New Haven, CT:HRAF Press.

Gerth, H., and C. Wright Mills.

1954   *Character and Social Structure.* London:Routledge & Kegan Paul, Ltd.

Ghalioungui, P.

1963   *Magic and Medical Science in Ancient Egypt.* London:Hodder and Stoughton.

Gifi, A.

1981   *Homals Users Guide.* Leiden, Netherlands:Department of Datatheory, University of Leiden.

Giorgis, B.

1981   *Female Circumcision in Africa.* U.S. Economic Communication for Africa, African Training and Research Centre for Women, Addis Ababa, Ethiopia.

Gluckman, M.

1955   *Custom and Conflict in Africa.* New York:Free Press.

Gluckman, M., ed.

1962   *Essays on the Ritual of Social Relations.* Manchester, UK:Manchester University Press.

Godard, E.

1867   *Egypte et Palestine.* Paris:Victor Masson et Fils.

Goldschmidt, W.

    1968   Theory and Strategy in the Study of Cultural Adaptability. In *Man In Adaptation: The Cultural Present.* 2d ed., edited by Y. Cohen, 297–301. Chicago:Aldine Publ. Co.

Goldsmith, G.

    1920   On Marriage Customs among the Beni Amer Tribe. *Sudan Notes and Records* 3, no. 1 (Notes):293–95.

Goody, J.

    1969   *Comparative Studies in Kinship.* London:Routledge and Kegan Paul.

    1976   *Production and Reproduction: A Comparative Study of the Domestic Domain.* Cambridge, UK:Studies in Social Anthropology, Cambridge University Press.

    1977   *The Domestication of the Savage Mind.* Cambridge, UK:Cambridge University Press,

Gordon, D.

    1990   Female Circumcision and Genital Operatons in Egypt and the Sudan: A Dilemma for Medical Anthropology. WHR Rivers Prize Essay 1990. *Medical Anthropology Quarterly*, New Series 5, no. 1:3–14.

Gottlieb, A.

    1988   Menstruation Cosmology among the Beng of Ivory Coast. In *Blood Magic: The Anthropology of Menstruation*, edited by T. Buckley & A. Gottlieb, 55–74. Los Angeles:University of California Press.

Granqvist, H.

    1947   *Birth and Childhood among the Arabs.* Helsinki:Soderstron and Co.

Grassivaro-Gallo, P.

    1986   Views of Future Health Workers in Somalia on Female Circumcision. *Medical Anthropology Quarterly* 17, 3:71–3.

    1986a   Female Circumcision in Somalia: Some Psychosocial Aspects. *Genus* 41, 1–2:133–47.

    1986b   *La Circoncisione in Somalia: una ricerca sul campo.* Milano:Franco Angeli.

Grassivaro-Gallo, P. and M. Abdisamed.

    1985   Female Circumcision in Somalia: Anthropological Traits. *Anthropologische Anzeiger* 43, 4:311–26.

Greeberg, J.

    1946   *The Influence of Islam on a Sudanese Religion.* New York:J.J. Augustin.

Gregory, J.

    1984   The Myth of the Male Ethnographer and the Woman's World. *American Anthropologist* 86, no. 2, June:316–27.

Grottanelli, V. Conte.

1947   Die Negerstaemme in Abessinien, Eritrea und Somaliland. In *Afrika*, edited by J. Bernatzik, 842-54. Innsbrück, Austria:Sluesselverlag Ges., M.B.H.

Grove, E.

1919   Customs of the Acholi. *Sudan Notes and Records* 2, no. 3:181-82.

Gruenbaum, E.

1979   *Patterns of Family Living: A Case Study of Two Villages on the Rahad River.* Development Studies and Research Centre, Faculty of Economic and Social Studies, University of Khartoum, Monograph no. 12.

1982   The Movement against Clitoridectomy and Infibulation in Sudan: Public Health Policy and the Women's Movement. W.H. Rivers Prize Paper; *Medical Anthropology Newsletter*, 13(2):4-12.

1988   Reproductive Ritual and Social Reproduction: Female Circumcision and the Subordination of Women in Sudan. In *Economy and Class in Sudan*, edited by N. O'Neill and J. O'Brien, 308-25. Aldershot:Avebury.

1991   The Islamic Movement, Development and Health-education: Recent Changes in the Health of Women in Central Sudan. *Social Science and Medicine*, (6):637-45.

Grunnet, N.

1962   An Ethnographic-ecological Survey of the Relationship Between the Dinka and Their Cattle. *Folk* 4:5-21.

Gulliver, P.

1965   *The Family Herds.* London:Routledge & Kegan Paul (especially pp. 223-43).

1974   The Jie of Uganda. In *Man In Adaptation: The Cultural Present.* 2d ed., edited by Y. Cohen, 323-45. Chicago:Aldine Publ. Co.

1974a   The Turkana. In *Man In Adaptation: The Cultural Present.* 2d ed., edited by Y. Cohen. Chicago:Aldine Publ. Co.

Haaland, G.

1972   Nomadisation as an Economic Career among the Sedentaries in the Sudan Savannah Belt. In *Essays in Sudan Ethnography*, edited by Cunnison & James, 149-72. London:C. Hurst and Co.

1984   The Fur. In *Muslim People, A World Ethnographic Survey.* 2d ed., edited by R. Weekes, 264-69. Westport, CT:Greenwood Press.

Haaland, G., ed.

1980   *Problems of Savannah Development: The Sudan Case.* University of Bergen, Norway:Department of Social Anthropology.

Haberland, V.

1963   *Galia Süd-Aethiopiens.* Band II of Völker Süd-Aethiopiens. Stuttgart, Germany:Kohl Hammer Verlag.

Hagerstrand, T.

1972   *The Impact of Social Organization and the Environment Upon the Time Use of Individuals and Households.* Stockholm, Sweden:Plan (International).

Hall, E.

1969   *The Hidden Dimension.* New York:Anchor Books.

1973   *The Silent Language.* New York:Anchor Books.

1977   *Beyond Culture.* New York:Anchor Books.

1984   *The Dance of Life: The Other Dimension of Time.* New York:Anchor Press, Doubleday.

Hall, M., and B. Ismail.

1982   *Sisters Under the Sun: The Story of Sudanese Women.* London:Longman.

Hallpike, C.

1972   *The Konso of Ethiopia.* London:Oxford University Press.

Hamer, J. The Sadama.

1984   In *Muslim People, A World Ethnographic Survey.* 2d ed., edited by R. Weekes, 647–52. Westport, CT:Greenwood Press.

Hamilton, A.

1911   *Somaliland.* London:Hutchinson and Co.

Harako, R.

1982   The Role of Abela in the Gabra Society: A Case Study of Gerontocratic Society of the Pastoralists. *African Study Monographs*, Supplementary Issue 1, March:63–69.

Hardin, G.

1969   *Population, Evolution, and Birth Control.* San Francisco:Freeman.

Harrell, B.

1981   Lactation and Menstruation in Cultural Perspective. *American Anthropologist* 83, no. 4, December:796–823.

Harries, L.

1964   The Arabs and Swahili Culture. *Arcia* 34:224–29.

Harris, M.

1974   *Cows, Pigs, Wars & Witches: The Riddles of Culture.* New York:Random House.

Hartmann, R.

1863   *Reise des Freiherrn Adalbert von Barmin Durch Nord-Ost Afrika in den Jahren 1859 und 1860.* Berlin:np.

Hasan, Y.

1967   *The Arabs and the Sudan.* Edinburgh, Scotland:University Press.

1980   The Penetration of Islam in the Eastern Sudan. In *Islam in Tropical Africa.* 2d ed., edited by I. Lewis. London:Hutchinson University Library for Africa.

Hasselblatt, G.

1979 *Aethiopien: Menschen, Kirchen, Kulturen.* Stuttgart, Germany:Radius Verlag.

Hayder, I.

1979 *The Shaiqiyya: The Cultural and Social Change of a Northern Sudanese Riverain People.* Wiesbaden, Germany:Franz Steiner verlag, GMBH.

Helander, B.

1991 The Somali Family. In *Somalia: A Historical, Cultural and Political Analysis*, edited by K. Barcik and S. Normark, 17-28. Uppsala, Sweden:Life and Peace Institute.

Henin, R.

1968 Fertility Differentials in the Sudan. *Population Studies* 22, no. 1, March:147-64.

1919 Some Data on Fertility from Sudan's 1955/56 Population Census. *Sudan Notes and Records* 50:97-105.

1969a The Patterns and Causes of Fertility Differentials in the Sudan. *Populations Studies* 23, no. 2, July:171-98.

1969b Marriage Patterns and Trends in the Nomadic and Settled Populations of the Sudan. *Africa* 39, July, no. 3:238-59.

Herskovits, M.

1962 *The Human Factor in Changing Africa.* New York:Routledge and Kegan Paul.

Hess, R.

1966 *Italian Colonialism in Somalia.* Chicago:University of Chicago Press.

Hillelson, S.

1935 Religion in the Sudan. In *The Anglo-Egyptian Sudan From Within*, edited by J. Hamilton, 207-24. London:Faber and Faber.

Hjärpe, J.

1983 The Attitude of Islamic Fundamentalism Towards the Question of Women in Islam. In *Women in Islamic Societies: Social attitudes and Historical Perspectives*, edited by B. Utas, 12-25. New York:Olive Branch Press.

Hofstee, E.W.

1976 *Differentiële Sociologie.* Deel I, II, III. Unpublished Collegedictaat. Wageningen:Afdeling Sociologie en Sociografie, Agricultural University, Wageningen.

Holt, P.

1961 *A Modern History of the Sudan.* London:Weidenfeld and Nicolson.

Holt, P., and M. Daly.

1979 *The History of the Sudan.* 3d ed. London:Weidenfeld and Nicolson.

Holy, L.

1972   Residence among the Berti. In *Essays in Sudan Ethnography*, edited by I.
        Cunnison and W. James, 58–70, London:C. Hurst and Co.

1974   *Neighbours and Kinsmen: A Study of the Berti People of Darfur.* London:C.
        Hurst and Co.

1984   The Berti. In *Muslim People, A World Ethnographic Survey.* 2d ed., edited
        by R. Weekes, 158–62. Westport, CT:Greenwood Press.

1988   Gender and Ritual in an Islamic Society: The Berti of Darfur. *Man,* n.s.
        23:469–87.

1991   *Religion and Custom in a Muslim Society: The Berti of Sudan.* Cambridge,
        UK: Cambridge University Press.

Horowitz, I.L., ed.

1972   *Power, Politics and People: The Collected Essays of C. Wright Mills.*
        (Reprint) London:Oxford University Press.

Horowitz, M. A.

1967   Reconsideration of the 'Eastern Sudan.' *Cahier d'etudes Africaines,* 27, vol.
        7, 3e cahier:381–98.

Horowitz, M. M.

1974   Barbers and Bearers: Ecology and Ethnicity in an Islamic Society. *Africa*
        44:371–82.

Horton, R.

1987   African Traditional Thought and Western Science. *Africa* 37:155–87.

Hosken, F.

1976   Genital Mutilation of Females in Africa. *Munger Africana Library Notes*
        36:1–24.

1977   Women and Health in Africa: Genital Mutilation. *Women Speaking* 4:15–18.

1978   The Epidemiology of Female Genital Mutilation. *Tropical Doctor* 8:150–56.

1979   *Women and Health Summary Facts.* Lexington, MA:Womens' International
        Network News.

1982   *The Hosken Report: Genital and Sexual Mutilation of Females.* 3d ed.
        Lexington, MA:Womens' International Network News.

Huber, A.

1966   Female Circumcison and Infibulation in Ethiopia. *Acta Tropica* 23 (1):87–91.

Hulsbosch, F.

1976   *Soedan.* Koninklijk Instituut voor de Tropen, Amsterdam. Nijmegen:Human
        Relations Area Files (HRAF) Universiteitsbibliotheek.

Hunt, J.

1951   *A General Survey of the Somaliland Protectorate, 1944–1950.* Colonial
        Development and Welfare Scheme D.

Huntingford, G.

1955   *The Galla of Ethiopia: The Kingdoms of Kafa and Janjero.* Northeastern
        Africa, Part II. London:International Africa Institute.

Ibrahim, H.

1979   *The Shaiquiya: The Cultural and Social Change of a Northern Sudanese
        Riverain People.* Wiesbaden, Germany:Frans Steiner verlag.

Inkeles, A.

1955   Social Change and Social Character: The Role of Parental Mediation. *Journal
        of Social Issues* 11, no. 2:12-23.

Irons, W., and N. Dyson-Hudson, eds.

1972   *Perspectives on Nomadism.* International Studies in Sociology and Social
        Anthropology, Vol. XIII, Leiden, Netherlands:Brill.

Ismail, E.

1982   *Social Environment and Daily Routine of Sudanese Women: A Case Study of
        Urban Middle Class Housewives.* Berlin:Dietrich Reimer verlag.

Ismail, E., and M. Makki

1990   *Women of the Sudan.* Bendestorf, Germany:Verlag Dr. Ellen Ismail-Schmidt.

Its, R.

1975   Ethnocultural Development in External and Internal Isolates. In *Population,
        Ecology, and Social Evolution,* edited by S. Polgar. Paris:Mouton.

James, F.

1888   *The Unknown Horn of Africa. An Exploration from Berbera to the Leopard
        River.* London:G. Philip and Son.

James, W.

1979   *'Kwanim Pa, The Making of the Uduk People.* Oxford:Clarendon Press.

1988   *The Listening Ebony: Moral Knowledge, Religion, and Power among the
        Uduk of Sudan.* Oxford:Clarendon Press.

Janata, A.

1984   The Afar. In *Muslim People, A World Ethnographic Survey* 2d ed., edited by
        R. Weekes, 14-8. Westport, CT:Greenwood Press.

Jelliffe, D., and E. Jelliffe.

1979   *Nutrition and Growth.* New York:Plenum Press.

Jensen, C.

1947   OstAfrika. In *Afrika, Handbuch der Angewandten Voelkerkunde.* Vol. 2,
        edited by H. Bernatzik. Innsbrück, Austria:Schluesselverlag Ges. M.B.H.

Johnson, A.

1978   *Research Methods in Social Anthropology.* London:Edward Arnold Ltd.
        (Stanford U. Press ed., 1978 entitled *Quantification in Cultural Anthropol-
        ogy: An Introduction to Research Design*).

Johnson, D.

1969   *The Nature of Nomadism: A Comparative Study of Pastoral Migrations in Southwestern Asia and Northern Africa.* Chicago:Univ. of Chicago, Department of Geography, Research Paper no. 18.

Johnson, G.

1983   Decision-making Organization and Pastoral Nomad Camp. *Human Ecology* 11, no. 2:175–99.

Johnston, H.

1903   *The Nile Quest.* London:Lawrence and Bullen, Ltd.

Jousseaume, F.

1889   Sur l'infibulation ou mutilation des organes génitaux de la femme chez les peuple des bords de la Mer Rouge et du Golfe d'Aden. *Revue d'Antropologie,* Paris:675–86.

Katakura, M.

1977   *Bedouin Village.* Tokyo, Japan:University of Tokyo Press.

Keane, A.H.

1884   Ethnology of Egyptian Sudan. *Journal Royal Anthropological Institute* 14:91–113.

Kennedy, J.

1970   Circumcision and Excision in Egyptian Nubia. *Man* 5 (2):175–91.

1977   *Struggle for Change in a Nubian Community: An Individual in Society and History.* Mountain View, CA:Mayfield publishing Co.

Kennedy, J., ed.

1978   *Nubian Ceremonial Life.* Berkeley:University of California Press.

Kenyon, S.

1984   *Women and the Urban Process: A Case Study from El Gal'a, Sennar.* Development Studies and Research Center, Seminar no. 46. Khartoum, Sudan:University of Khartoum.

Kenyon, S. ed.

1987   *The Sudanese Woman.* Khartoum, Sudan:University of Khartoum, Graduate College Publications no. 19.

Kers, W.

1985   HOMALS Application to Infibulation Data. Faculteit der Sociale Wetenschappen, Erasmus Universiteit, Rotterdam. Unpublished.

Kesby, J.

1977   *The Cultural Regions of East Africa.* London:Academic Press.

Khattab, A., and A. Hadari

1969   Nutritional Evaluation of Diets in Gezira and Managil. *Sudan Notes and Records* 50:160–64.

King, J.S.

1890   On the Practice of Female Circumcision and Infibulation among the Somali
        and Other Nations of Northeastern Africa. *Journal of the Anthropological
        Society of Bombay* 2 (2):2-6.

Kirk, J.

1904   The Yibirs and Midgans of Somaliland, Their Traditions and Dialects.
        Journal of African Soc. 4, 13, October:91-108.

Klima, G.

1970   *The Barabaig: East African Cattle-Herders.* Chicago:Holt, Rinehart and
        Winston.

Kloos, H.

1982   Farm Labor Migrations in the Awash Valley of Ethiopia. *International
        Migration Review* 16, no. 1, Spring:133-68.

Koso-Thomas, O.

1987   *The Circumcision of Women: A Strategy for Eradication.* London:Zed Books.

Kouba, L.J., and J. Muasher.

1985   Female Circumcision in Africa: An Overview. *African Studies Review* 28
        (1):95-110.

Krader, L.

1959   The Ecology of Nomadic Pastoralism. *UNESCO, Intnational Social Science
        Journal* 11, no. 4:499-510.

Kronenberg, H.

1958   Nyimang Circumcision. *Sudan Notes and Records* 39:79-82.

Kunstadter, R.

1950   The Nutritional and Endocrine Control of Growth in Children. In *Progress
        in Clinical Endocrinology*, edited by S. Soskin. New York:Grune and Strat-
        ton.

Kwaak v.d., A., I. Haaijer, and K. Bartels.

1991   Besnijdenis bij Somalische vrouwen: De stilte doorbroken? *Medische An-
        tropologie* 3 (2):210-35.

LaFargue, P.

1887   Sur la circoncision, sa signification sociale et religieuse. *Bulletin Sociologie
        d'Anthropologie de Paris*, 10 4e série:420-36.

Lampen, G.

1928   Short Account of the Meidob. *Sudan Notes and Records* 11:55-68.

1933   The Baggara Tribes of Darfur. *Sudan Notes and Records* 16, pt. 2:97-118.

1935   The Cattle Owning Tribes. In *The Anglo-Egyptian Sudan From Within*, edited
        by J. Hamilton, 130-39. London:Faber and Faber.

Lancaster, W.

1981   *The Rwala Bedouin Today.* London:Cambridge University Press.

Lange, W.

1982   *History of the Southern Gonga (S.W. Ethiopia).* Wiesbaden:Frans Steiner verlag.

Lapidus, I.M.

1988   *A History of Islamic Societies.* Cambridge, UK:Cambridge University Press.

Larrey, D.

1803   *Relation historique et chirurgicale de l'Expedition de l'Annee d'orient.* Paris:np.

Lattimore, O.

1979   Herdsmen, Farmers, Urban Culture. In *Pastoral Production and Society, Equipe Ecologie et Anthropologie des Societes Pastorales.* Proceedings of the international meeting on nomadic pastoralism, Paris. London:Cambridge University Press.

Layish, A.

1975   *Women and Islamic Law in a Non-Muslim State.* New York:John Wiley and Sons, (and Israel Universities Press, Jerusalem).

Leakey, L.

1931   The Kikuyu Problem of the Initiation of Girls. *Journal of the Royal Anthropological Institute* 61:277-85.

LeBeuf, A.

1959   *Les Populations du Tchad.* Paris:Press Universitaires de France.

LeBeuf, J.

1947   Die Staemme Zwischen Schari und Nil. In *Afrika, Handbuch der Angewandten Voelkerkunde.* Vol. 1, edited by H. Bernatzik, 427-71. Innsbrück, Austria:Schuesselverlag Ges.

Lessner-Abdin, D.

1980   Die Frau in der Sudanesischen Oeffentlichkeit. *Afrika Spectrum* 1, 15:5-18.

Levi-Strauss, C.

1949   *The Elementary Structures of Kinship.* London:Eyre & Spottiswoode.

Levin, T.

1980   Unspeakable Atrocities: The Psycho-sexual Etiology of Female Genital Mutilation. *Journal of Mind and Behavior* 1, no. 2, Autumn:197-210.

Levy, R.

1931   *An Introduction to the Sociology of Islam.* Vol. 1. London:Williams and Norgate, Ltd.

1962   *The Social Structure of Islam.* London:Cambridge University Press.

Lewis, H.

1966   The Origins of the Galla and Somali. *Journal of African History* 7, nos. 1, 2, and 3:27–43.

1984   The Oromo. In *Muslim People, A World Ethnographic Survey.* 2d ed., edited by R. Weekes, 590–96. Westport, CT:Greenwood Press.

Lewis, I.

1960   The Galla in Northern Somaliland. *Rassegna di Studi Etiopici* 15:21–38.

1960a   The Somali Conquest of the Horn of Africa. *Journal of African History* I, 2:213–20.

1961   *A Pastoral Democracy: A Study of Pastoralism and Politics among the Northern Somali of the Horn of Africa.* London:Oxford University Press.

1961a   Notes on the Social Organisation of the Clise Somali. *Rassegna di Studi Etiopici* 17:69–82.

1962   Historical Aspects of Genealogies in Northern Somali Social Structure. *Journal of African History* 3, no. 1:35–48.

1962a   *Marriage and the Family in Northern Somaliland.* East African Studies no. 15. Uganda:East African Institute of Social Research.

1965   *The Modern History of Somaliland.* London:Weidenfeld and Nicolson.

1969   From Nomadism to Cultivation. In *Man in Africa,* edited by M. Douglas and P. Kaberry. London:Tavistock publications.

1969a   *Peoples of the Horn of Africa. Ethnographic Survey of Africa, North Eastern Africa, Part I.* London:International African Institute, (first published 1955).

1973   The Somali of Somalia and North-Eastern Kenya. In *Cultural source Materials for Population Planning in East Africa: Beliefs and Practices.* Vol. 3, edited by A. Molnos, 428–35. Institute of African Studies. Nairobi:University of Nairobi, East African Publ. House.

1980a   Conformity and Contrast in Somali Islam. In *Islam in Tropical Africa* 2d ed., edited by I. Lewis. London:Hutchinson University Library.

1991   The Recent Political History of Somalia. In *Somalia: A Historical, Cultural and Political Analysis,* edited by K. Barcik and S. Normark. Uppsala, Sweden:Life and Peace Institute.

Lewis, I. ed.

1980   *Islam in Tropical Africa.* 2d ed. London:International African Institute and Hutchinson University Library for Africa.

Lightfoot-Klein, H.

1989   *Prisoners of Ritual: An Odyssey into Female Genital Circumcision in Africa.* New York:Harrington Park Press.

Linden, v.d., J.

1977   *L'Ethiopie et ses populations.* Bruxelles:Editions Complexe.

Lipsky, G.

1962   *Ethiopia: Its people, its Society, its Culture.* New Haven:HRAF.

Lipton, M.

  1970   Interdisciplinary Studies in Less Developed Countries. *The Journal of Development Studies* 7, October no. 1:5–18.

Lobban, R.

  1977   Class, Endogamy, and Urbanization in the Sudan. Paper presented at the Joint Annual Meeting of the African Studies Association, Houston, Texas, November.

Loewenstein, L.F.

  1978   Attitudes and Attitude Differences to Female Genital Mutilation in the Sudan: Is There a Change on the Horizon? *Social Science and Medicine* 12:417–21.

Longrigg, S.

  1945   *A Short History of Eritrea.* Oxford:Clarendon Press.

Loria, L.

  1936   Usi matrimoniali assortini. *Archivia per L'Antropologia e la Etnologia* 66:7–24.

Lorimer, F.

  1954   *Culture and Human Fertility.* Paris:UNESCO publication.

Lovejoy, P., and S. Baier.

  1975   The Desert-side Economy of the Central Sudan. *International Journal of African Historical Studies* 8, 4:551–84.

McAdam, D.

  1992   Gender and the Activist Experience. *American Journal of Sociology* 97, no. 5, March:1211–40.

MacCormack, C.

  1982   Biological, Cultural and Social Adaptation in Human Fertility and Birth: A Synthesis. In *Ethnography of Fertility and Birth*, edited by C. MacCormack, 9–13. London:Academic Press.

MacDonald, J.

  1893   East Central African Customs. *Journal of the Royal Anthropological Institute* 23:99–123.

Mack, D.

  1984   The Beni Amer. In *Muslim People, A World Ethnographic Survey.* 2d ed., edited by R. Weekes, 143–46. Westport, CT:Greenwood Press.

McLean, S., and S. Graham.

  1985   *Female Circumcision, Excision and Infibulation: The Facts and Proposals for Change.* 2d ed., Report No. 47. London:Minority Rights Group.

MacMichael, H.

  1912   Notes on the Zaghawa and the People of the Gebel Meidob. *Journal of the Royal Anthropological Institute* 52:288–335.

  1923   Sudan Arabs in Nigeria. *Sudan Notes and Records* 6:109–10.

1935   The Coming of the Arabs to the Sudan. In *The Anglo-Egyptian Sudan From Within*, edited by J. Hamilton. London:Faber and Faber.

1954   *The Sudan.* London:Ernest Benn, Ltd.

1967   *A History of the Arabs in the Sudan.* 2 vols. London:Frank Cass and Co. Ltd.

1967a   *The Tribes of Northern and Central Kordofan.* London:Frank Cass and Co. Ltd.

Magos, T.

1981   Women and the Eritrean Revolution. *Horn of Africa* 4, no. 2:32–36.

Malina, R., C. Chuumlea, C. Stepick, and G. Lopez.

1977   *Age of Menarch in Oaxaca, Mexico, Schoolgirls, with Comparative Data for Other Areas of Mexico.* No. 194 Offprint Series. Austin:Institute of Latin American Studies, The University of Texas at Austin.

Malmberg, T.

1980   *Human Territoriality: Survey of Behavioural Territories in Man with Preliminary Analysis and Discussion of Meaning.* The Hague, Netherlands:Mouton publishers.

Mansaray, K.

1988   Female Circumcision, Fertility Control, Women's Roles, and the Patrilineage in Modern Sierra Leone: A Functional Analysis. *International Journal Sierra Leone Studies* 1:114–21.

Marcus, H.

1972   *The Modern History of Ethiopia and the Horn of Africa. A Selected and Annotated Bibliography.* Stanford:Hoover Institute Press.

Marx, E.

1977   The Tribe as a Unit of Subsistence: Nomadic Pastoralism in the Middle East. *American Anthropologist* 79:343–63.

Maududi, a'la, A.

1972   *Purdah and the Status of Women in Islam.* Translated and edited by Al-Ash'ai. Pakistan:Islamic Publ. Ltd.

Mayer, P., ed.

1970   *Socialization: The Approach from Social Anthropology.* A.S.A. Monographs. London:Tavistock.

McLoughlin, P.

1962   Economic Development and the Heritage of Slavery in the Sudan Republic. *Africa* 32, October, no. 4:353–90.

Mehan, H., and W. Houston.

1975   *The Reality of Ethnomethodology.* New York:J. Wiley and Sons.

Mernissi, F.

1975   *Beyond the Veil: Male Female Dynamics in a Modern Muslim Society.* Cambridge, UK:Schenkman Publ. Co. Inc.

1982   Virginity and Patriarchy. In *Women and Islam*, edited by A. al-Hibri, 183–92. Oxford:Pergamon Press.

1991   *Women and Islam: An Historical and Theological Enquiry.* Translated by M.J. Lakeland. Oxford: Basil Blackwell.

Messing, S.

1973   The Somali of the Ogaden, South-east Ethiopia. In *Materials for Population Planning in East Africa, Beliefs and Practices.* Vol. 3, edited by A. Molnos, 436–41. Institute of African Studies, University of Nairobi. Nairobi:East African Publ. House.

Minces, J.

1980   *La femme dans la monde arabe.* Paris:Mazarine.

1982   *The House of Disobedience: Women in Arab Society.* (Orig. French ed. publ. in 1980). Translated and reprinted by Zed Press, London.

Moghissi, K., and T. Evans.

1977   Nutritional Impacts on Women: Throughout Life with Emphasis on Reproduction. Bethesda, MD:Medical Dept. Harper and Row.

Mohsen, S.

1970   Aspects of the Legal Status of Women among Awlad' Ali. In *Peoples and Cultures of the Middle East.* Vol. 1, edited by L. Sweet, 220–23. New York:The Natural History Press.

Molnos, A.

1968   *Attitudes towards Family Planning in East Africa.* München:Weltforum verlag.

Molnos, A., ed.

1973

        Materials for Population Planning in East Africa. Beliefs and Practices. Vol. 3 (of 4 volumes). Institute of African Studies, University of Nairobi. Nairobi:East African Publ. House.

Montandon, G.

1912   Le Ghimirra. *La Geographie* 5, 25:1–20.

Monteil, V.

1959   The Evolution and Settling of the Nomads of the Sahara. UNESCO, *International Social Science Journal* 11, no. 4:572–88.

Morrison, G.

1971   *The Southern Sudan and Eritrea: Aspects of Wider African Problems.* Report No. 5. London:Minority Rights Group.

Muhsam, H.

1959   Sedentarization of the Bedouins in Israel. UNESCO, *International Social Science Journal* 11, no. 4:539–49.

Münzinger, W.

    1864   *Ostafrikanische Studien.* Schaffhausen, Germany:Fr. Hurtersche Buchhandlung.

Murdock, G.

    1949   *Social Structure.* New York:Macmillan.

    1959   *Africa, Its Peoples and Their Culture History.* New York:McGraw Hill.

    1967   Ethnographic Atlas: A Summary. *Ethnology* 6 (2).

Murphy, R.

    1968   Social Distance and the Veil. In *Readings in Anthropology. Cultural Anthropology.* Vol. 2, 2d ed., edited by M.H. Fried, 351–69. New York:Thomas Y. Crowell, Co.

Murphy, R., and L. Kasdan.

    1959   The Structure of Parallel Cousin Marriage. *American Anthropologist* 61:17–29.

Murray, G.

    1924   Circumcision Festivals in Arabia and East Africa. *Man*, No. 39.

    1927   The Northern Beja. *Journal of the Royal Anthropological Institute* 57:39–54.

    1935   *Sons of Ishmael: A Study of the Egyptian Bedouin.* London:George Routledge and Sons, Ltd.

Murray, M.

    1934   Female Fertility Figures. *Journal Royal Anthroropological Institute* 64:93–100.

Musil, A.

    1928   *The Manners and Customs of the Rwala Bedouins.* American Geographical Society, Oriental Explorations and Studies No. 6, New York.

Mustafa, G.

    1971   Female Circumcision and Infibulation in the Sudan. *Journal of Obstetrics and Gynaecology of the British Commonwealth*:73.

Nachtigal, G.

    1971   *Sahara and Sudan.* 4 vols., translated by A. & H. Fisher, reissue and translation of German publications 1879, 81, and 89. London:C. Hurst and Co., Ltd.

Nadel, S.

    1943   *Races and Tribes of Eritrea.* Asmara, Eritrea:British Military Administration.

    1947   *The Nuba: An Anthropological Study of the Hill Tribes in Kordofan.* London:Geoffrey Cumberlege, Oxford University Press.

Naisho, J.

    1982   Health Care for Women in the Sudan. *World Health Forum* 3, no. 2, W.H.O.

Nalder, L.

   1935   Folklore and Fable in the Sudan. In *The Anglo-Egyptian Sudan*, edited by J.
            Hamilton, 225-43. London:Faber and Faber, Ltd.

Nelson, C., ed.

   1973   *The Desert and the Sown: Nomads in the Wider Society.* Research Series no.
            21, Institute of International Studies. Berkeley:University of California Press.

Nelson, H.

   1973   Area Handbook for the Democratic Republic of Sudan. DA. Pam. 550-27,
            Washington, DC:U.S. Govt. Printing Office.

   1980   *Ethiopia, A Country Study.* Area Handbook Series. Washington, DC:U.S.
            Govt. Printing Office.

   1982   *Somalia, a Country Study.* Area Handbook Series. 3d ed. Washington,
            DC:U.S. Government Printing Office.

Nelson-Richards, M.

   1982   *Social Change and Rural Development: Intervention or Participation, A
            Sambian Case Study.* Washington, DC:University Press of America.

Netting, R., R. Wilk, and E. Arnould.

   1984   *Households: Comparative and Historical Studies of the Domestic Group.*
            Berkeley:University of California Press.

Newbold, D.

   1935   The Beja Tribes of the Red Sea Hinterland. In *The Anglo-Egyptian Sudan
            From Within*, edited by J. Hamilton, 140-64. London:Faber and Faber.

NGO Report.

   1985   Seminar on Traditional Practices Affecting the Health of Women and Chil-
            dren in Africa. Organised by Ministry of Public Health, Senegal and NGO
            working group in collaboration with W.H.O., UNICEF, and UNFPA (see
            especially pgs. 55-180), Africa.

Nicolaisen, J.

   1963   *Ecology and Culture of the Pastoral Tuareg.* Denmark:The National Museum
            of Cophenhagen.

Nordenstam, T.

   1968   *Sudanese Ethics.* New York:Africana Publ. Co.

O'Fahey, R.

   1980   *State and Society in DarFur.* London:C. Hurst and Co.

Olayinka, K.T.

   1987   *The Circumcision of Women.* London:Zed press.

Oldfield-Hayes, R.

   1975   Female Genital Mutilation, Fertility Control, Women's Roles, and the Patri-
            lineage in Modern Sudan: A Functional Analysis. *American Ethnologist* 2,
            no. 4, Nov.:617-33.

Owen, T.

1927   The Hadendowa. *Sudan Notes and Records* 20, pt. 2:183–208.

Paine, R.

1970   Lappish Decisions, Partnership, Information Management and Sanctions—a Nomadic Pastoral Adaptation. *Ethnology* 9:52–68.

Pallme, I.

1844   *Travels in Kordofan.* London:J. Madden and Co.

Pankhurst, R.

1974   The History of Prostitution in Ethiopia. *Journal of Ethiopian Studies* 12, 2:159–78.

Paoli, S., and S. Puccioni.

1931   *Resultati Scientifici Delle Missioni Stefanini Paoli (1913), e Stefanini Puccioni (1924) in Somalia.* Bologna, Italy:Nicola Zanicchelli.

Parkinson, J.

1936   Customs in Western British Somaliland. *Journal of the Royal African Society* 39:241–45.

Parkyns, M.

1851   The Kubbabish Arabs between Dongala and Kordofan. *Journal of the Royal Geographical Society* (of London) 20:254–75.

Parsons, T.

1977   *The Evolution of Societies*, edited by J. Toby. Englewood Cliffs, NJ: Prentice-Hall.

Pastner, S.

1984   The Afar. In *Muslim People, A World Ethnographic Survey.* 2d ed., edited by R. Weekes, 10–14. Westport, CT:Greenwood Press.

Patai, R.

1951   Nomadism: Middle Eastern and Central Asian. *Southwest Journal of Anthropology* 7:401–14.

1976   The Goddess Cult in the Hebrew-Jewish Religion. In *The Realm of the Extra-Human. Agents and Audiences*, edited by A. Bharati, 197–210. Paris:Mouton.

Paul, A.

1950   Notes on the Beni Amer. *Sudan Notes and Records* 31, pt. 2, Dec.:223–45.

1954   *A History of the Beja Tribes of the Sudan.* London:Frank Cass and Co., Ltd.

Paulitschke, P.

1880   *Beiträge zur Ethnographie und Antropologie der Somal, Galla um Harar.* Leipzig, Germany:np.

1893   *Ethnographie Nordost-Afrikas: Die Materielle Culture der Danakil, Galla, und Somal.* 2 vols. Berlin:Geographische Verlagshandlung Dietrich Reimer.

Peristiany, J.
  1966   Honour and Shame. In *The Values of Mediterranean Society*, edited by J.
          Peristiany, 9-19. Chicago:University of Chicago Press.

Peters, E.
  1980   Aspects of Bedouin Bridewealth among Camel Herders in Cyrenaica. In *The
          Meaning of Marriage Payments*, edited by J. Comaroff, 125-60. New
          York:Academic Press.
  1984   The Paucity of Ritual among Middle Eastern Pastoralists. In *Islam in Tribal
          Societies: From the Atlas to the Indus*, edited by A. Ahmed and D. Hart,
          187-219. London:Routledge and Kegan Paul.

Petherick, J.
  1861   *Egypt, the Soudan and Central Africa*. Edinburgh, Scotland:np.
  1869   *Travels in Central Africa, and Explorations of the Western Nile*. 2 vols.
          London:Tinsley Bros.

Phillips, A., and H. Morris.
  1971   *Marriage Laws in Africa*. London:Oxford University Press.

Plog, F., C. Jolly, D. Bates, and J. Acocella.
  1980   *Anthropology, Decisions, Adaptation, and Evolution*. 2d ed. New York:Al-
          fred A. Knopf.

Ploss, H.
  1871   Die Operative Behandlung der weiblichen Geschlechtstheile bei ver-
          schiedenen Völkern. *Zeitschrift für Ethnologie* 3:381-97.

Population Studies.
  1964   *Population Growth and Manpower in the Sudan*. Study no. 37, Dept. of
          Statistics, Council of Ministers, the Republic of Sudan, Khartoum, U.N., New
          York.

Pouwells, R.L.
  1987   *Horn and Crescent: Cultural Changes and Traditional Islam on the East
          African Coast 800-1900*. Cambridge, UK: Cambridge University Press,
          African Studies Series 53.

Prins, A.
  1962   *The Swahili-Speaking Peoples of Zanzibar and the East African Coast
          (Arabs, Shirazi and Swahili)*. London:International African Institute, East
          Central Africa, Part 12.

Puccioni, N.
  1931   Antropologia e ethnografia delle genti della Somalia. Vol. 1, *Antropometria*,
          p. 384; Vol. 3 of *Ethnografia e paletnologia*. Bologna, Italy:Zanichelli.

Purves, W.
  1935   Some Aspects of the Northern Provinces (The Northern Riverain Provinces).
          In *The Anglo-Egyptian Sudan From Within*, edited by J. Hamilton, 165-80.
          London:Faber and Faber.

Rayne, H.

    1921   *Sun, Sand and Somals.* London:H.F. and G. Witherby.

Rehfisch, F.

    1964   A Sketch of the Early History of Omdurman. An Unrecorded Population Count of Omdurman. *Sudan Notes and Records* 45:33-47.

Reid, J.

    1935   The Nomad Arab Camel-Breeding Tribes. In *The Anglo-Egyptian Sudan From Within,* edited by J. Hamilton, 113-29. London:Faber and Faber.

Reyners, M.M.J.

    1989   Circumcisie bij vrouwen en infibulatie. *Nederlandse Tijdschrift voor Geneeskunde* 133, no. 51:2557-61.

Roberts, R.

    1980   *The Social Laws of the Qoran.* 5th ed. London:Curzon Press.

Robertson, A.F.

    1991   *Beyond the Family: The Social Organization of Human Reproduction.* Berkeley:University of California Press.

Robertson-Smith, W.

    1903   *Kinship and Marriage in Early Arabia.* London:Adam and Charles Black.

Rodd, F.

    1926   *People of the Veil.* London:Macmillan and Co., Ltd. (especially pp. 168-78).

Rodney, W.

    1971   *How Europe Underdeveloped Africa.* London:East Africa Publ. House.

Roles, N.C.

    1966   Tribal Surgery in East Africa During the XIXth Century. Part 1: Ritual Operations. *East-African Medical Journal* 43 (12) Dec.:579-94.

Roper, E.

    1927   Poetry of the Hadendiwa. *Sudan Notes and Records* 10:147-59.

Rubel, P.

    1969   Herd Composition and Social Structure: On Building Models of Nomadic Pastoral Societies. *Man* 4:268-76.

Rüppell, E.

    1829   *Reisen in Nubien, Kordofan un dem petraeischen Arabien.* Frankfurt A.M., Germany:F. Wilmans.

Rüssegger, J.

    1843   *Reisen in Europa, Asien und Afrika.* Stuttgart, Germany:np.

Rushwan, H., C. Slot, A. el Dareer, and M. Bushra.

1983   *Female Circumcision in the Sudan: Prevalence, Complications, Attitudes and Change.* Khartoum, Sudan:University of Khartoum (Faculty of Medicine).

Saadawi, N.

1980   *The Hidden Face of Eve: Women in the Arab World.* London:Zed Press.

1982   Women and Islam. In *Women and Islam*, edited by A. al-Hibri,193–206. Oxford:Pergamon Press.

Sagar, J.

1922   Notes on the Religion and History of the Nuba. *Sudan Notes and Records* 5, no. 1:137–56.

Sahlins, M.

1968   The Segmentary Lineage: An Organization of Predatory Expansion. In *Man In Adaptation: The Cultural Present.* 2d ed., edited by Y. Cohen, 203–30. Chicago:Aldine Publ. Co.

1968   *Tribesmen.* Englewood Cliffs, NJ:Prentice Hall.

Salah, Abu Bakr.

1982   *Circumcision and Infibulation in the Sudan.* WHO/EMRO Technical Publication 2/2:138–44.

Salih, K.

1982   The British Administration in the Nuba Mountains Region of the Sudan, 1900–1956. Ph.D. thesis. London:SOAS, University of London.

Salzman, P.

1968   Political Organization among Nomadic Peoples. In *Man in Adaptation: The Cultural Present.* 2d ed., edited by Y. Cohen. Chicago:Aldine Publ. Co.

1978   The Study of Complex Society in the Middle East: A Review Essay. *International Journal of Middle East Studies* 9:539–57.

Sandars, G.

1933   The Bisharin. *Sudan Notes and Records* 16, pt. 2:119–50.

Sanday, P.

1973   Toward a Theory of the Status of Women. *American Anthropologist* 75, no. 5, Oct.:1682–700.

Sanderson, L.

1981   *Against the Mutilation of Women: The Struggle to End Unnecessary Suffering.* London:Ithaca Press.

1981a   Female Genital Mutilation: Possible Break-through for the Ultimate Abolition of the Practice in the Sudan. *Women Speaking* 5:15–16.

Santandrea, P.

1964   *A Tribal History of the Western Bahr el Ghazel.* Bologna:Editrice Nigrin.

Saucier, J.

1972   Correlations of the Long Postpartum Taboo: A Cross-cultural Study. *Current Anthropology* 13, April, no. 2:238–49.

Scaramucci, F., and E. Gigliolo.

1884   Notizia sui Danakil. *Archivio per L'Antropologia e la Etnologia* 14: 2–44.

Schacht, J.

1964   *An Introduction to Islamic Law.* Oxford:Clarendon Press.

Schneider, H.

1971   Romantic Love among the Turu. In *Human Sexual Behavior*, edited by D. Marshall and R. Suggs. New York:Basic Books Inc.

Schneider, J.

1970   Of Vigilance and Virgins: Honor, Shame and Access to Resources in Mediterranean Societies. *Ethnology* 10:1–24.

Schneider, P.

1969   Family Patrimonies and Economic Behavior in Western Sicily. *Anthropological Quarterly* 42:100–30.

Seligman, C.

1913   Some Aspects of the Hamitic Problem in the Anglo-Egyptian Sudan. *Journal of the Royal Anthropological Institute* 43:593–705.

Seligman, C.G., and B. Seligman.

1918   The Kabâbish, a Sudan Arab Tribe. *Harvard African Studies* 2:105–84.

1930   Note on the History and Present Condition of the Beni Amer (Southern Beja). *Sudan Notes and Records* 13, pt. 1:83.

1932   *Pagan Tribes of the Nilotic Sudan.* London:Routledge and Kegan Paul, Ltd.

Shack, W.

1963   Religious Ideas and Social Action. *Africa*, 33, no. 3:198–208.

Shandall, A.

1967   Circumcision and Infibulation of Females. *Sudan Medical Journal* 5:178–212.

Silberman, L.

1959   Somali Nomads. UNESCO, *Intnational Social Science Journal* 11, no. 4:559–71.

Simmel, G.

1955   *Conflict.* Translated by Kurt H. Wolff. Glencoe, Ill.:The Free Press.

Simoons, F.

1960   *Northwest Ethiopia.* Madison:University of Wisconsin Press.

Sisaye, S.

1978   The Role of Social Sciences in Rural Development Planning: The Case of Ethiopia. *African Studies Review* 21, no. 3, December:75–85.

Sjoberg, H.
  1955   The Preindustrial City. *American Journal of Sociology* 60, March:438–45.

Skinner, E.
  1980   Islam in Mossi Society. In *Islam in Tropical Africa*. 2d ed., edited by I. Lewis, 173–93. London:Hutchinson University Library for Africa.

Slack, A.T.
  1988   Female Circumcision: A Critical Appraisal. *Human Rights Quarterly* 18 (10):439–84.

Slatin, R.
  1896   *Fire and Sword in the Sudan.* 3 vols. Leipzig, Germany:Bernhard Tauchnitz.

Slavin, L. and J. Slavin.
  1973   *The Tuareg.* London:Gentry Books.

Smart, Carol and Barry, eds.
  1981   *Women, Sexuality and Social Control.* London:Routledge and Kegan Paul.

Smith, C., ed.
  1976   *Regional Analysis.* 2 vols. New York:Academic Press.

Smith, J., and Y. Haddad.
  1982   Eve: Islamic Image of Woman. In *Women and Islam*, edited by A. al-Hibri, 135–44. Oxford:Pergamon Press.

Southall, A.
  1960   On Chastity in Africa. *Uganda Journal* 24, no. 2, September.:207–17.

Spence, B.
  1949   Female Circumcision in Sudan. *Lancet*:457.

Statistik des Auslandes.
  1982   *Länderkurzbericht, Sudan.* Statistisches Bundesamt Wiesbaden. Stuttgart, Germany:W. Kohlhammer GMBH.
  1982   *Länderkurzbericht, Aethiopien.* Statistisches Bundesamt Wiesbaden. Stuttgart, Germany:W. Kohlhammer GMBH.
  1984   *Länderkursbericht, Somalia.* Statistisches Bundesamt Wiesbaden. Stuttgart, Germany:W. Kohlhammer GMBH.

Stenning, D.
  1958   Household Viability among the Pastoral Fulani. In *Developmental Cycle in Domestic Groups*, edited by J. Goody. Cambridge, UK:Cambridge University Press.
  1959   *Savannah Nomads.* London:Oxford University Press.
  1965   The Pastoral Fulani of Northern Nigeria. In *Peoples of Africa*, edited by J. Gibbs, 363–401. Chicago:Holt Rinehart and Winston.

1980   Cattle Values and Islamic Values in a Pastoral Population. In *Islam in Tropical Africa*. 2d ed., edited by I. Lewism 194-205. London:Hutchinson University Library for Africa.

Stephens, W.N.

1963   *The Family in Cross-cultural Perspective.* New York:Holt, Rinehart and Winston.

Stevenson, R.

1984   *The Nuba People of Kordofan Province. An Ethnographic Survey.* Graduate College Publ. Monography 7. Khartoum, Sudan:University of Khartoum.

Stott, D.

1969   Cultural and Natural Checks on Population Growth. In *Environment and Cultural Behavior*, edited by A. Vayda. Austin:University of Texas Press Source Books in Anthropology.

Strauder, J.

1971   *The Majangir: Ecology and Society of a Southwest Ethiopian People.* Cambridge, UK:Cambridge University Press.

Sudan: Background Notes.

1982   Washington, DC:U.S. Dept. of State, Bureau of Public Affairs.

Sudan: Merkblätter für Auslandtaetige und Auswanderer.

1982   Köln, Germany:Bundesverwaltungsamt.

Suggs, R., Marshall, D.

1971   Anthropological Perspectives on Human Sexual Behavior. In *Human Sexual Behavior*, edited by R. Suggs, and D. Marshall. New York:Basic Books Inc.

Sundstrom, E., and I. Altman.

1976   Interpersonal Relationships and Personal Space: Research Review and Theoretical Model. *Human Ecology* 4:47-67.

Sweet, L.

1969   Camel Pastoralism in North Arabia and the Minimal Camping Unit. In *Environment and Cultural Behaviour*, edited by A. Vayda, 157-80. Austin:University of Texas Press, Texas Press Source Books in Anthropology.

1970   Camel Raiding of North Arabian Bedouin: A Mechanism of Ecological Adaptation. In *Peoples and Cultures of the Middle East*. Vol. 1, edited by L. Sweet, 265-90. New York:The Natural History Press.

Swift, J.

1979   The Development of Livestock Trading in Nomad Pastoral Economy: The Somali Case. In *Pastoral Production and Society, Equipe Ecologie et Anthropologie des Societes Pastorales*. Proceedings of the International Meeting on Nomadic Pastoralism, Paris. London:Cambridge University Press, pp. 447-66.

Taba, A.

1980   Female Circumcision. *Tropical Doctor* 10, no. 1:21-24.

Tanaka, J.

1982   Adaptation to Arid Environment: A Comparative Study of Hunter-gatherers and Pastoralists in Africa. *African Study Monographs*, Supplementary Issue 1:1-12.

Tapper, R.

1984   Holier than Thou: Islam in Three Tribal Societies. In *Islam in Tribal Societies, From the Atlas to the Indus*, edited by A. Ahmed and D. Hart, 244-65. London:Routledge and Kegan Paul.

Tetzlaff, R., and K. Wohlmuth.

1980   *Der Sudan, Probleme und Perspektiven der Entwicklung.* Frankfurt a.m.:Alfred Metzner Verlag GmbH.

Thelwall, R.

1984   The Meidob. In *Muslim People, A World Ethnographic Survey.* 2d ed., edited by R. Weekes, 504-08. Westport, CT:Greenwood Press.

Thompson, V., and R. Adloff.

1968   *Djibouti and the Horn of Africa.* Stanford, CA:Stanford University Press.

Thurnwald, R.

1929   Social Systems of Africa. *Africa* 2, no. 3, July:221-53; and continued in *Africa* 2, October, 1929, no. 4:352-78.

1940   *Völkerkunde von Afrika, mit besonderer beruchsichtigung der Koloniale aufgabe.* Essen, Germany:Essener Verlagsanstalte.

Tornay, S.

1979   Generations, classes d'ages et superstructures: A propos de l'etude d'une ethnie du cercle karimojong (Afrique orientale). In *Pastoral Production and Society, Equipe Ecologie et Anthropologie des Societes Pastorales.* Proceedings of the International Meeting on Nomadic Pastoralism, Paris. London:Cambridge University Press.

Torry, W.

1973   *Subsistence Ecology among the Gabra: Nomads of the Kenya Ethiopia Frontier.* Columbia University Ph.D. dissertation. University Microfilms International, Ann Arbor, MI.

Trimingham, J.

1949   *Islam in the Sudan.* London:Geoffrey Cumberlege, Oxford University Press.

1952   *Islam in Ethiopia.* London:Oxford University Press.

1968   *The Influence of Islam upon Africa.* London:Longmans.

1964   *Islam in East Afica.* Oxford, UK:Clarendon Press.

1980   The Phases of Islamic Expansion and Islamic Culture Zones in Africa. In *Islam in Tropical Africa.* 2d ed., edited by I. Lewis, 99-111. London:Hutchinson University Library for Africa.

Tubiana, J.

1984   The Tunjur. In *Muslim People, A World Ethnographic Survey.* 2d ed., edited
         by R. Weekes, 796-99. Westport, CT:Greenwood Press.

Tubiana, M.

1977   *The Zaghawa from an Ecological Perspective. Food Gathering, the Pastoral
         System, Tradition and Development of the Zaghawa of the Sudan and Chad.*
         Rotterdam:A.A. Balkema.

Tubiana, M-J.

1964   *Survivances préIslamique en pays Zaghawa.* Paris:Institute D'Ethnologie,
         Musée de l'Homme.

1984   The Beri. In *Muslim People, A World Ethnographic Survey.* 2d ed., edited by
         R. Weekes, 154-58. Westport, CT:Greenwood Press.

Tubiana, M-J., and J. Tubiana.

1968   *Fieldwork in Darfur.* Dossiers de la R.C.P. no. 45, Paris.

Tully, D.

1984   The Masalit. In *Muslim People, A World Ethnographic Survey.* 2d ed., edited
         by R. Weekes, 499-504. Westport, Connecticut:Greenwood Press.

Turner, V.

1962   Three Symbols of Passage in Ndembu Circumcision Ritual. In *Essays on The
         Ritual of Social Relations*, edited by M. Gluckman, 124-73. Manchester,
         UK:Manchester University Press.

U.S. Dept. of State Background Notes: Sudan.

1982   Washington, DC:U.S. Dept. of State, Bureau of Public Affairs, November.
         *United Nations Economic and Social Council, Country Programme Profile—
         Sudan.*

1981   *University of Khartoum.*

nd   Institute of African and Asian Studies—3d International Conference on the
         Central Bilal al-Sudan.

Utas, B. ed.

1983   *Women in Islamic Societies: Social Attitudes and Historical Perspectives.*
         New York:Olive Branch Press, Interlink Publ. Group, Inc.

Van Gennep, A.

1960   *The Rites of Passage.* Chicago:Chicago University Press.

Verzin, J.

1975   Sequelae of female circumcision. *Tropical Doctor* 5:163-69.

Vizedom, M.

1976   *Rites and Relationships: Rites of Passage and Contemporary Anthropology.*
         London:Sage Publications.

Wai, O.

1981   *The African-Arab Conflict in the Sudan.* London:Africana Publ. Co.

Weinstein, D., H. Shugart, and C. Brandt.

    1983   Energy Flow and the Persistence of a Human Population: A Simulation Analysis. *Human Ecology* 11, no. 2:201–24.

Weissleder, W.

    1978   *The Nomadic Alternative.* Paris:Mouton.

Werne, F.

    1852   *Reise durch Senaar nach Mandera, Noeseb, Cheli, in Lande zwischen dem blauen Nile und dem Atbara.* Berlin, Germany:np.

Wessing, R.

    1984   The Sudanese. In *Muslim People, A World Ethnographic Survey.* 2d ed., edited by R. Weekes, 727–32. Westport, CT:Greenwood Press.

White, R.

    1920   Notes on the Turkana tribe. *Sudan Notes and Records* 3:217–22.

Whiting, J.

    1969   Effects of Climate on Certain Cultural Practices. In *Environment and Cultural Behavior,* edited by A. Vayda, 416–55. Austin, TX:University of Austin Press Source Books in Anthropology.

W.H.O./EMRO Technical Publication no. 2.

    1979   Traditional Practices Affecting the Health of Women and Children: Female Circumcision, Childhood Marriage, Nutritional Taboos, etc. Report of a Seminar Khartoum, 10–15 Feb. W.H.O. Publ., Alexandria, Egypt.

W.H.O. Report on Ad-Hoc Survey.

    1981   Infant and Early Childhood Mortality in Relation to Fertility Patterns. (Survey in Greater Khartoum and in the Blue Nile, Kassala and Kordofan provinces, 1974–1976.) Geneva, Switzerland.

W.H.O., 12th Annual Report.

    1983   Special Programme of Research Development Training in Human Production. Geneva, Switzerland.

W.H.O. Chronicle.

    1986   A Traditional Practice that Threatens Health: Female Circumcision. WHO Chronicle, 40 (1):31–36.

W.H.O. Report.

    1987   Regional Seminar on Traditional Practices Affecting the Health of Women and Children in Africa. 6–10 April, Addis Ababa, Ethiopia.

Widstrand, C.

    1964   Female Infibulation. *Studia Ethnographica Uppsalensia* 20, Varia I:95–124.

Wilder, W.

    1970   Socialization and Social Structure in a Malay Village. In *Socialisation: The approach from Social Anthropology,* edited by P. Mayer. A.S.A. Monographs 8. London:Tavistock Publ.

Wilmsen, E.

 1979 Diet and Fertility among Kalahari Bushmen. Boston, MA:African Studies
 Center, Boston University, Working papers, no. 14.

Wilson, D.C.

 1955 Female Circumcision and the Age of the Menarch. *British Medical Journal*
 1:1375.

Wolff, K.H.

 1950 *The Sociology of Georg Simmel.* New York:The Free Press.

World Health Forum.

 1982 *International Journal of Health Development.* W.H.O. publication, vol. 3,
 no. 4, Geneva, Switzerland (especially pages 357-64, 376-79, 423-28,
 450-51).

 1984 *International Journal of Health Development.* W.H.O. publication, vol. 5,
 no. 1, Geneva, Switzerland (especially pages 49-53, 59-60, 76-78).

Worsley, A.

 1938 Infibulation and Female Circumcision: A Study of a Little Known Custom.
 Journal of Obstetrics and Gynaecology of the British Empire 45:686-91.

Wright Mills, C.

 1945 *The Sociological Imagination.* Middlesex, UK:Penguin Books Ltd.

Wynne-Edwards, V.

 1962 *Animal Dispersion in Relation to Social Behavior.* New York:Hafner.

Young, F.

 1962 *Initiation Ceremonies: A Cross-cultural Study of Status Dramatization.* New
 York:Bobbs-Merrill.

Youseff, N.

 1973 Cultural Ideals, Female Behavior and Kinship Control. *Comparative Studies
 in Society and History* 15, 3:326-47.

Yuzbashi, N.

 1922 Notes on the Baggara and Nuba of Western Kordofan. *Sudan Notes and
 Records* 5, no. 1:200-07.

 1924 Notes on the Kuku and Other Minor Tribes. *Sudan Notes and Records* 7, no.
 1:1-42.

Zabrowski, M.

 1894 La circoncision, ses origines et sa répartition en Afrique et à Madagascar.
 Bulletin sociologie d'Anthropologie 18, January:654-75.

Zenkovsky, S.

 1945 Marriage Customs in Omdurman. *Sudan Notes and Records* 26, pt. 2:241-56.

Zimmerman, C.

 1947 *Family and Civilization.* New York:Harper and Bro.

Zito, G.
   1975   *Methodology and Meanings.* New York:Praeger.

Index